Happy 10th
Anniversary as
a MOM !
Love Karen

Mothers Day
1988

By Joyce Maynard

LOOKING BACK

BABY LOVE

DOMESTIC AFFAIRS

For Children (with Steve Bethel)

CAMPOUT

NEW HOUSE

DOMESTIC
AFFAIRS

Joyce Maynard

DOMESTIC AFFAIRS

*Enduring the
Pleasures of
Motherhood
and
Family
Life*

Times
BOOKS

The material included in this book has appeared in
different form in Joyce Maynard's column "Domestic Affairs,"
which is syndicated by The New York Times Syndication
Sales Corporation, Inc.; in *The New York Times*; *Redbook*;
Family Circle; and *Harrowsmith*.

LIBRARY OF CONGRESS CATALOGING-IN-PUBLICATION DATA
Maynard, Joyce, 1953–
Domestic affairs.
1. Mothers—United States—Anecdotes, facetiae,
satire, etc. 2. Working mothers—United States—
Anecdotes, facetiae, satire, etc. 3. Parent and
child—United States—Anecdotes, facetiae,
satire, etc. I. Title.
HQ759.M395   1987   306.8'743   86-30033
ISBN 0-8129-1244-6

Book design by Beth Tondreau
Drawings by Naomi Osnos

Manufactured in the United States of America
9   8   7   6   5   4   3   2
First Edition

For my mother, Fredelle Maynard, who inspired me with a
longing to raise children, because it was so clear
she loved doing it

ACKNOWLEDGMENTS

I want to recognize and thank all the women who have loved and cared for my children over the past eight and a half years: Mary Walker, Joanne Marziano, Minerva Roque, Irma, Beverly Dumais, Cathy Cartagena, Denise Blanchette, Shari Sudsbury, Victoria Whitten, Dulce Donovan, Joanie Laidley.

Because so much of this book first appeared as newspaper columns, a number of editors have contributed their guidance and sound judgment to the work that appears here. Dona Guimares and Nancy Newhouse of *The New York Times*; Max Horowitz of the New York Times Syndicate; and especially Ann Harnagel, also of the Times Syndicate, who has made the weekly escapades of my family a part of her life for a long time now.

Thanks also to Amy Gash, who read and reread, and helped to organize this book. To my friend and editor, Elisabeth Scharlatt, goes gratitude and deep affection, for her patience and faith, and her wonderful editorial eye. To my agent and friend, Bob Cornfield, love and thanks go always. And to my husband, Steve, who would so much have preferred having a wife who wrote historical novels, or science fiction—or anything that didn't mention him, my heart.

CONTENTS

DOMESTIC
AFFAIRS

INTRODUCTION

Sometimes the sun rises first. More often, it's my two-year-old, Willy, who does. And that's when my day begins.

I roll out of bed and put on water for coffee, and Willy opens the cupboard to choose his cereal. (Maybe a combination of Kix, Honey Nut Cheerios, and Rice Krispies. Maybe oat flakes, Shredded Wheat, and Raisin Bran, with sliced banana, because that's what they show on the front of the cereal box. Or he wants the toy pictured on the back, that you have to send away for. Or he may put in a bid for his Halloween candy, in which case, when I tell him no, he'll cry and swear that if he can have just one, he'll be good forever.)

He wants to pour the milk, and I always let him, and he always spills it. We turn on *Sesame Street*. He wants to carry his bowl into the living room himself. He spills cereal on his pajamas and demands a fresh pair. I say, reasonably, that once we're changing him anyway, we might as well put on his shirt and overalls. But my son is two years old: This kind of logic does not apply. He wants different pajamas—for the ten minutes that remain before daybreak. He wants his Superman pair that are in the wash. And he wants to put them on himself. Which (after I retrieve them from the dirty clothes) he does, with two feet in one leg hole, and inside out.

Now my son is angry, indignant. And because just about everything in his life right now is involved with me, his current problem is all my fault. He cries. He says he doesn't like me anymore. He hates this cereal. He wants to put the peel back on the banana. He wants cartoons, and the fact that this isn't Saturday is immaterial, because (once again) I should be able to conjure up a few Smurfs if I really try. "No cartoons today," I say, in a calm, level voice—though I am in fact nearing the breaking point. And now Willy's wailing has roused my son Charlie, who thumps down the stairs, with his bear in his hand and his thumb in his mouth, requesting oatmeal with maple syrup and raisins to look like a face, while from her bed my daughter Audrey is weeping that I let her sleep in too late and now she's missed everything.

It's five minute to seven. The coffee water has just come to a boil.

I make the peanut butter sandwiches for Audrey's lunch and get to work braiding Audrey's hair while my husband Steve attempts to round up the right number of shoes, socks, hair clips, mittens, and little boxes of juice. Steve warms up the car, Audrey searches frantically for her piano book. Willy insists on putting his own boots on. Charlie wants help with his. Mr. Rogers is just placing his suit coat on a hanger and lacing up his sneakers as I zip up the last pair of snow pants. My coffee sits on the counter, cold.

At times, in the middle of the chaotic morning rites of getting everybody up and dressed (some out the door, some not) my mind flashes to an image of the old *Donna Reed Show* that I used to watch when I was my daughter's age: Donna Reed, in her immaculate starched apron and her perfect hairdo, standing at the door of her tidy home, handing out the lunch bags and kissing her husband and children good-bye as they head out to face the day. Her husband forgets to kiss her, and Donna looks vaguely distressed, but in the end he always comes back and gives her a peck on the cheek. Then she smiles contentedly and gets on with her day. Which is what I try to do also, although sometimes, by eight A.M., I feel more like taking a two-hour nap. I might have been climbing a mountain or competing in a triathalon, but in fact all I've been doing is arbitrating disputes over mittens, pouring out cereal, and sponging off counters. Some adventure.

I was a newspaper reporter in New York City once, and I wrote about fires and elevator operators' strikes and dog shows and murders. It was a pretty exciting line of work for a young single woman who'd grown up in a small New Hampshire town. I loved having a job that allowed me to earn my living doing what I like best anyway, which is ob-serving life and asking questions. But I knew from the first that it was no life for a married woman with young children, and so when I met the man I wanted to marry and with whom I wanted to raise children, I quit my job and left the city. We moved back to my home state of New Hampshire, to this two-hundred-year-old farmhouse at the end of a dirt road with no neighbors in sight, five miles outside of a small town with no stop light or movie theater, no elevator oper-ators' strikes or, for that matter, elevators. Steve, my hus-band, is a painter, who sometimes paints canvases and sometimes houses. He built himself a studio; I got pregnant. At first it was enough simply to be together in our new home, and having a baby.

But when, after the first idyllic months up here, the reality began to hit us that we'd both have to do something about earning a living, I fell into despair. Truthfully, I guess I also missed the excitement and adventure of my former career in this new life of mine, in which the big news of the day might be the ripening of our first tomato or a trip to the town dump. I was a reporter without a story—and where once I could always hop on the subway and find one, now I was seven months pregnant, with the snow piled so high I couldn't see out my kitchen windows and our only car buried deep in the drifts.

I made bold plans that as soon as our baby was born I'd get right back to business as usual, and from a tip I'd picked up I even got myself an assignment to do a story about houses of prostitution in midtown Manhattan. Six weeks after her birth, I strapped Audrey into the infant seat beside me and drove to New York to conduct my research. I made phone calls to an underworld character who could be reached only between three and four A.M. I even made it to one East Side town house, whose shades were all drawn—where, I was told, there was a woman who would talk to me round about the same hour of night, if I'd meet her at a certain corner.

Only Audrey didn't cooperate: She needed to be nursed when I was supposed to be taking notes. She cried in the background while I attempted to carry on my interview with the underworld character. The problem wasn't confined to Audrey, either. I realized, once I left my hearth and home, that by my hearth, in my home, was really where I wanted to be with this new child of mine. By day two of work on my assignment I knew the whole thing was impossible. Not simply this particular project, but also the notion that having a baby would change nothing in my life but the number of exemptions on our income tax return. Walking down a particularly fashionable section of downtown the day before returning home, with my empty notebook and Audrey strapped on my chest in her corduroy front pack, I saw a chic-looking woman stare at us, stop, and then do a double take. "Oh," she said, seeing that I'd observed her. "I was just surprised to see you had a real baby in there. At first I thought it was just an accessory."

I had a real baby all right. And I had learned something from my ridiculous, impossible attempt at combining investigative reporting with mothering a newborn. Having a child changes everything. If I was still going to write, I'd do better to acknowledge and adapt to my child's existence than to pretend she wasn't there.

So I made my child and my home my new beat. I set up my typewriter on my kitchen table and I began reporting on my own life and the little dramas that happened in the sandbox and the supermarket, and discovered that there was in fact plenty of action to be found without having to venture past the end of our driveway. Over the years there have been more characters added to the scene (Audrey's two brothers, plenty of friends, and strangers passing through). A few summers back, Steve built a little house for me to work in, out behind our own bigger one and his studio, so I no longer work surrounded, as I used to, by the smells of dinner cooking and the sight of laundry in need of sorting. But my situation remains in many ways the same: My mind is always on the home front. I could get on a plane to New York City, by myself, and write about the goings-on of the big world beyond our little town a little more easily these days than I could have nine years ago. But the fact is, the adventure that occupies me now is making a home, making a marriage work, trying to have a career. And central among them all: the difficult, exhausting, humbling, and endlessly gratifying business of raising children, of ensuring the health of both body and soul.

For nine years now, I have been reporting on and ruminating about domestic affairs. This book is the result: nine years' worth of stories and reflections on the things I care about and think about, the things that move my heart. Finally, though, this is not a book about me or about my children. Because the reason for telling these stories, I have come to believe, is not that they're so rare and amazing—headline material—but that they're not. In my newspaper days I wrote chiefly about isolated events and extraordinary phenomena. Now I document ordinary daily life. And I think one of the chief pleasures in doing that comes from the knowledge that what's going on here is not unique or rare. What I went through this morning to get my son's sneakers on and my daughter's hair braided was probably the same thing a million other mothers were going through at exactly the same moment. And while it's often said that parenthood—motherhood, anyway—is a pretty isolating experience (and it's true, I have never felt so lonely as I used to sometimes, home alone with a new baby), the opposite can also be said. Having children is one way of feeling a connection with the human race, and all the other inhabitants of this planet, who—however else their lives may differ from your own—are doing precisely the same thing you are.

I was in New York with Audrey a while back, and we were riding a crowded bus. Audrey (eight years old now) was carrying the turquoise purse she takes with her everywhere, that contains all of her greatest treasures. A mother and a little girl who looked just about Audrey's age got on the bus and sat down next to us in the only two vacant seats. The little girl was also carrying a scaled-down shoulder bag, although hers was purple.

We had fifty blocks to travel. Audrey unzipped her bag,

then (partly, I think, as a way of establishing silent communication with the child beside her) began taking items out to examine them. A handful of jelly bracelets, a couple of ribbon barrettes, a miniature Cabbage Patch doll, a bottle of pink sparkly nail polish. Her birthstone (amethyst), her address book, featuring the names of several dozen pen pals. Scissors, hair bows, glue, a Chinese fan, an eraser in the shape of a banana.

And then an interesting thing happened. The girl opened her bag, and without saying anything, began to do the same thing Audrey had been doing. It turned out she had a handful of jelly bracelets and a couple of fancy barrettes too. She also had nail polish and a little plastic figure, and a notepad, and a shell, and an eraser in the shape of a watermelon slice. The two girls (still feeling no need to converse) began to giggle. I found myself catching the eye of the other child's mother, knowing the two of us had the same impulse: To see if we resembled one another as closely as our daughters did. And what I felt, observing the similarities between us, was not the kind of panic I can remember (when you discover someone else bought the same prom gown you did, in the same color), but a reassuring sense of kinship. We never spoke, that other mother and I—we didn't have to. I knew some things about her life. She knew about mine. We are both adventurers in the same mysterious territory of parenthood.

I seldom feel like much of an adventurer—standing in this kitchen, pour cereal into bowls, refilling them, handing out paper towels when the inevitable cry comes: "Uh-oh. I spilled." But sometimes at night the thought will strike me: There are three small people here, breathing sweetly in their beds, whose lives are for the moment in our hands. I might as well be at the controls of a moon shot, the mission is so grave and vast.

CUT FROM THE SAME CLOTH

There is no way to be somebody's mother without having been, first, someone's child; and the kind of mother I am is all wrapped up with the kind of mother I had. Some of what my mother did is precisely what I've chosen not to do. Some of what she did is imprinted on me so strongly that now and then I'll hear myself saying to my children the very words that were once said to me. (Of cookies on a plate: "What you touch you take." Or, to a child wailing over being sent to bed: "That just shows me you're overtired.") Some of those lines probably go back a generation or two before me, and probably one or two will survive, through my children, into the twenty-first century. I think it wasn't until I had children myself that I understood the power of inheritance and the meaning of heritage.

Of course I've rejected, railed against, and even cursed

parts of my heritage, as most daughters have. But in the end, I guess I never for a moment questioned the essential belief my mother possessed (and possesses still): that there could be nothing more worthwhile and challenging than having and raising children. Fashions in raising of children dictate, now, that women leave their litle girls more free to choose or reject childbearing. But my mother raised me to be a mother, and (though I'm always quick to say not "when you have children," but only "if") the truth is I am probably passing on a good deal of the same pattern to my children too. Patterns are hard to break. If I had to name one occasion on which I learned that, it would be this one. The year was 1979. Audrey had just turned one. I was twenty-five, my mother fifty-seven, my grandmother eighty-six. One day there were four generations. The next day there were only three.

My mother called to tell me that my grandmother was dying. She had refused an operation that would postpone, but not prevent, her death from pancreatic cancer. She could no longer eat, she had been hemorrhaging, and she had severe jaundice. "I always prided myself on being different," she told my mother. "Now I *am* different. I'm yellow."

My mother, telling me this news, began to cry. So I became the mother for a moment, reminding her, reasonably, that my grandmother was eighty-six, she'd had a full life, she had all her faculties, and no one who knew her could wish that she live long enough to lose them. In the last year or so my mother had begun finding notes in my grandmother's drawers at the nursing home, reminding her, "Joyce's husband's name is Steve. Their daughter is named Audrey." She rarely saw her children anymore, had no strength to cook or garden. Just the other week she had said of her longtime passion, Harry Belafonte, "I gave him up." She told my mother that she'd had enough living.

My grandmother's name was Rona Bruser. She was born

in Russia, in 1892, the eldest daughter of a large and comfortable Jewish family. But the comfort didn't last. She used
to tell stories of the pogroms and the Cossacks who raped her
when she was twelve. Soon after that her family emigrated
to Canada.

My mother has shown me photographs of my grandmother in the old days. Today a woman like her would be
constantly dieting, but back then her stout, corseted figure
was the ideal. She had a long black braid and the sort of
strong-jawed beauty that would never be described as frag-
ile. She was pursued by many men, but most ardently by
Boris Bruser, also an immigrant from Russia, who came
from a much poorer country family and courted her through
the mail, in letters filled with his watercolor illustrations and
rich, romantic prose. "Precious Rona!" his letters begin. "If
only my arms were around you." "Your loving friend," they
end (as little as one week before the wedding), "B. Bruser."

My grandfather, like the classic characters in Isaac
Bashevis Singer stories, concerned himself with heaven
more than earth. He ran one failing store after another,
moved his family from town to town across the Canadian
prairies, trusting the least trustworthy of customers, invest-
ing in doomed businesses, painting gentle watercolors, while
his wife balanced the books and baked the knishes.

Their children, my mother in particular, were the center
of their life. The story I loved best as a child was of my
grandfather opening every box of Cracker Jacks in his store,
in search of the particular tin toy my mother coveted.
Though they never had much money, my grandmother saw
to it that her daughter had elocution lessons and piano
lessons, and the assurance that she would go to college.

But while she was at college my mother met my father,
who was not only twenty years older than she was, and divorced, but blue-eyed and blond-haired and not Jewish.
When my father sent love letters to my mother, my grand-

mother would open and hide them, and when my mother told her parents she was going to marry this man, my grandmother said if that happened, it would kill her.

Not likely, of course. My grandmother was a woman who used to crack Brazil nuts open with her teeth, a woman who once lifted a car off the ground when there was an accident and it had to be moved. She had been representing her death as imminent ever since I could remember and had discussed, at length, the distribution of her possessions and her lamb coat. Every time we said good-bye, after our annual visit to Winnipeg, she'd weep and say she'd never see us again. But in the meantime, while every other relative of her generation, and a good many of the younger ones, had died (nursed in their final illness, usually, by her) she kept making borscht, shopping for bargains, tending the most flourishing plants I've ever seen, and most particularly, spreading the word of her daughters' and granddaughters' accomplishments.

On the first real vacation my grandparents ever took, to Florida—to celebrate their retirement, the sale of their last store and the first true solvency of their marriage—my grandfather was hit by a car. After that he began to forget his children's names and could walk only with two canes. After he died my grandmother's life was lived, more than ever, through her children, and her pride, her possessiveness, seemed suffocating. When she came to visit, I would have to hide my diary. She couldn't understand any desire for privacy. She couldn't bear it if my mother left the house without her. Years later, in the nursing home, she would tell people that I was editor of *The New York Times* and my cousin was the foremost artist in Canada. My mother was simply the most perfect daughter who ever lived.

This made my mother furious (and then guilt-ridden that she felt that way, when of course she owed so much to her mother). So I harbored the resentment that my mother, the dutiful daughter, would not allow herself. I, who had always performed specially well for my grandmother—danced and sung for her, offered up my smiles and kisses and good report cards and prizes, the way my mother always did—stopped writing to her, ceased to visit.

But when I heard that she was dying I realized I wanted to go to Winnipeg to see her one more time. Mostly to make my mother happy, I told myself (certain patterns being hard to break). But also, I was offering up one more particularly successful accomplishment: my own dark-eyed, dark-skinned, dark-haired daughter, whom my grandmother had never met.

I put Audrey's best dress on her for our visit to Winnipeg, the way the best dresses were always put on me for visits twenty years before. I made sure Audrey's stomach was full so she'd be in good spirits, and I filled my pockets with animal crackers in case she started to cry. I scrubbed her face mercilessly (never having been quite clean enough myself to please my grandmother). In the elevator going up to her room, I realized how much I was sweating.

For the first time in her life, Grandma looked small. She was lying flat with an IV tube in her arm and her eyes shut, but she opened them when I leaned over to kiss her. "It's Fredelle's daughter, Joyce," I yelled, because she didn't hear well any more, but I could see that no explanation was necessary. "You came," she said. "You brought the baby."

Audrey was just one year old, but she had already seen enough of the world to know that people in beds are not meant to be so still and yellow, and she looked frightened. "Does she make strange?" my grandmother asked.

Then Grandma waved at her—the same kind of slow, finger-flexing wave a baby makes—and Audrey waved back. I spread her toys out on my grandmother's bed and sat her down. There she stayed, most of the afternoon, playing and humming and sipping on her bottle, taking a nap at one point, leaning against my grandmother's leg. When I cranked her Snoopy guitar, Audrey stood up on the bed and danced. Grandma couldn't talk much anymore, though every once in a while she would say how sorry she was that she wasn't having a better day. "I'm not always like this," she said.

Mostly she just watched Audrey. Over and over she told me how beautiful my daughter is, how lucky I am to have her. Sometimes Audrey woud want to get off the bed, inspect the get-well cards, totter down the hall. "Where is she?" Grandma kept asking. "Who's looking after her?" I had the feeling that, even then, if I'd said, "Audrey's lighting matches," Grandma would have shot up to rescue her.

We were flying home that night, and I had dreaded telling her, remembering all those other tearful partings. But in the end, when I said we had to go, it was me, not Grandma, who cried. She had said she was ready to die. But as I leaned over to stroke her forehead, what she said was "I wish I had your hair" and "I wish I was well."

On the plane flying home, with Audrey in my arms, I thought about mothers and daughters, and the four generations of the family that I know most intimately. Every one of those mothers loves and needs her daughter more than her daughter will love or need her someday, and we are, each of us, the only person on earth who is quite so consumingly interested in our child. Sometimes, when she was a baby, I would kiss and hug Audrey so much she starts crying— which is in effect what my grandmother was doing to my mother all her life. And what made my mother grieve, I knew, was not only that her mother would die in a day or two, but that once her mother was dead, there would never again be someone to love her in quite such an unreserved, unquestioning way. No one to believe that fifty years ago, she could have put Shirley Temple out of a job, no one else who remembers the moment of her birth. She would be only a mother, then, not a daughter anymore.

As for Audrey and me, we stopped over for a night in Toronto, where my mother lives. In the morning we would head for a safe deposit box at the bank to take out the receipt for my grandmother's burial plot. Then Mother would fly back to Winnipeg, where, for the first time in anybody's memory, there was waist-high snow on April Fool's Day. But that night, she fed me a huge dinner, as she always does when I come, and I ate more than I do anywhere else. I admired the Fiesta-ware china (once my grandmother's) that my mother set on the table. She said (the way Grandma used to say to her of the lamb coat), "Someday it will be yours."

□

Steve traveled light into our marriage. (Few childhood possessions remain. His parents moved often while he was growing up, and always, when they moved, held yard sales to dispose of excess baggage.) I move through life weighted down with possessions: every Barbie doll I ever played with, and all of their outfits. Junior-high poems. Letters from camp. My collection of fifty-odd salt and pepper shakers. The family Christmas ornaments, including a virtually shattered, nearly forty-year-old egg with a Santa face drawn on that my mother made in the first year of her marriage to my father. (When my parents divorced, the Christmas decorations all came to me.) Like her, and like her mother, I cannot bear to part with things.

Still, it occurs to me, it isn't things, chiefly, that will be my inheritance (or my bequest). When I am most likely to think of my mother, when my mother is most likely to think of her mother (and when my children will be most apt to think of me, I suspect), is in the kitchen. Baking. Baking pies, especially.

I make a good pie crust. I make pies fast, and often; my freezer's full of last summer's berries, and I'm never without a backup can of Crisco on the pantry shelf. At six o'clock on a Thursday afternoon, if I suddenly get the idea to invite a couple of friends over for dessert, pie is what I'll bake; forty-five minutes later I'm ready, and all the guests need to do is maybe pick up the whipping cream on their way over. I particularly like the moment when I take the pie out of the oven and set it on the table, cut the first slice, watch the steam rise.

Later, as we're sitting with our coffee, picking bits off the edges of the crust to straighten it, or forking up stray raspberries from the bottom of the pan, someone is likely to ask for my pie crust recipe. I could write it down for them, of course, but the truth is, there's no such thing as a recipe for good pie crust. There are the novelty crusts, made with cream cheese or spun up in a Cuisinart. There are the classic debates—vegetable shortening or butter?—and there are state-of-the-art tools: rolling pins you fill with ice cubes, acrylic slabs on which to roll out the dough. But really, the secret to good pie crust is all in the hands, and not something any cookbook I've ever read has properly conveyed. I guess it must be possible to make good pie crust without having had a mother who makes good pie crust, whose mother before her made good pie crust. It's just a little hard to picture.

I use one of my mother's rolling pins when I make a pie, and a 1940s Pyrex dish of a weight and design she has always claimed superior to modern equivalents, and a wooden-handled pastry blender meant to duplicate hers. In my mind my mother is inseparably linked with her pies—the smell, the taste, the score of little rules she laid out for me long ago, beginning with how she assesses the baking day's climatic conditions, right on through to the unthinkableness of serving a cold pie or failing to have whipped cream or vanilla ice cream on hand to accompany it.

It's sometimes a mixed blessing, this maternal heritage of flaky pie crust and soup from scratch. I remember a day, a few years back, when my friend Kate was up from New York visiting for the weekend, and we sat together on stools at the kitchen table while she sipped a beer and I made pie crust. She took notes, said she'd never been able to bake a decent pie, and when I asked about her mother's cooking (because therein hangs the tale) she laughed, describing a childhood full of cold cuts and canned tuna.

We had spent the earlier part of that day climbing a nearby mountain—she and the man she eventually married, my husband, our daughter and I. There had been a moment, coming back down, when we were sitting in a grove of trees and Kate's boyfriend, Greg, had picked her up, was throwing pine needles in her hair and down her shirt, and the two of them were rolling down the mountain, while I (in that early stage of pregnancy when one looks merely plump) sat watching, bearing a backpack filled with the remains of a seven-course picnic lunch. And our daughter, just three (but linked to me, it sometimes seems, directly through the nerve endings), put her arms around me and started singing "Zip-a-dee-doo-dah" with a faintly forced mirth designed to be contagious.

My friend—aged thirty-one, plenty of love affairs, and no children or pies behind her—swims a mile a day and plays championship tennis. Having had a mother far less domestically defined than my own—one who had positively neglected her children, it often seemed, from my friend's stories—left my friend freer than I, in some ways, to define her self. At that moment, in my kitchen, she seemed to me, suddenly, to be not so much lacking a crucial piece of knowledge about cooking as she was in possession of a precious and enviable ignorance. She wanted to learn how to make pie crust like mine, she said. And I felt hesitant to teach her. Not out of any proprietary sense about my pie crust, only a reluctance to see such a free spirit with a ten-pound bag of flour on her shelf.

It should be possible, of course, to know how to make good pies without necessarily having to produce them. But in my case, at least, the one goes with the other. My domestic training brought with it a certain bondage to domesticity. If my mother is, in some sense, defined for me by her pies, well, so am I (not to my husband or my friends, only to myself) too much defined by what comes out of my oven. I can't even say I'd choose another woman's life over my own: The truth is, I like and feel at home in kitchens, I enjoy stitching doll clothes and sewing colored plastic animal buttons on children's cardigans—and certainly I love to cook. What I don't like is the sense I have, sometimes, that this was not so much a course I chose as the route laid out for me from earliest childhood, and one I have to alert myself to avoid laying out for my daughter. We spend some of our happiest times baking together. She has her own cookie cutters and a scaled-down pie pan and rolling pin, and already she knows some things about pie crust a person won't find in *The Joy of Cooking*. She has heard my running commentary on the process often enough that she can, and does, instruct her brother.

The danger comes when a person invests too much of her identity in her pie crust (or her sewing, or, I suppose, her backhand), so that without those performances, at the stove or on the tennis court, she ceases to exist. I'm getting better, but it's hard for me, still, to put a simple meal on the table for friends, or (as my husband regularly urges me) to buy a

birthday cake or simply cut up a pineapple for dessert—
which would allow me to spend more time swimming and
rolling down mountainsides, for sure.

I have another friend, Betty, whose mother died when she
was very young, and her father not long after that—leaving
her, at around age ten, an orphan whose real life resembled
pretty closely the orphan dramas I loved to act out with my
dolls when I was that age. Foster homes, brothers and sisters
wrenched apart, cardboard suitcases, a pair of socks for
Christmas, and birthdays passing altogether unnoticed. No
steaming pies on the tables of her childhood, no mother
brushing floury hands on her apron. My friend asks me,
now, how it is that I make that good pie crust, and I say I'll
show her.

What Betty had to do was piece together, from a hundred
different women, and men too, a thousand little ways of doing things: which direction you put the toilet paper on the
roll (the loose sheet in, or out); how you thread a needle,
treat a burn; the rhymes you recite as you bounce a baby on
your knee. I learned them all in a single kitchen, on one lap,
at one woman's side. Sometimes, as a result, her stamp upon
me seems so indelible it's hard to be as separate and new a
person as I'd like. And still I teach my children the recipe for
pie crust I learned twenty-five years ago, and my mother
twenty-five years before that: 2 cups of flour to 1 teaspoon of
salt, ⅔ cup shortening, ice water strictly by the feel of
things. And that's not the half of it.

□

My father was many things in his life. The youngest son
of strict British missionaries, born in India, raised to believe
the Bible was the one book worth reading. He was an artist.
(And to his missionary parents that constituted a sin.) He
was a radio announcer who courted my mother by reading

poetry to her over the airwaves of Canada. After my parents marrried—and he had a family to support—he was a teacher who painted only on weekends and late at night, in our attic. He was fifty-one years old when I was born—a man who'd always claimed he never wanted children. He loved us with fierce, proud, and utter devotion.

My father was a lover of the outdoors who took my sister and me hiking and sketching nearly every weekend of our childhood, and always (to our mortification) carried a walking stick, in the best British tradition. He would sometimes raise his stick and point it dramatically at some bird or cloud formation, commanding us to freeze and observe. "I see it," I would say, impatient. No, really look, he would tell me. And there we would stand, for whole minutes at a time, until he put down his stick and we could move on.

One day, walking across a field full of cows, I was attacked by a bull (or maybe just a large cow), and my father beat that cow so hard his stick broke. I have always remembered that day, not only because it was so scary (the animal looming over me with its hot breath and its swatting tail), but because that was just about the only time I can remember when I felt as if it was my father who took care of me, and not the other way around.

My father was an alcoholic. The word was never spoken in our house in all the years of my growing up. (Other words we avoided: Liquor. Drunk. Vodka.) We lived with the myth of my father's delicate digestion, his artistic temperament, his tendency toward moodiness. If my father was tilted on his axis, it was our job (my mother's, my sister's and mine) to shift the rest of the universe so everything appeared to be in place. Enormous as that task was, it seemed more possible than changing him.

Now I know that's a classic pattern in alcoholic families. Back then, I didn't believe there were any other families in the world like mine. I spent hour after hour, watching reruns of *Father Knows Best* and *Leave It to Beaver*, confessing in my diary how much I wished I had a father like the ones I saw on TV. Someone who'd sit in a La-Z-Boy rocker and wear aftershave, instead of careening across our living room floor, conducting a scratched record of Mozart horn concertos in the middle of the night.

My father was my terrible secret. And it wasn't just the midnight telephone calls he used to make or wild drives down the wrong lane of Main Street, or the unpredictable tirades against unsuspecting boyfriends or repairmen. My other, and much worse, secret (I believed) was that I had failed. I couldn't make my father happy. If I could only be good enough, smart enough, funny enough, kind enough, he wouldn't go up to our attic and take out the vodka. It was up to us, to me, to save him. And we—I—just couldn't do it.

My father's drinking shaped my view of him in all sorts of ways, of course. I knew I couldn't count on him. I worried about him all the time. And I knew he would embarrass me. (Calling up my English teacher to rail at the mediocre poem she'd assigned us to study. Asking my sixteen-year-old boyfriend to give him a definition of Beauty.) The one thing I never did was to stop loving him. You don't blame an alcoholic for getting drunk any more than you blame a pneumonia sufferer for running a fever. The blame is all with the doctor, who cannot make him well.

So the more my father floundered, the more I rescued, and the more I rescued, the more he floundered. And always, always, always, I worried about him, and always I held out the hope (like the King and Queen, parents of the infant Sleeping Beauty, burning every spinning wheel in the kingdom to keep her from pricking her finger) that if I could just get rid of every bottle, hide every pair of car keys, take him on enough walks, he wouldn't drink any more. I might just as well have tried to hold back the tide.

When I was nineteen, and safely gone from home, my

mother gave up and ended what all the rest of us had always imagined to be a marriage that would last (however unhappily) forever. A wife can divorce a husband, after all. Even if a child can't divorce a parent.

There came a point, though, when I stopped trying to rescue my father—not because he was getting better, but because things looked so bad that there seemed no hope at all. I thought there was nothing more I could do to save him. He was seventy-five years old. He had no home, no money. His health was failing fast, and I thought he would die soon.

Instead, he got himself to Alcoholics Anonymous, and he got sober. He packed up the paints and paintings he'd put aside more than forty years earlier and headed back to Canada, where he'd lived as a young man. He lived five good years there, before a painting trip to Alaska laid him up with pneumonia that locked his joints, made it impossible for him to paint, and sent him off into one last, self-destructive round of vodka drinking, from which he never recovered. Nine months pregnant with my second child, I got a middle-of-the-night phone call, telling me my father was dying. I felt violently ill then and began to shake and lay down on our bed and didn't know, until the moment Charlie's head appeared, that it wasn't simply my father's death my body was registering after all. I had grown so used to thinking of my father as my chief source of pain. Lo and behold, this time it was my son. (Who came out, not dark like my daughter and me, but blond-haired and blue-eyed, like his grandfather.)

My father's death, and my son's birth, freed me, I think, to look at the man without guilt, or frustration, or embarrassment, or regret over all he never could give me. I think of my father very often, of course: sometimes when I hear a particular bird call, or catch sight of an interesting cloud formation, sometimes when I spot a field of cows. I hear him quoting me poetry or a line from the Bible, or instructing me on the correct cultivation of tomato plants. I hear him railing at mediocre art, immoral politics, and the way you can never find Scotch tape, when you need it. I think with regret of my loneliness, all those years not knowing the world was filled with alcoholic parents, and their children trying desperately to save them. And I grieve over how great his misery must have been—loving us, and knowing what his drinking cost us, and having to go out and buy another bottle anyway.

But I no longer wish I'd had a different father, because if I had, I would be a different person myself. And I no longer wish I'd been a different daughter (one who might have been able to stop the drinking), because I no longer believe such a daughter could have existed. I couldn't keep him from drinking. He couldn't keep me from loving him anyway. And no family should keep the truth from one another.

☐

I've known only two homes in my life: the one I live in now, with my husband and children, and another one, just sixty miles from here, where I grew up. My father's dead now, and even before that, my parents were divorced and my mother moved away from our old house. But though she rents the house out nine months of the year and hasn't spent a winter there for thirteen years, she hasn't sold our old house yet. It's still filled with our old belongings from our old life. And though my mother has another house now, and a good life, with another man, in a new place, she still comes back to the old house for a couple of months every summer. Every year I ask her, "Have you considered putting the house on the market?" And every summer the answer is "not yet."

My children call the place where I grew up the yellow door house. They love the place, with its big, overgrown yard, the old goldfish pond, the brick walkway, the white picket fence. On the front door there's a heavy brass knocker my sons like to bang on to announce their arrival for visits with their grandmother, and French windows on either side that I was always cautioned against breaking as a child. (As now I caution my children.) There's a brass mail slot I used to pass messages through to a friend waiting on the other side. Now my daughter Audrey does the same.

It's a big house, a hip-roofed colonial, with ceilings higher than anybody needs, and a sweeping staircase rising up from the front hall, with a banister that children more adventurous than my sister and I (mine, for instance) are always tempted to slide on. There are plants everywhere, paintings my father made, Mexican pottery, and a band of tin Mexican soldiers—one on horseback, one playing the flute, one the tuba. We bought those soldiers on the first trip I ever made to New York City. They cost way too much, but my mother said we could get them if we took the bus home instead of flying. So we did.

One room of the yellow door house is wood paneled and lined with books. There used to be a big overstuffed armchair in it that I'd settle into with my cookies and milk, when I came home from school, to do my homework or watch *Leave It to Beaver*. (That chair is in my house now.) There's a porch with a swing out back, and a sunny corner in the kitchen where I always ate my toast—grilled in the oven, sometimes with cinnamon sugar and sometimes jam, but always the way my mother made it, buttered on both sides. My mother is a wonderful, natural cook, who would announce, on a typical night, three different dessert possibilities, all homemade. Now I wouldn't think of eating a third piece of blueberry pie. But the old habits return when I walk into my mother's kitchen. The first thing I do is go see what's in the refrigerator.

It's been fourteen yars since I lived in the yellow door house, but I could still make my way around it blindfolded. There are places where the house could use some work now, and my mother never was the best housekeeper. I open a drawer in the big Welsh dresser in the dining room, looking for a safety pin, and so much spills out (though not safety pins) that I can't close it again. A person can choose from five different kinds of cookies in this house. There's a whole closetful of fabric scraps and antique lace. Eight teapots. But no yardstick, no light bulbs, no scissors.

My children's favorite place in the house is the attic. The front half used to be the studio where my father painted, at night, when he came home from his job as an English teacher. The paintings and paints are long gone now; but my father was a lover of art supplies and hopelessly extravagant when it came to acquiring them, so every once in a while, even now, thirteen years since he's been here, I'll come upon a box of unopened pastels, or watercolor pencils, or the kind of art gum eraser he always used. I'll pick up a stub of an oil pastel and hold it up to my nose, and a wave of feeling will wash over me that almost makes my knees weak. Cadmium yellow light. Cerulean blue. Suddenly I'm ten years old again, sitting on the grass in a field a couple of miles down the road from here, with a sketch pad on my lap and my father beside me, drawing a picture of Ski Jump Hill.

Beyond the room that was my father's studio is the part of our attic where my mother—a hoarder, like me—has stored away just about every toy we ever owned, and most of our old dresses. A ripped Chinese umbrella, a broken wicker rocker, a hooked rug she started and never finished, an exercise roller, purchased around 1947, meant to undo the damage of all those blueberry pies. Songs I wrote when I was nine. My sister's poems. My mother's notes from college English class. My father's powerfully moving proclamations of love to her, written when she was eighteen and he was thirty-eight, when she was telling him she couldn't marry him and he was telling her she must.

Every time we come to the yellow door house to visit,

Audrey and Charlie head for the attic—and though we have
mostly cleaned out my old Barbies now (and a Midge doll,
whose turned-up nose had been partly nibbled off by mice),
we never seem to reach the end of the treasures: My homemade dollhouse furniture (I packed it away, room by room,
with notes enclosed, to the daughter I knew I would someday have, describing how I'd laid out the rooms.) An old
wooden recorder. A brass doll bed. Wonderfully detailed
doll clothes my mother made for us every Christmas (at the
time, I longed for store bought). One year she knit a sweater,
for a two-inch-tall bear, using toothpicks for knitting needles. Another year she sewed us matching skirts from an old
patchwork quilt.

The little town where I grew up (and where I used to
know just about everyone) has been growing so fast that my
mother hardly knows anyone on our street anymore. A
house like hers has become so desirable that within days of
her arrival this summer, my mother got a call from a realtor
asking if she'd be interested in selling. He named as a likely
asking price a figure neither one of us could believe. My parents bought the house, thirty years ago, for a fifth of that
amount, and still, they sometimes had to take out loans to
meet the mortgage payments.

For years now, I have been telling my mother that it
makes little sense to hold on to the yellow door house (and to
worry about tenants, make repairs, put away the Mexican
tin soldiers every Labor Day and take them out again every
Fourth of July). But I suddenly realized, hearing about this
realtor's call, that when the day comes, that my mother sells
the house, I will be deeply shaken. I doubt if I will even
want to drive down our old street after that, or even come
back to the town, where I scarcely know anybody anymore.
I don't much want to see some other family inventing new
games, new rituals, in our house. Don't want to know where
they put their Christmas tree, or what sort of paintings they

hang on their walls. It would be crazy—impossible—to pack up and haul away all those dress-up clothes and bits of costume jewelry and boxes of old book reports and crumbs of pastels. But neither do I relish the thought of someday having to throw them out.

My mother's yellow door house is a perfect place to play hide-and-seek, and last weekend, when I was there visiting with my three children, that's what my two sons and I did. I found a hiding place in the wood-paneled room, behind the couch. I scrunched myself up so small that several minutes passed without my sons' finding me, even though they passed through the room more than once.

Many families have rented the house since my mother ceased to make it her full-time home, but the smell—I realized—hasn't changed. Listening to my children's voices calling out to me through the rooms, I studied a particular knothole in the paneling, and it came back to me that this knothole had always reminded me of an owl. I ran my finger over the wood floors and the upholstery on the side of the couch, and noted the dust my mother has always tended to leave in corners. I heard the sewing machine whirring up-stairs: my mother, sewing doll clothes with Audrey. I smelled my mother's soup on the stove. And for a moment, I wanted time to freeze.

But then I let myself make a small noise. "We found you, we found you," my boys sang out, falling into my arms. And then we all had lunch, with my mother's chocolate chip cookies for dessert—and headed back to the house I live in now. Whose door is green.

———

OTHER
CALLINGS

- □ *Babysitter Problems*
- □ *Tuning in to Ozzie and Harriet*
- □ *Getting Off the Plane*
- □ *Death of the Full-Time Mother*
- □ *Mother of Nine*

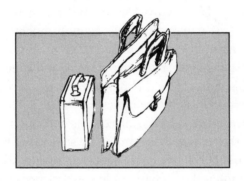

We were having babysitter problems—again. Our sitter had quit, I was spending my days placing ads in the Help Wanted columns and interviewing replacements. As many as four women a day were taking a tour of our house and our life. Every one had to hold Willy, play blocks with Charlie, meet Audrey's dolls, inspect the changing table, take a look at our bathroom. Dinnertimes I quizzed the children: What did they think of Liz? Bonnie? How did they like Roxanne? How did the walk with Susan go? We were all exhausted— not just physically, though there was that too. (For every visit, the house had to be neat, the children clean and rested.) It was the emotional weight of projecting so many different strangers into our life that was hardest, though—

the weight of making such an important decision, knowing
what a wrong choice would cost us: namely, another period
in our lives like the one we were presently going through.

I wonder all the time whether it's worth the struggle.
Every morning I wake up having to assess the situation
anew, asking myself (based on the current day's information)
whether it makes sense to have three children and not spend
one's days being their full-time mother. Why—given how
much time and energy I go through in searching for a suit-
able replacement for me—I don't simply fill the job myself
and be done with it. There are many days when I feel like
throwing in the towel.

Of course I know why I work. Beginning with the fact
that I have to, if we're to have enough money. "Enough"
meaning—naturally—the amount we've become accustomed to having since I've been working full time. You earn
more, you spend more. Then you have to keep earning. I
know that much about economics, anyway.

There are other reasons, of course, and one is the work
itself, and the way it allows me to be something besides my
children's mother. I love being a mother, admire women who
can do that job full time without losing patience or spirit, but
I'm also a little frightened of what uninterrupted, all-day
seven-day-a-week motherhood of our three children would
be like for me after so many years of another kind of life. I
wonder whether—without my quiet, solitary cup of morning coffee at my desk, and the moments I give myself, sometimes, to just put on a record and look out the window;
without the chance for a quiet adult conversation, and unbroken reading, and unbroken thought—I might become so
frayed I'd unravel.

A whole day of painting with my children, playing cars,
making boats, dressing dolls, reading out loud, taking
walks—there'd be no problem with that. It's all the things in
between: wiping off the counters, sponging up the juice,

folding the laundry, picking up the blocks, tying the shoes, wiping the counters again, never doing any one task longer than the time it takes for a two-year-old to lose interest in his ball and need help finding his truck.

There's a rhythm mothers—successful mothers, anyway —get into. The pace is slower. You might move pretty fast (you'll do plenty of running), but you never get anywhere fast. You have to be prepared to stop and study a caterpillar for five minutes, or hop up three times in the middle of a conversation to pour juice. Walks are seldom taken in straight lines. Children move as if they had all the time in the world—and the best full-time mothers I know act that way too.

While a mother with another job besides mothering—if she's to survive—has to be forever rushing. And switching gears, going from child-pace to work-pace and back again. Never wholly in either one place or the other. Always knocking herself out to give her children what they need, to make up for her absences. Dealing with childhood illnesses, middle-of-the-day crises. And then, on top of everything, coping with the periodic and recurrent problem of child care; filling the unfillable job of part-time mother, when a good part of her longs to be doing it herself.

I've been sitting here close to an hour, trying to figure out whether it makes sense trying to do what I attempt, and I have no answer. I do believe some women can manage to work outside their homes and raise children, and do both well. But never without a struggle.

I keep looking for an absolute solution myself: the perfect babysitter. The right ages of children. The right type of work, the right work schedule. Women keep lobbying for better day care, longer maternity leaves (and paternity leaves), child care on the job, more flexible hours—and those are all good things. But as for ultimate solutions, I don't believe, anymore, that they exist. It should be a struggle to

leave one's children. It should be hard to give them everything they need, because they need a lot. Eventually, I know
I will find and hire a new babysitter. (A woman who will be
willing to perform a job I can't imagine taking on: caring,
forty hours a week, for somebody else's children. Taking on
the kind of responsibility that I myself am able to shoulder
for one reason only: because these children are mine.) And
still I know I'll be filled with reservations about the whole
thing and with a sense of compromise. She will buy the
wrong kind of apples. She'll chew gum. She will mix the
Legos in with the Bristle Blocks. When of course the real
problem will simply be, as it always is, she's not me.

□

We rented a video of *Ozzie and Harriet* the other night.
Two episodes, from back around 1960, complete with commercials for Pepto-Bismol and Aunt Jemima Pancake Mix. I
would've been eight the first time I saw those shows. That's
how old my daughter is now.

So there they were: the Nelson family. A family, not just
on television, but in real life too. (Knowing that added an
odd dimension to the show. Contributed to the notion that
television can be like life, and life can be like television. Not
that mine, back in 1960, bore much resemblance.) You never
knew what sort of job Ozzie had. (Did they maybe sometimes refer to his being a bandleader, or am I getting television confused with life again?) As for Harriet, you didn't
have to ask her about her career aspirations. She was Mom,
and Honey (as in, "Honey, I'm home"). She must've had
those aprons permanently stitched onto her dresses. She was
always sponging off her kitchen counters, even though they
were spotless to begin with. Always pouring coffee. Passing
out the Aunt Jemima pancakes. Nobody in that family
needed Pepto-Bismol, you could just tell.

The first show we watched was about a fishing trip Ozzie and his friend and next-door neighbor, Thorny, are planning to take up to Rainbow Lake. Then they lock themselves out of their houses with their pajamas on. (Is this why I'm always trying to talk my husband, who favors T-shirts and shorts for nightwear, into checked flannel PJs? Is it Ozzie Nelson I've been after all this time?)

Anyway, the two men end up falling asleep in the Nelsons' station wagon. Harriet and the boys, David and Ricky, wake up, imagining that Dad must be reeling in trout by now. Harriet (whose hair looks about as messy as Nancy Reagan's) announces she's getting her hair done and drives off to the beauty parlor with Oz and Thorny still asleep in the back. The men wake up in the parked car and skulk around Main Street, trying to call someone to come pick them up. Harriet drives off in the station wagon. They're stranded in their PJs.

It was all pretty amusing stuff—though I guess I'd have to say Steve and I enjoyed the shows somewhat more than our kids did. "Didn't you have anything else besides Pepto-Dismo, back in the olden days?" said Charlie, after the fourth commercial. Sure we did, I say. There was Alka-Seltzer.

I'm trying hard to remember what else we had back then. Looking at the words flash across the screen, knowing I must have seen all this before. Trying to put myself back into the head of the little girl who used to sit there on the green TV-watching chair, eating Fritos, taking it all in.

Even in 1960, the life of the Nelson family (and all those other television families whose escapades I followed every week) seemed pretty far removed from my own. Pretty far, too, from the life I lead now (the life—I remind myself—that I have chosen). Because in addition to being Mom and Honey, what I am, frequently, is Gone. Sitting at my desk, trying hard to put my children and home out of my mind and attend to my work. If they made a TV show of our life, it would have to feature our babysitter, Vicky, as a key character. A typical line at the breakfast table—delivered almost every day by my son—would be, "Is it a Mommy day or a Vicky day?"

I do believe I am a good mother to my children—though not the same kind of good mother Harriet Nelson was. I'm definitely more concerned with personal fulfillment than Harriet ever seemed to be: which doesn't mean I'm more fulfilled, only (often) more frustrated. I want the kitchen table and the children gathered round, but I also want important conversations to be taking place there. I want my husband to tell me what he's feeling, I want to tell him what I'm feeling. As for the feelings themselves: I take a reading on my emotional well-being at least as often as Harriet used to get her hair done—though my head is seldom as well under control as hers. I want to grow old with my husband; I want passion and romance. I want to have babies; I want to write books. I want my home to be a safe haven for my husband and children; then again, I want to go trekking in Nepal.

I'm no fool. I know it's not all possible. Left to choose, I do, consistently, opt for family well-being over complete and utter personal gratification. I mean to say only that I suspect I feel the pull more keenly than wives and mothers did in 1960, when options were more limited, possibilities fewer. Of course, times have improved. I keep in mind the fact that right about the same time that Harriet Nelson was probably taking yet another batch of rolls out of her oven, Sylvia Plath—a wife and a mother and a poet too—was sticking her head into hers. Today, maybe, it would be a little easier for a woman like that to follow a different path.

Steve and I won't ever pull off an Ozzie and Harriet routine. Naturally, we'd both say, we're after something different. There are bigger problems than finding yourself downtown with your pajamas on. You won't find me wearing an apron or sitting across the table from Steve talking about the bridge club.

There's no telling, either, what it was really like for the Nelsons after the cameras stopped rolling and the lights were turned out. Maybe Ozzie was tormented by the thought that he was a bandleader and not a symphony conductor. Maybe Harriet really longed to run off with the milkman. Then again, maybe they were all just as happy as they seemed. As for Ricky, we all know he ended up divorced from the beautiful wife he married (on the show and in real life). And died in a plane crash, heading to a singing engagement.

But back in 1960, that life looked good. I may have tuned out the commercials, but I bought the stuff about Mom and Dad and the kids. Getting into scrapes, sure—even fighting sometimes. But being—more than anything else, more than they were themselves, maybe—a family. That first.

"I wish they lived next door to us," says my daughter dreamily, as the credits on the video roll. (My son has already expressed a preference to live on Sesame Street.) And both of those do look like nice places to be.

Now sometimes I think I'd like to be Tina Turner or Margaret Mead. Amelia Earhart. Sarah Bernhardt. Madame Curie. Sometimes I just want to run off to a little cottage in the mountains and write a novel and learn to play the flute.

And then sometimes all I want to be is Harriet Nelson, sponging off her counters, ruffling the tops of her sons' crew-cut heads, giving her husband a peck on the cheek and flipping the pancakes.

□

I was supposed to go to New York City and work. Fly in on a morning commuter plane, put in an eight-hour day at the office of a magazine I sometimes write for, get on another commuter plane, and be home by midnight. That was the plan.

I awoke early. I took my shower, washed my hair. I hunted for panty hose, and made some, finally, by combining the good leg from two different pairs. I put on makeup, earrings, a squirt of my new Christmas perfume. I set out juice for my sleeping children, gave Willy a bottle, compiled a list of instructions and reminders for Steve. Audrey was going to her friend Sage's house. Charlie was having a friend over. We needed to call a babysitter for the weekend, and we were almost out of coffee and paper towels. All of that happened before the sun came up.

Then I assembled my papers. I took out my city boots and arranged a pin over the orange-juice stain on my blouse. Charlie woke up; I changed his diaper, read him *Where the Wild Things Are* and the special issue of *People* magazine devoted exclusively to Michael Jackson. I fixed him his bowl of Cheerios; he wanted strawberries in the bowl, like the ones they show in the photograph on the front of the Cheerios box. I took some strawberries from the freezer.

Audrey woke up, tousled and bleary. Steve got up, and I ran outside to warm up the car. I ran back into the house to check on the children, discovering Wheat Chex all over the floor and Willy eating dog chow. I gulped down my coffee, stuck my eyeliner pencil in my pocket for some future quiet moment, and raced out the door, calling out the babysitter's phone number.

And then I was alone, driving down our road, just as the sun was coming up. I put a tape of jazz piano into the tape player. I stopped at the foot of our hill to put on my eyeliner. Heading for the highway, I sang.

Forty-five minutes later I was at the airport, buying my ticket. There were two men wearing suits and carrying real leather briefcases; one had a lock, even. There was a woman with a perfect manicure, and a purse coordinated to match her boots. Frequent flyers; the man at the ticket counter knew their names.

We were experiencing a slight delay, he told us. Icy runway conditions, low visibility. He wouldn't know for another half hour whether the plane would be flying.

It was over an hour before they told us we could go and led us out to the ten-seater commuter plane on the runway. I climbed the steps, found my seat, buckled my seat belt, picked up an issue of *Savvy* magazine. The propellers were just starting to spin.

And then I did something I have never done before. I unbuckled my seat belt and called out to the pilot, "Excuse me, I'm getting off."

When I got home, Charlie was still in his sleeper suit and Willy had just overturned another bowl of Wheat Chex. "You're back," said Audrey. Nobody seemed that surprised to see me, standing at the counter again, loading plates into the dishwasher.

I took off my silk blouse. I took off my stockings. I took off my high-heeled boots and put on my slippers.

I know what the people on that plane thought. That I'm afraid of flying. That icy runway, that fog. That comment someone made as we stood outside waiting to board: "Got your parachute?"

The truth is, I'm accustomed to navigating treacherous skies: I am trying to be a mother and a career woman, both in the same one lifetime, and it's probably the hardest thing I'll ever do. I don't want to suggest, for a moment, that women who have young children can't handle a career or that they'll end up doing their jobs less well than undistracted men. Only that it's hard, finding the babysitter, keeping up with the laundry, baking at midnight, getting up at dawn. It's hard scheduling dentists' appointments and car inspections and immunizations. It's hard, when there are three little mouths all asking for three different brands of

cereal, catching what that other adult, halfway across the
kitchen table, has to say, and hard having something to say to
him besides "Can you take the compost out?"

It's hard to walk out the door, when there's a two-year-old
boy standing there behind you, stretching out his arms and
saying, "I want you." But the hardest part comes after.

Out the door, down the road, on the plane. You've made
your escape, and now you can open your briefcase, plug in
your computer, make your summation to the jury. Buckle
your seatbelt and soar . . .

Only all you can think of is their faces. Did you remember
to set out his Masters of the Universe training pants? Are we
out of peanut butter? Does she know one of her winter boots
is underneath the living-room couch, with a dinosaur stuck
inside?

□

"When you were growing up," I asked Steve the other
day, "how many of your friends' mothers worked?" At jobs
outside the home, I was careful to add, as always, knowing
all the things a stay-at-home mother does, that make the life
of a woman sitting at a desk seem pretty uncomplicated by
comparison.

He thought a moment. His own mother never held a job,
until her four children were in high school and college. She
is one of those women (that dying breed) who made running
a home her art. More than once, over the years, I've heard
my mother-in-law say, "I loved being a housewife. Those
were the best years of my life." Since then she has returned
to school, worked as a librarian, run her own bookstore. But
the job she loved best was (what I have never really been)
full-time mother. At the executive level, and irreplaceable.

Back to my question. As I said, Steve had to think about it
for a while. Finally he gave up. He couldn't think of a single

mother he had known, in those years from the early fifties to the mid-sixties, when he grew up, who'd held a full-time job. Of course, he'd lived in a pretty middle-class suburb. But try finding a community anywhere, today, without one employed mother.

Well, my mother held jobs when I was growing up, but I remember what an oddity that was, how torn she felt, and how unfair it seemed to me. There were no day-care centers or after-school programs back then. And somehow my mother always managed to make pies and keep our cookie tin filled, to sew dresses for us and our dolls, in spite of her jobs. There was no model, yet, of that other sort of mother who's become pretty commonplace today—the one who comes home, at six, with a pizza or a box of fried chicken. The one who serves cookies from a package that says Almost Home.

Now, among the mothers of my daughter's classmates at school, nearly every one holds down a job. I know, because Audrey's teacher has told me how hard it is, these days, to find a mother who's able to help out with the class field trips or type up the children's stories or volunteer to make cupcakes. When the first grade held their Pilgrim banquet, half the mothers signed up to supply juice and no one came forward with home-baked cornbread. As for me, I sent paper cups.

There are still a handful of these other mothers in our town, and because there are so few of them now, they're in big demand. I know all their names, because they're always the ones at the Friends of the School meetings and the fundraising yard sales. Sometimes their children come over to play, and they wear hand-knit sweaters, or a home-sewn dress identical to the one on their Cabbage Patch doll. I hear little things about them: They have ruffled curtains in their rooms, to match the bedspread. Their houses have windowboxes filled with pansies. Their socks match. They wear their hair in French braids. The stockings they hang on the mantle at Christmas feature their names embroidered on the toe. While around here we're always scrambling. The dress Audrey needs got washed but not dried, or dried but not sorted. Charlie's sneakers are too tight, but we haven't got around to buying new ones. There are items in the back of my refrigerator that are so far gone they could bypass the compost pile and go directly into the garden.

Of course I know about the other side of it: the boredom and isolation many of those women felt, back in the days my husband remembers so fondly, when the children came home from school to find their mothers waiting with the milk and cookies. I know about the Feminine Mystique, and the importance of financial independence from husbands, and the crisis that can occur, for women who have spent fifteen or twenty years feathering a nest, when that nest becomes empty. I know how lucky I am to have all sorts of freedoms my mother's generation missed.

But I inhabit a state of perpetual ambivalence too: part homemaker, part career person. Not as ambitious or successful as lots of childless women I know in New York City. Not as free as my children would like, either, to be there with the chocolate chip cookies when they come home from school ready to play Old Maid. Of course these days they show working mothers on television, but there is nobody I see on the screen whose life looks remotely like mine. There is no name for what I do. With one foot in the door and one foot out, I often feel wistful, looking at the lives of women who know precisely where they stand.

□

Ten years ago, when I was single and living in a studio apartment on the East Side of Manhattan—wearing silk blouses to work and picking up my dinners from a gourmet shop around the corner—I bought myself a pair of couches covered in Haitian cotton. Nine years ago, when I met Steve, those couches were among the few possessions we moved with us to New Hampshire, where we live now, and where I never put on a silk blouse or buy dinner at gourmet shops. And the truth is, the white couches, with their hard, streamlined edges, always did look a little out of place in our house.

But over the years the couches got beat up enough to fit in a little better. The Haitian cotton ripped, Charlie built forts with the pillows, Audrey took to practicing her gymnastics routine on the sofa back, and balancing her cereal bowl on a sofa arm, while she watched her cartoons. An extended family of mice set up residence inside the hide-a-bed a couple of years back (Steve and I would be sitting on the couch sometimes, after the children were in bed, and I'd say, "Do you hear something?" and he'd say, "It's just my stomach rumbling." But in the end, it turned out to be a whole mouse city, coming out among the increasingly unsprung springs. They had pulled out the cotton batting, stored acorns under the seats, and gnawed on the strings of loose threads of the Haitian cotton. Which, as you might guess, was no longer even close to being white).

So this fall we finally decided to get some slipcovers. Steve—who had the kind of mother who would have taken it upon herself to make them—commented that it might make a wonderful fall project for me, sewing those slipcovers. I said no thanks and started asking around for the name of someone who'd make them.

This morning she showed up. Her name is Peg. She's a small, trim woman in her early fifties. She was at our door at seven-thirty sharp.

But because I was still pretty busy getting the children out the door to preschool and second grade, getting the lunch boxes packed, the library books gathered up, I had to ask Peg to wait a minute. There was just too much going on, it seemed, even to run upstairs for my bolt of fabric.

Then finally the children were gone, and I spread out the material while Peg got her scissors. "I'm sorry," I said. "It's pretty hectic around here in the mornings. Getting three children dresssed and out the door . . ."

"I know," she said. "I had nine."

I thought about that for a moment, then asked their ages. She put down the box of straight pins so she could use her fingers to count.

"There's Alice, she's—let's see—thirty-one. Mary. She's thirty. Bob, twenty-nine. Douglas—no, not Douglas. Roger, twenty-eight. *Then* Douglas. Then Noreen . . ." It went pretty much like that (with a few more years between the last couple of children), all the way down to Joseph, who was seventeen and just finishing up his senior year in high school.

"Caring for all those children was no big deal," Peg said. "Everybody pitched in, and everyone behaved, because they just had to." When it was time to bathe the baby, the others would all gather around, and it would be "go get the powder" to this one and "go get the diaper" to that one. Every night Peg made a list of everybody's jobs for the next day. "Every one of my children knows how to cook, clean, do laundry, and sew," said Peg, scrambling around my living room floor, cutting fabric and drawing chalk lines as she spoke, while I stood there, feeling awkward and guilty at having nothing but a cup of coffee in my hands. Still, I wanted badly to talk to this woman. "Forget about the slipcovers," I wanted to say. "Just sit down and tell me how you did it."

She made all her children's clothes, of course—usually out of her husband's worn-out shirts and pants (because the sleeves went first, and that left lots of good fabric in the middle). It would be nothing for her to put up two hundred quarts of beans, she said. Every day she baked bread. Every night they ate meat—casseroles mostly. Plus, her husband did a lot of hunting.

For Christmas there'd be doll beds made out of old oatmeal boxes, and knitted yarn balls, and necklaces of old wooden spools, painted in bright colors. "You should see our house at the holidays," she said. "My supper table seats twenty-two. But sometimes we'll feed up to thirty-five people in my dining room."

What about when she went places, I asked her.

"Well," she said, "except for grocery shopping and church, mostly we stayed home. We raked leaves and jumped in them in the fall. We made snow angels and snow forts in winter. My kids had a two-story tree house. They always had each other. What else did they need?"

Peg was pinning fabric together on my couch as she spoke. She never stopped moving. I told her she made it look easy. "This is nothing," she said.

But surely she didn't sew slipcovers when the children were small, I asked (I who can't get a page of a newspaper read until after all three children are in bed). "Of course I did," said Peg. "Even with my husband working two shifts, we needed the money. The children always knew just how to entertain themselves. Anytime they were idle, I'd just tell them to pick up my washcloth and start scrubbing something."

Weren't there times, I asked her, when it was all just crazy? Out of control? Times you just wanted to throw up your arms and scream?

Peg looked at me, thought for a moment, took the pins out of her mouth, and shook her head. "No," she said. "I can't say there were."

"I don't know how you did it," I told her.

"Maybe you don't have enough kids," she suggested. "When there's only three there might be too much leeway. These women who only have one now—I don't know how they do it."

"Of course," she said, "you young girls are different, and I'm not criticizing. You've got your own needs. You want to go jogging. Want to go out at night. Me, I never knew anyone, besides my husband and my kids. I hardly even knew who was president. My children were everything: my career, my friends, my exercise program, my hobby. I guess I was sort of a child myself: down on my hands and knees half the day, playing with them. Your mind goes a little funny. But I'll tell you, I had fun."

I asked Peg what the hardest times were, raising her nine children. One, she said, was when her oldest daughter left home to go to nursing school thirty miles away. "I cried and cried to lose her," she said.

Then she told me this story:

She only gave birth to seven children. But one day a neighbor called, asking if Peg would watch a friend's two babies (a girl and a boy, both under two). Just for a few hours. Peg said no problem, which was true. Two more babies fit in just fine.

A few hours later the neighbor called again, asking whether Peg could keep the babies overnight. Once again Peg said no problem. The mother didn't come the next day, or the day after that. After a few months Peg had the children baptized. After five years she and her husband decided they'd better file papers to adopt the kids. That's when the mother finally showed up, and took the boy and girl away.

Did she ever see them again?

Not until Roxanne's funeral. The girl was eighteen years old. Running with a bad crowd. Killed in a car accident. The boy was deeply into drugs too.

So now she has just seven children. Plus one of her sons is divorced; the ex-wife doesn't have anything to do with their three-year-old daughter, and the son has to work all the time. So the little girl lives with Peg and her husband. She keeps Peg company, drawing or looking at books beside her, while she sews or scrubs the appliances.

This morning now, Peg got up at three o'clock to finish up a set of slipcovers for a customer. Then she made blueberry muffins. Then she did a load of wash and hung it up to dry. Then she got her granddaughter up and fed her breakfast. Then she mixed up a batch of bread dough and set it out to rise. By the time she got home, she told me (picking up the last of her pins, packing to go), she figured it would be about ready to pop into the oven.

I told her I was a writer. I explained to her that now I would be leaving my house, too, leaving my littlest son with Vicky, our babysitter, and heading out to my office, to sit at my typewriter all day. I asked if she'd mind my writing about her.

"Why would you want to do that?" she said. "There's nothing special or interesting about me. I just did what I knew. Fed my children, loved them, kept them busy. Made sure they said their prayers every night. That's all I ever wanted."

But just before she left, Peg noticed the old pink piano we got recently from my friend Ursula. She sat down at the keyboard. "Do you play?" I asked her. "No," she said. "Not really. Not for forty years." But suddenly she was playing a tune with both hands, not badly at all. From memory.

"It's good I don't have one of these around my house," she said a few minutes later, closing the piano firmly. "I'd spend all my time playing it. But it sure would've been nice to have, for the children. Your little girl must love it."

I didn't tell her that as a matter of fact, the one who's taking the beginning piano lessons in this family is me. I just shook her hand, circled the date on the calendar when the slipcovers would be ready. Headed out to my office, and looked out my window at Vicky, pushing Willy on the swings.

———

BABY LOVE

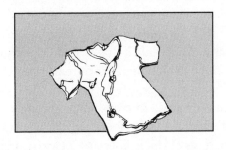

Of course life with young children has its surprises. (Sometimes it's the child himself who is the surprise.) But our days around here are probably more defined by repetition. If I have read *Scat Scat Cat* once, I bet I've read it five hundred times. I've sung "Hush, little baby, don't say a word" nearly every night for the last eight years. Made ten thousand peanut butter sandwiches. Kissed five million places where it hurt.

There's no denying some of the tasks of parenthood are simply tedious. But in fact I guess I also love and need the familiarity of the territory. (At best, we have rituals. At worst, ruts.) I love ending my day with a tour of my sleeping children in their beds. Setting out the cereal bowls for morning. I even like folding my sons' pajamas, still warm from the dryer. I know by heart the *Joy of Cooking* recipe for blueberry muffins and the names of all seven dwarfs and eight reindeer. I guess they add up to a kind of household rosary, and I can't imagine ever forgetting any of it, though women older than I assure me I will.

So much of life remains uncertain. But I always know the punch line to Charlie's one joke. (What kind of car does Humpty Dumpty drive? A yolkswagen.) I know Audrey will always make a face out of her meatballs, arranged on top of her spaghetti. Willy will always claim his pants are dry. Charlie will always, before settling down to read a book with me, run to get his bear, whose string he likes to twirl in his ear.

For years now, the routine around here has included looking after a baby. And while living with an adolescent may be more emotionally demanding, for pure physical rigor there's nothing to match those first few years with a young child.

Now, even as the end of baby tending comes into view, I find myself feeling not only liberated, but ensnared, looking back as much as I look forward. Partly, perhaps, my wistfulness comes simply from not wanting to see a stage I have loved come to an end. Maybe I'm also scared. (When my children were all very young, my life was clearly laid out. There was not so much room to question what I should be doing. There was little opportunity for experiment and adventure, but also that meant less opportunity for failure.) And partly I am wistful simply because there is not much I like better than holding a baby in my arms.

I have been spending my evenings this past week watching Olympic skaters spin around the ice. In my dreams, and anytime I find myself on a smooth frozen pond with no one watching, I am Tiffany Chin. I hum myself a soundtrack. I rely heavily on hand gestures rather than triple jumps and camels. Because the truth is, I'm not much of a skater—even when I'm not, as I am now, nine months pregnant, with thirty extra pounds and a sore back.

For the first eight and a half months of this third pregnancy of mine I have been carrying on my life pretty much as usual. It's the two children with us already who demand the attention I once gave to childbirth manuals and nursery decoration. Also, I tell myself I know all about babies and having them. When people inquire how I am, I tend to register surprise at the question and then say "How about you?" I have almost forgotten that around March 1 a baby is going to be born here.

But there comes a point—and it's here—when the body and the mind get pretty much overtaken by a pregnancy and every inch is occupied territory. (With even my hair no longer normal, I am advised to hold off getting a permanent.) Three times in the past six years, I've reached that point in a New Hampshire winter. (My son's and daughter's birthdays coincide with the full moons of one February and one March.) And now here I sit once more, staring out a window at nothing but mud and snow, putting off taking the ten steps between my chair and the door, where our dog is scratching to be let out, because the task just seems too tiring. I've spent the last twenty minutes drawing moustaches on the models in the annual *Sports Illustrated* bathing-suit issue. I might as well belong to a separate species from those flat-bellied, golden-skinned women in their silver bikinis.

It's an odd state to be in, this period just before the birth of a baby. The mind empties. I see my true self slipping away, being replaced by a person who behaves, not like me, but like full-term pregnant women everywhere. Unexplainable tears. A ravenous appetite for salt one night and sweet the next. A need—as real as an artist's for paint or a keyboard—to wax the floors and repaint the kitchen. I want to hold not only babies, kittens, puppies, but a nearly full-grown Irish setter. "That letter you wrote had the word tiny in seven places," a friend tells me.

So I bake cookies and stare for half an hour into the tropical-fish tank, watching a cobra-skin guppy circle a plastic model of a scuba diver, who endlessly raises and lowers a piece of plastic buried treasure. I fold laundry and sort old

baby clothes, bury my face in the little T-shirts, remembering the one (my "middle child," "the older brother," people
have already started calling my toddler son) who wore them
last. And I read to Charlie the story of *Babar and His Children*—chronicle of the triple birth, to Queen Celeste, of
baby elephants named Pom, Flora, and Alexander—and try
to explain an illustration that shows Babar watering a flower
and seeing in its center the image of a baby elephant. (Babar
sitting down to read and seeing, on the pages of his book, a
baby elephant. Poised over his royal stationery to write proclamations and producing a drawing of a baby elephant. I
know the feeling.)

The strange part is what follows. That what this is, really,
is the original calm before the storm. That as the full-term
pregnant woman sits, face to the sun, in a calm tidal pool,
staring out to a sea with not a whitecap in sight, suddenly,
she never knows when, there comes a tidal wave. I have
known plenty of women to dread the birth and afterward to
curse the agony they went through. For myself, I look forward to the event with the anticipation of a passionate surfer.
More accurately, with the anticipation of one who never
could surf, or ski, or stay on a skateboard, even. The last one
chosen for every school field hockey and basketball team she
ever played on. Before I had children I always wondered
whether their births would be, for me, like the ultimate in
my gym class failures. And discovered instead that I'd finally found my sport.

My son Charlie was two days overdue the night a call
came from Canada to tell me that my father, in a Victoria
hospital with pneumonia, was not likely to live through to
morning. Not much to be done about it: He couldn't have
heard me if I tried to speak to him, and I wouldn't have
known what to say anyway. I put down the receiver and told
Steve, who had been watching the Boston Celtics play Los
Angeles. Then I felt the sickest I have ever been in my life,

and my legs began to shake so badly that I lay down on the bed and he lay across my shins to steady me. We had seen a baby of ours born, on that same bed, four years before, and still I didn't recognize the symptoms I was feeling as the transition stage of labor. Just to be safe we called the midwife, a forty-minute drive away, suggesting that she come over. But things happened very fast then, and five minutes later I heard a sound in the room, coming from me, that I had heard only one other time in my life—when I pushed our daughter out into the world. Steve felt for the cord around the baby's neck and guided him as he corkscrewed out—our ten-pound boy. The next morning when our daughter came downstairs to find the top of her brother's head sticking out from under the covers of our bed, where he slept between us, what she said was, "My dream came true." And the thing that always strikes me with amazement is how, in a house where there had been three people a few hours earlier, there were now four, although no one had come in the door.

I think of my children's births—carry them around with me—every day of my life. Sometimes it will be just a fleeting image: My friend Stephanie coming into the room, the day our daughter was born, with a bagful of oranges I'd asked her to bring over; seeing them spill out in all directions on the bed. Steve holding out a towel he'd warmed on our woodstove to wrap around a baby who would be born before the towel had time to cool off again. Audrey's thick tuft of black hair that I saw and touched before I even knew the sex of the still unborn person it belonged to. Her hands on her cheeks, like some vaudeville chorus girl pantomiming surprise, as she shot out. The feeling of a newborn baby's skin. Eyes wide open, looking at light for the first time.

One more thing I want to say: If I had been unable to have babies myself, I would have grieved over never having known what it's like to carry a baby, to feel movement inside my own body, and most of all I would have missed, terribly, watching my child born. But the world is full of adoptive parents and people who had their babies before the return of natural childbirth and the acceptance of fathers in the delivery room, and though I have heard some of those men and women speak with regret over having missed out on their children's births, they didn't miss out on their children. As for me, I will never know what it's like to ride on a hang glider or execute a triple toe loop in Sarajevo. I love riding the wave of childbirth—love even how hard it is—and when the moment comes that I know I've done it for the last time, I'll mourn. But birth is an experience and parenthood is a state of being; the one passes, the other never ends.

□

It's happening again: that old baby-longing. And the fact that I already have three children doesn't matter. Doesn't matter that I'm so tired at the end of every day, I haven't stayed awake through the end of a movie in months. Doesn't matter that I have rubber bands on all my cupboard doors to keep Willy out, and that we have to hide the egg cartons in the back of the refrigerator, covered in aluminum foil, now that he's discovered the joys of taking out and breaking eggs, a dozen at a time. It doesn't matter that I also dream of taking off for a weekend alone with Steve, that I long to do a kind of serious, uninterrupted work that's simply not possible for the mothers of young children. It doesn't matter that we can't afford another child—financially, emotionally, or physically. All I know is, last week my friend Alice had a baby, and when I hold her, I want one too.

I guess there are some women around who manage simply to give birth to the number of children that's practical and appropriate for their situation, and then stop, with not a backward glance toward pregnancy, childbirth, and the world of newborn infants. Women who, given the choice between a bottle of Chanel No. 5 or the smell you find on a newborn's head (and nowhere else on earth), would go for the Chanel. As for me, I don't suppose I'll ever reach the stage where the sight of a new baby no longer gives me pangs.

It's irrelevant how many children you have: I could have a dozen, and still, if one of them wasn't a baby, there'd be an empty place in my life, a vacancy. Because having children is not the same—simply not the same—as having an infant.

I'm not the only one I know who's addicted. My friend Rachel—divorced, the mother of three marvelous children—waited three days before heading over to check on Alice's baby. "I had to steel myself," she said. "I knew once I picked her up, I'd never want to put her down."

Then there's my friend Sally, the mother of four children. Two complete generations of them, she has, with two daughters by her first marriage, in their early twenties, and two sons from her second marriage, both in preschool. And still, though she's forty-four now, and though she runs a successful toy store, though her life is full and good, she longed for one more baby. Even after her miscarriage two years ago, she kept hoping. Even after the second miscarriage, she hoped. After the third miscarriage, when her doctor told her it looked as if she was simply too old to carry a fetus to term successfully, she had to try again. She's six months pregnant now. By the time the baby's born she'll be forty-five.

As for me, I've passed on the maternity jumpers, but kept the one pair of stretch-front jeans that always were my favorites. I'm only thirty-two, I remind myself. We could hold off for seven years, and still there'd be time for one more baby before I'm forty. If it isn't going to happen, I'd rather not know now—I'd rather harbor the hope for a few years, anyway, that I haven't met all of my children yet.

You have to quit sometime. There's no such thing as never

having a last baby, it's only a question of when, and which one. Because though the capacity for loving children may be infinite, the capacity for raising them has its limits.

When I was eighteen, I thought everything was possible: thought I could have a wonderful, successful career, an exciting, uninterruptedly romantic marriage, a perfect home, good food on the table every night with flowers from my garden, and six children too. I see it still in young women starting out today: that innocent belief not only in themselves, but in the world, too. Life will be kind. Money will be plentiful. Babies will sleep. In-laws will take the kids for weekends. The sun will shine. Every generation has to learn, all over again—as if for the first time, as if all the others hadn't learned this already—just how hard it all is, and that along with all sorts of good things, every year also brings with it a narrowing of possibilities. Every month there's a child who could have been born, who would've been loved—the one who might've been an artist, might've been a major-league pitcher—and there is simply no way in the world to give birth to every one of them. And even if you did manage to have every potential child, you'd lose something else—which is the time and space to know and savor them. And even if you managed that—to have the children, and to raise them right—there would be other doors closed. Books unread or unwritten. Trips not taken. A husband or a self not sufficiently tended.

"I want to be something else in life besides a dad," says my husband, who is a very good dad, and doesn't ever want to be a less good one. As for me, I rail all the time at the frustrations of taking care of little children. I wish I could swim clear across the lake in summer instead of doing my laps always parallel to shore, where I can keep an eye on my sons. But still, in spite of all that, I hold on to a little hand-knit blue sweater with a yellow duck on the front (size three months) and a pink rabbit-fur-trimmed baby hat, and even when I hand over to my friend Laurie a boxful of Audrey's outgrown dresses, I say (trying to sound casual), "If you get around to it, you might give them back when Leah doesn't need them anymore." I don't want to burn my bridges yet.

□

Today we had one of those mornings when I would have given my three best pairs of salt and pepper shakers (two china bananas, the miniature baseball mitt and ball, the plastic penguins), plus my entire freezer's worth of frozen raspberries, my favorite eight-year-old pink chenille bathrobe, and our last jar full of homemade maple syrup, for a half hour more of sleep.

We stayed up late last night. Came home past midnight, fixed ourselves a snack, had (crazily) a cup of coffee. Got to bed around two A.M. (The staying up part is never what's hard. What's hard comes later.)

Six-fifteen A.M. A yelp from upstairs: Willy. And then a crash (he leaps out of his crib unassisted now, but you wouldn't want to watch). Followed by: a few bars of "Zip-a-dee-doo-dah." "Go-bots. More than meets the eye!" *Thump, thump, thump* on the steps. (He skids down, on his bottom, one riser at a time.) Then the familiar sound of footed pajama bottoms scuffing across the kitchen floor. The refrigerator door opening. (He gets his own bottles now, too.) The bedroom door opening. Little feet rushing across the floor. The sound of a toy chain saw, buzzing in my ear. (Directly overhead, in fact. And to think that last December, Steve and I actually went to five toy stores to locate this item.)

And finally, as he pounces on top of us, the words "I want my breakfast!"

Of course I prolong this stage, of being half awake but still at least prone and under my quilt, as long as possible. Willy brings me a book to read in bed (dumps it on my head, usually), and if I'm lucky it will be one I know so well that I can recite the words without opening more than one eye. At which point he will reach over to the night table for my glasses and put them on my face. Upside down, generally.

In my eight years of rude awakenings, I have developed a few tricks, of course. Feigning sleep is one. Sighing dramatically, then flopping onto my stomach, head under the pillow. Toddlers know how to handle that one, though: by sitting on your face. Particularly effective when the toddler in question is still sporting last night's diaper.

I may give my child an errand to run, to the farthest reaches of the house. ("Go bring me a purple marker." "Have you seen your bulldozer lately?") Then he'll —briefly—dash off. (More scurrying of footed PJs on floorboards, bumping back upstairs, rummaging in toy bins.) But now I know that my reprieve is only momentary; I get no peace: I lie there like a patient waiting for the dentist, who has stepped out for a moment only to return with the drill.

Sometimes I try to toss the ball to my husband's court—a dirty trick, no question. "Dad will read you that book," I say. "Go ask Dad to slice up your banana." Feet scuffing around to the other side of the bed. Pouncing. The sound of book jacket hitting skull. Followed by, "Ask Mom."

So I adjust my glasses on my nose—right side up—and open this morning's selection, which, if I'm lucky, will be *The Pokey Little Puppy* or Curious George. And if I'm not so lucky, an ancient but well-loved comic book, *The Adventures of the Incredible Hulk*, or a three-year-old program from Disney World on Ice. I may, after the second reading, try my final ploy: "Now why don't you read it to me, Will?" (Then I can close my eyes for two more precious moments.) But by now I know the game is up. Six-thirty finds me out of bed and in the kitchen, making coffee. Rounding up Charlie and Audrey. Packing the school lunches. Pouring out the cereal.

Now the truth is, even before I had children I was never one to loll around in bed till some scandalous hour like eight-fifteen. I always believed in getting a good early start on the day (and on the rare occasions when I'd sleep in, I invariably felt guilty). But nowadays, my fantasies turn not so much to desert islands, moonlit cruises, romantic interludes by candlelight, as they do to sleep. Unbroken sleep. Eight hours. Maybe even twelve. I can't remember the last time I had a night like that.

As parents, we are always quick to point out to our children, "You're overtired," and remind them, "That's why you're cranky." (Even now, a quarter century later, I can still remember the terrible frustration I used to feel, as a child, hearing my mother speak those words. "I AM NOT!" I would scream. "See," she would say calmly, as I do now to my children. "That just shows what I mean.") But nobody gets more overtired than the grown-ups (mothers in particular). I'll bet it's the number one occupational hazard of parenthood.

What most of us discover, I think (when we reach the stage of life that calls for rising in the night to feed the baby or comfort him out of his nightmares or greet him with the sun, ready to play blocks), is that we have strength and stamina we never before knew about. Inner resources we wouldn't have guessed at. (Maybe it was childbirth that revealed them to us.) I look back on my old days—when I sometimes sat down just to think, went to bed when I felt like it, and got up when the spirit moved me—and wonder why I didn't, back then, make it to the Fortune 500 club or at the very least come up with a vaccine against chicken pox. Give a mother of young children seven days in which she is not required to make a single peanut butter sandwich or get out of bed before seven, and she could (I bet) accomplish just about anything.

But this is what we want to be doing. Best, probably, not to calculate so far ahead, but this is most likely what I will be doing for the next five years, at the very least. Fifteen hundred more mornings spent burrowing under the covers while one or another of my children announces, directly into my eardrum, "Time to get up!" Someday, no doubt, the time will come when they fix their own breakfasts (or when they get too busy with their lives to sit down for a morning meal at all), and of course then I will miss the warm, faintly damp presence of a baby in our bed.

> Good morning to you.
> Good morning to you.
> We're all in our places, with bright shining faces.
> Good morning to you. Good morning to you.
> Good morning to you.

□

I've been buying diapers, nearly without interruption, for eight and a half years now. There was a period of around eighteen months, after Audrey was trained and before Charlie was born, when we lived diaper free, but we made up for it, a couple of years later, when Willy was born and Steve and I found ourselves with two children in diapers. Using the rough figure of 6 a day, 365 days a year, multiplied by 8, I come to somewhere in the neighborhood of 16,000 diapers we've gone through. As for what they cost us—I don't even want to figure that one out. If we'd been using cloth, all these years, I would at least have one terrific collection of cleaning rags to show for it all. As it stands, all I can say is, you won't find many people who change a diaper faster than I can.

Diapers aren't that significant, really, but you might notice how often they tend to come up in discussions of babies and the decision to have children. When people try to sum up the experience of parenthood they probably don't mention watching one's twelve-month-old discover her toes, or giving a two-year-old a bath, or the look on her face the first time she tastes ice cream. They don't go into the supreme pleasure of holding a toddler on one's lap, reading him *Goodnight Moon*, and when he gets to the page with the quiet old lady, hearing him whisper "Hush." What people talk about, when they attempt to reduce the whole thing to twenty-five words or less, is apt to be: diapers.

What can you say about them? Some brands are a lot better than others, and it's seldom true economy to buy the cheap ones. Some children are a lot easier to change than others—and I have had both kinds. A daughter who used to lie still on the changing table, peel back the tapes obligingly, and say, as if the two of us were just sitting down with our best china for tea, "Please pass the powder" or "How are you doing today, Mom?" And a son who liked to break dance while I changed him, and one who, the moment I had his diaper off, would bound like a stunt man from the changing table (three feet off the ground) and race out the door—naked from the waist down, no matter what the season. "Don't say *ick* and don't say *ugh*," he would instruct me as I carried him off again to clean him up.

It hasn't just been my children I've tussled with over the issue of diapers, either. I couldn't begin to count the number of arguments Steve and I have had over who'd attend to the diaper this time. Same arguments, really, same words—all that changed were the children. Foolish fights, that would sometimes reduce me to tears or him to stony silence. And what they were about, of course, was never really changing diapers at all. (I know there are people who can't stand the job, but it has never really bothered me.) I argued with my husband over who got up to change the baby, mostly out of principle. "You never ask me to change the diaper. Why is it I have to ask you?" I would say. "When did you last change the oil in our car?" he'd reply. Round and round we went— ending up nowhere. With about as much to show for all our battles on the subject as I have to show for all those sixteen thousand disposable diapers now lying somewhere at the bottom of our town dump.

During our daughter's babyhood, when we were at our most broke, I harbored the fantasy (shared by half the mothers in America, I'll bet) that she might make diaper commercials. Where was there a cuter, more adorable baby? Who could resist her—or whatever brand of diaper she'd wear? If she would just do—in front of a camera—what she did for me in our living room (putting the diaper on her head, kissing the baby on the diaper box), she might earn herself a college education. But we lived in the country—no ad agencies, no talent scouts within a hundred-mile radius. So her antics in diapers went unrecorded by everyone but her father and me. And I'm sure it was all for the best.

Then one by one our children left diapers behind them. I am a sentimentalist about every aspect of our children's lives, and a historian of their days, whose tendency it is to save physical artifacts (a baby tooth, the first scrawl that could be said to resemble a human face, even the plastic clip from Audrey's umbilical cord), and if I could have known, when I was putting it on, that this particular diaper would be the last one this child ever wore, I might even have shed a tear over its absorbent quilted layers. But of course that's never how it is when a child is giving up diapers. One day he stays dry. Then another. And suddenly it occurs to you, it's been three days since you've bothered to put a diaper on him, even when you go out. And the next thing you know, you've got marigold seedlings on what used to be the chang-

ing table and you're buying a six-pack of Alvin and the Chipmunks briefs, size 2.

A few months ago that moment arrived at our house with
our youngest son Willy. And though I never go so far as to
say he is our last child, and I always harbor the hope that
sometime there will again be energy and space in our lives
for one more, this particular round of toilet training certainly
feels like a particularly momentous one. The end of an era.
A graduation, not just for Willy, but for Steve and me too. It
seems totally appropriate, then, that the moment should be
marked by a rather extraordinary event, and it was. Here is
the story:

I am a believer in the idea of rewarding children, during
the early stages of toilet training, with prizes for peeing in
the pot. In the past, I have used goldfish crackers, balloons,
plastic farm animals, and once—when I was really desperate—M&M's. This time around, Willy's prizes were tiny
pink plastic figures currently much coveted by little boys
across the nation, called Muscle Men. Every time he made it
to the toilet on time, he got one; and though Muscle Men
carry the fairly hefty price of around a quarter apiece, until
one particular day when he was two years and a few months
old, Willy's performance in the bathroom wasn't putting
much of a strain on our budget. All day long I was mopping
up puddles on the floor, while Willy smiled sorrowfully,
commenting, "That's life."

Then in a single day everything changed. He woke up
announcing that he wanted to go to the bathroom, and all
morning long he kept his pants dry. That afternoon I took
him shopping—wearing briefs, not diapers—and there were
no accidents. On the ride home, a trip of about thirty miles,
Willy suddenly piped up, "I need to pee." So naturally I
slammed on the brakes and pulled over into the breakdown
lane of Interstate 93. "I'm going to get another Muscle Man,"

Willy sang happily as I unbuckled his seat belt and led him down the embankment in some tall grass by the side of the highway. And my heart sank, because I had left home without my supply of Muscle Men. I had no reward.

He pulled down his pants. And just as he was finishing, and we were both studying the ground, we spotted it. Nearly buried in the dirt, in the precise spot along Route 93 where my son had chosen to pee, was a pink plastic figure who looked as if he could give Arnold Schwarzenegger a run for his money. "Oh, there's my Muscle Man," he said with total casualness, bending to pick it up. He put the figure in his pocket. I put my son back in the car. That was six months ago, and he's been dry ever since.

———

DAY IN, DAY OUT

□ *Mess*   □ *The La-Z-Boy Lounger*
□ *Counting Heads*   □ *Swamped*

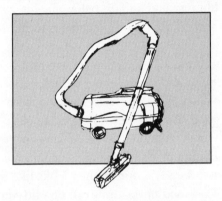

I work. I raise children. I think about large subjects like how to raise a moral child, how to stay married, how to prevent nuclear war. These things are deeply important to me—and if I sound flip, I surely don't mean to.

But what occupies my mind, as I set out the cereal bowls, as I pull on my sweat pants, as I tromp out to the car to drive Audrey, who has just missed the bus, to school—a dozen other moments of my day and as the sixty seconds before sleep comes—is very often how, how, how, how to keep this house neat.

Not spotless, mind you, or even clean. Just how to avoid being totally buried in Matchbox cars, GI Joe figures, half-eaten fruit roll-ups, and glitter.

I never used to care so much about tidiness. Before I was married, I used to keep a whole room (with the door securely latched) filled with nothing but boxed-up junk. I didn't even own a mop. I had taken my vacuum cleaner to be repaired and six months later still hadn't picked it up. I had enough changes of clothes that I could go two weeks—sometimes as long as a month—between trips to the laundromat. If I was having a friend over for dinner, I'd sometimes put a few dirty dishes in the closet.

Then I got married. Steve isn't one of those compulsively tidy types. He just had so few belongings it would've been impossible to mess them up. He came into my life with five cartons of possessions—three of which were paints and brushes. About those, especially, he was and is inordinately fastidious. You would never know, to look at his hands or his work pants, what colors he was working with that day. It takes him a good half hour, every night, to clean his brushes to his satisfaction. Always take good care of your tools, he has been teaching our children ever since they could talk.

When I cook, he says, our kitchen looks like the site of an explosion. Good food never came out of a tidy kitchen, I tell him. Clean the counter, overcook the rice. Wash the pans, burn the onions. You need only look at my kitchen to know I'm a good cook.

And then—this is what breaks us—there are our children. Who, like their mother, do not travel light through life. I think Audrey still owns, and keeps tabs on, all but maybe twelve of the toys she's been given in her nearly seven years of life. Now and then I wade through the stuff and eliminate something, burying it deep at the bottom of the trash. A few hours later she confronts me suspiciously: "Have you seen the purple brush that goes to My Little Pony? I can't figure out what happened to that pillow I had in my Barbie Town-house." (Now the tea bag on the doll bed makes sense. And all those little tea leaves leaking out onto her floor).

Audrey believes, and tells me regularly, that toys have feelings. Not just toys, either, but also three-year-old Happy

Meal boxes (collectibles of the future?), barrettes, broken china. A pair of red patent-leather pointy-toed shoes her godmother Kate gave her—that she can't fit, but likes to use as cars for Barbie and Skipper to drive around in. Many large, interesting sculptures made out of cigar boxes, cardboard wrapping-paper tubes, pipe cleaners, and Styrofoam trays. None of these things can be thrown out, as long as she lives within state lines.

Willy goes less for details, more for broad strokes. He likes to take every pillow from the couch and all the beds, dump out the contents of every large box I have just filled with toys, sorted by category. And then stretch our eight-foot-long expandable tunnel across the living room to make a spaceship. He heads directly for the nucleus of whatever activity is going on at the moment and scatters whatever has been assembled there (the marbles from Chinese checkers, the tracks of our new train, two cups full of chocolate chips) in all directions.

All of this makes it sound as if I make no effort to exercise control or discipline, but I do. I post signs, aimed at both the literate and preliterate members of our household, listing both tasks and reminders. ("STOP! Have you put your bowl in the dishwasher?" Or simply a picture of me, looking mad, standing over a pile of blocks.) I confiscate un-picked-up toys. I buy brightly colored plastic boxes, tubs, and bins; I label them "Legos," "Smurfs," and "Superheroes." We start a new leaf at least once a month.

The truth is, I suppose, that whatever rules and threats I lay down for my children, my own ambivalence about mess and cleanup must somehow have communicated itself to them. Partly, I love and am proud of their crazy, impossible pillow constructions. How—walking into the kitchen and finding yarn and ribbon strung from the refrigerator door to the knobs on the stove to the rungs on all five chairs, hung with dandelions and toilet paper roses and signs that say "I love you xoxoxo"—how can a person look at that and say anything besides "Isn't that beautiful"?

If my children are accumulators, well, I don't have to think very hard to know where they got it from. One reason Audrey owns twelve Barbies is because nine of them were mine when I was little, and of those, probably seven still have their original bathing suits and heels. The stuffed animals Charlie lines up in a parade across the living-room rug were mine too. I was never any good at throwing things out either.

But every once in a while I do sweep through the house, tossing into a couple of garbage bags every doll with less than half its hair, every car with no more than one wheel. I load the children in the car, and we drive solemnly to the dump. We stand at the edge, and I give each of them a bag to throw in. Audrey might shed a tear. "Bye-bye, broken squirt gun," says Charlie.

And then one of them spots it: not at the edge of the garbage, of course, but about ten feet out, and twenty feet down. A GI Joe doll with only one leg missing. A pair of gold curtains that would be perfect for dress-ups. A stack of carpet samples. . . . Lucky I wore my boots.

□

I was in a furniture store the other day, looking at carpeting for my children's playroom, when something made me stop in the chair department. In my whole married life, I've bought exactly one piece of furniture new, but something made me sit down in a big, ugly, and indescribably comfortable chair, the kind with the extending foot rest and the lever on one side to tilt it backward. I laid my head back, put my feet up, closed my eyes. I could hardly bring myself to get up.

"I want this chair," I told Audrey. (Though the price tag made the purchase unlikely.) But of course what I really wanted was something money can't buy. To sit down. To lie down, even. Something I haven't done much of for the last few years.

Now, I'm seldom one to concede the commonly accepted notions of how men and women differ. (That men are more mechanically minded. Women are more sensitive. Men are more rational. Women are more emotional. I've known men and women who broke all of those stereotypes.) But there's one overwhelming and universal sex difference I'll grant you: Men take naps. Men know how to make use of a chair like that. Who ever heard of a woman stretched out in the middle of the day in a La-Z-Boy lounger?

This is not to say that men are lazier. I've never met a more hard-working person than my husband Steve. When he's awake, he's never idle. He puts in long, hard days—far more arduous than mine—without complaint. He can repair a car, build a shed, clear an acre of land, do fifty chin-ups. But his ability to put out huge amounts of energy is matched in equal measure by another aptitude I lack completely. He can stretch out on a couch, open a magazine, and sixty seconds later be sound asleep.

And once he is, it doesn't matter what's going on. His children may be crying. The phone may ring, our dog may need to be put out. I may be (almost certainly will be) clanging pans in the kitchen, as loudly as possible. None of it makes any difference. Steve remains dead to the world.

Of course, it's not as if I've never taken a nap myself. But mostly I catch up on my sleep in other places: at the movies (where I seldom make it to the rolling of the final credits of a second show). Driving home from our standing Saturday night out. And once, during what was supposed to be another of our romantic evenings alone together at an expensive restaurant we'd treated ourselves to, halfway through dinner, my head simply dropped to the table, missing my swordfish steak by inches. The waiter doubtless thought I'd had too many glasses of wine, but the truth is, it was only too many children.

What I can't do, though, and what no woman I know can do (no woman with children at home, anyway) is stretch out somewhere in my own house, during the middle of the day, and take a nap. You might as well ask a fireman to eat a sandwich in the middle of a burning building. Even if the children were all somehow, mysteriously, being attended to. (Off playing Monopoly somewhere, or doing puzzles. Not asking for glasses of water. Not fighting over who gets to use the garlic press with his Play-doh, or who gets the purple marker.) Even if my children were all over at friends' houses. (When in fact, invitations for Willy do not exactly tie up the phone lines around here.) Even then I couldn't spend my precious free time sleeping. I would want to take advantage of the opportunity to sort through old toys or wash the bathroom floor.

Maybe there is a physiological basis for this fundamental difference between the napping abilities of men and women. (Because this isn't just a pattern I observe in Steve and me. I've seen the same tendency in the males of countless other families as well.) I wonder if men are more prone to sudden, extraordinary bursts of adrenaline output (the kind required to lift a piano or jack up a car), whereas women keep a steadier, less intense, but unbroken energy level. I think there's something psychological there too, though: My husband can block things out when he wants to, while my antennae are permanently, irreversibly tuned to pick up every piece of household static. If Charlie has a friend over, my ear is cocked, listening for any sound of trouble. If Willy's out in the sandbox, I'm hovering near the window.

In my more mellow moments, I can look into our living

room, catch sight of my sleeping husband stretched out with an open copy of *Sports Illustrated* on his chest, and simply smile lovingly. At other times, I see him sleeping, think how nice that would be (and how equally impossible), and then I start slamming doors or turn on the vacuum cleaner. Eventually he'll wake up, get up, and give me a hand. Looking at those moments from an objective distance I can see they never really serve to make me feel better. They only ensure that he'll feel worse.

When I'm tired and grouchy, and the dishes are stacked up on the counter and one of my sons has just spilled granola all over the kitchen floor and my daughter is in tears because she can't find her jelly shoes, and there lies Steve, peaceful as Rip Van Winkle, I can't rouse much affection or understanding when it comes to his naps. At the moment—from a tranquil distance—I can say (or would say, to a young bride with five hundred nap arguments not yet under her belt) that men and women are simply different here. You can't fight it—although the impulse to try is just about unavoidable. But if you have yourself a fundamentally good and fair man, the moments when you rest and he works, and the moments when you work and he rests, will all even out in the end. Spend all your time scorekeeping, and you're almost sure to fall behind in the game.

□

Hardly a day goes by around here in the summertime that we don't head for the beach—not the ocean, but one of the several lakes and ponds and swimming holes in our town, where the children can make sand castles and splash in the water, while the mothers stretch out on the sand, catching up on everything that's happened in the twenty-four hours since they were last at the beach. Over this past summer, we have been following the progress of one mother's pregnancy and another's divorce, one woman's struggles with her visiting stepchildren and another's kitchen renovations. We talk about what teachers our children are going to have in the fall and what to do with the last few inches of an old permanent wave. When one little boy (a known troublemaker) calls one of our sons a Care Bear (this particular boy is nine years old, and there is evidently no worse name to call a nine-year-old boy), and when that son responds with a punch, we compare notes on appropriate disciplinary action. In between all of this, we pass out nectarines and granola bars, peanut butter sandwiches and fruit roll-ups. When one of our children announces, loudly enough for everyone to hear, that he needs to go to the bathroom, we take him. When he simply asks, quietly, what he should do, we may simply whisper, quietly, that he can do it in the water.

Some people, driving quickly past this beach we're spread out on (with our buckets and shovels, our coolers and floaters and suntan lotion and trucks), might imagine that we live the life of leisure, these women and I—and it's true, there aren't many better ways to spend a summer afternoon. But as any parent of young children will tell you, it's hard work too: arbitrating every dispute over who gets the green tractor; being there to applaud every time one's child does a handstand, every time he jumps off the big rock. And all the while, of course, knowing just where the very littlest ones are, the ones who have only recently got secure footing on dry land.

Because it only takes one little wave from a passing motorboat, one wrong step, and a child the size of Willy can be underwater and unable to find his way up again. Even with a four-year-old like Charlie, even with an eight-year-old like Audrey (who's swimming over her head now, but so anxious to keep up with her friends that she won't always come in when she's tired), there is danger, danger, danger.

Well, our friends Robert and Suzanne (a pianist and an opera singer) were visiting from out of town last week with their two daughters, Victoria and Claire, and I wanted some time to see them. At my favorite place—the beach.

Suzanne is a good and dear friend. We are also (as she would admit, as readily as I) very different in our approaches to child raising. She peels the grapes her children eat and stands behind baby Claire when she mounts the stairs, while I give Willy whole chicken bones to gnaw on and let him climb the ladder to the slide alone. Suzanne worries about germs and chills, while I let my children swim on all but the coldest, darkest days, and if somebody drops his cookie on the floor, there's no question somebody will still eat it. And though I think Suzanne is a wonderful and loving mother, it's also true, I've always felt she makes a mistake in worrying over her children as much as she does. Privately, I have to admit, I have occasionally congratulated my husband and myself for having raised our children to be a little tougher and more resilient.

So this particular afternoon we were standing by the shore, watching our children play. Suzanne's older daughter, Victoria, didn't want to go in the water because it was cold and the bottom was muddy, but she did want to play with Audrey, who was looking for tadpoles on a little island a few feet out. So she began, cautiously, wading to the island. She got halfway out and stepped on a rock. Then she let out a really bloodcurdling scream and called for her mother to come carry her across. And Suzanne, who had been digging in the sand with Claire and Willy, rushed to Victoria's side, calling out to me, as she went, to watch the baby.

I thought I was watching. But I was also thinking about the scene, with Victoria screaming, and Suzanne running, and Audrey standing there, holding her tadpole bucket, watching everything.

And for a moment I forgot about watching Suzanne's baby—I let down my guard. Then suddenly there was Suzanne's voice. (She is an opera singer. Her soprano can fill a concert hall. She can blow up an inner tube with a single breath.) "Get the baby!" she screamed. "The baby's drowning."

I whirled around then, of course, and saw Claire—just Willy's age—floating underwater, with her hair fanned out in all directions, and her arms and legs flailing, not touching ground. In half a second Suzanne was there with her arms around the baby, and she was safe—not even crying, in fact, just a little dazed looking.

There was nothing to say, really, though of course I said everything, and kept on saying it all that day and night. How sorry I was. How I had just been looking at Claire— just a moment before—and she was fine. How I got distracted and turned my head. Just for a second.

We didn't leave the beach right away after that. I paced the sand, hovering over my children—everybody's children —like a cat. I kept coming back to Claire, touching the top of her head. All through that afternoon I kept returning to Suzanne on her towel, going over it all again. She must have forgiven me a dozen times. "It's all right," she said. "I'm always watching, even when I ask someone else to watch." A true friend, she even asked me to keep an eye on Claire again for a moment while she packed up their car to leave.

It's a few weeks later now. Robert and Suzanne and their children have left for the summer. Although my mouth still goes dry, thinking about that afternoon, I'm able to stretch out on my towel again, at the beach, looking relaxed and easy, talking with my friends. Anybody driving past would think, "Boy, those women sure have it easy."

But oh, are we ever watching. Our eyes are fixed on that beach as if it were Normandy and this were D day. We never stop counting heads.

☐

Things had been pretty crazy around our house. Steve was finishing up the illustrations for a children's book we wrote together, which had to be at the publishers by Friday. In his off hours, he was down in our woods chainsawing up a lot of trees he felled last spring, in a place where we're about to have a pond dug. The bulldozer's due in five days, and there are still about thirty trees to get out of the way. He hauls the wood in our 1960 Jeep, whose engine needs a jump-start every time you drive it. The car he uses to jump it is a 1966 Valiant, because our other, newer vehicle has been in the repair shop. I was given a loaner car to use, but halfway home it burst into flames in the middle of the highway and I had to hitchhike back to the shop. That's how things have been going lately.

And our new bunk beds had just been delivered (unassembled) and were sitting in the middle of our kitchen. Willy had just lifted the porcelain top off our toilet and dropped it on the bathroom floor, where it landed in about fifteen pieces. ("A puzzle!" he said happily.) And we had friends visiting for the week. And our blackberries had all come ripe and needed picking. And Charlie had suddenly remembered that I'd never got around to holding his fourth birthday party, last March, and that I'd promised I would as soon as things quieted down around here. ("Is it time for my birthday yet?" he asked the day I came back from the repair shop.)

There are times in my marriage when I am angry at my husband, and times when I'm hurt. I have stalked out the door, on occasion, cried, poured dinner down the sink, and sometimes, when we've had a bad argument, I have simply stopped talking to him altogether. Nothing like that has happened lately. Only, we have both been so busy these last few weeks that it may be Friday before I get around to telling him about a phone call we got from an old friend the Monday before. Last Saturday (the night we try to reserve for going out together) Steve started our evening alone together with a discussion of the broken toilet and went on to the bunk beds and the question of what to do about our septic system. "I don't want to talk about it," I told him. "I'm not your business partner." And then I said some things about how we were in danger of forgetting what it is we're about here. That our relationship is supposed be the foundation of our household. Not the other way around.

The expression I'd use to describe how it was when Steve and I met, nine and a half years ago, is "head over heels in love." Although maybe heels over head describes it better. Heart over head, anyway. My feeling about this man standing on my doorstep was immediate, instinctual, and absolute. And it was all that romantic feeling, that weakening in the knees, that made me want to settle down with him. Have children. Make a home.

The catch is, the very impulse that drives so many people to domesticity and child raising sometimes allows them to drift apart. Before you know it, you're kissing the baby all the time (instead of each other). He's working overtime; your fantasies have to do with dishwashers and a new washing machine. Overrun as a person gets with the thousand little details required to make the household function, it's not hard to lose sight of what it was about your partner that got the two of you into this in the first place. By the time you get an evening out, away from the children, you may look at each other across the restaurant table in the candlelight and think of nothing better to say than that you found a terrific buy in high-top sneakers today and your daughter got an A+ in spelling.

None of this is news to anybody who's been married a while, especially if they're raising young children. But I think it's important simply to acknowledge the syndrome now and then, because when it's happening to you it's sometimes hard to remember that this doesn't mean the situation is hopeless. (You're nothing but a cook and a babysitter. Romance is gone from your life. He gave you a frying pan for your birthday. That's it: the marriage is finished.) It's hard to step back and take the long view when all you can see is unfolded laundry, unwashed dishes, and the crusts of three children's peanut butter sandwiches lying in the sink.

Now (speaking of the sink), we've had another problem around our house these past few days. There was a cup stuck in our sink. A very hard plastic cup, whose diameter (it turned out) matched precisely the diameter of the opening to our garbage disposal. When it first happened, I wasn't too concerned (I was sure Steve would know what to do about this). But by that night, after watching him struggle for over an hour, trying to dislodge the cup, we were both pretty fed up. You couldn't get a hammer into the opening to smash the cup. You couldn't get a pair of pliers around the edges of the cup to pull it out. You could take the whole disposal out, of course, but you'd be talking major plumbing work then. So since there were so many other things going on in our lives at the time, we just left the cup for another three days or so. It began to collect apple peelings and bits of eggshell and old yogurt and soggy Kix. It was depressing to see that cup in there. I'd pound away at it with a screwdriver for a few minutes every few hours, then get frustrated and give up. Eventually I covered that half of our double sink with a cutting board and tried to ignore the whole thing.

But I missed my garbage disposal, and the kitchen started smelling funny. One night I dreamed about the stuck cup (dreamed I tried pulling it out using the suction from my vacuum cleaner and got electrocuted). In the morning I got out my turkey baster and suctioned all the old yogurt and water out of the cup and tried the vacuuming method (wearing rubber-soled shoes), but it didn't work. What was going on in our sink began to look like a metaphor for my whole life. Clogged. Murky. Becoming stagnant.

Then this morning Steve's sheetrocking partner, Dave, came by with a pair of incredibly strong snips, and after spending another half hour hacking away at the cup, we pulled it out. The water gurgled down the drain, the children cheered, I hugged my husband, and we decided life was bearable after all. (It's often this way. When we're having rough times together, our breakthrough is more likely to involve getting our car back from the repair shop, or an efficient new babysitter coming on board, than the discovery of some whole new way of relating.)

And tonight (this being Saturday) I'm putting on my fanciest dress and the silk stockings Steve bought me for my birthday (following the one we'd all just as soon forget, on which he gave me the can opener), and we are going out to celebrate. And we are not going to mention plumbing or children or car repairs. To look at us you wouldn't even know we're married.

———

FAMILY
EXPANSION

□ *Audrey Gets a Brother* □ *The Third Child*
□ *Willy Walks* □ *Night at the Ramada Inn*

I was twenty-four years old when Audrey was born. And of all the things that were strange and new and frightening about becoming a parent at a time when I was in many ways a child myself (starting with the sight of one small body emerging from another that's one's own—something that's never wholly real, during all those endless months of pregnancy, until you see it happen), the one familiar part was her being a girl. She looked, people said, like me. And I felt like her. When she cried, my eyes filled with tears. When she was frustrated or angry (looking for her thumb, waiting the thirty seconds it took between when she cried and when I fed her), my own impatience was as real as a baby's empty belly. If I was sitting down, waiting for Steve to pick her up and bring her to me, and he hesitated first, just long enough to tie his shoe or throw a log on the fire, I would feel like screaming. Come on, come on, come on.

She grew, of course—cut first from the cord, then from the breast, and then (and still) an endless succession of further separations. Her first night away from home. The first (far from the only) time she said to me, "I don't like you. I'm going to find another mother." Four weeks when Steve and I went to China as teachers with a group of American high-school students and left Audrey with her grandparents, during which time my night was her day and the whole globe stood between us. By the time she was six she was choosing her own clothes every morning (seldom the ones I would have put her in) and heading out into the world for eight hours at a stretch, carrying a Strawberry Shortcake lunchbox and a pocketful of friendship pins. And though I would ask her every afternoon at three how her day had gone, she seldom gave me more than a sentence's worth of information.

With all of that, though, we're alike. I know which of a caseful of dolls will be her favorite. I know, when we meet a woman carrying an alligator bag in an airport lounge, that at the first opportunity she'll pull me aside and whisper disapprovingly, "Endangered species!" I hear about the birthday party of a girl at her school, to which she wasn't invited, and though I don't cry, I easily could. Like me, Audrey loves to talk, so that now (at times more than my often silent husband) she is my companion and confidante who, settling into the front seat of the car beside me or reaching for the fanciest china teacup at the kitchen table, says with a happy, expectant sigh, "What are we going to discuss today?"

You have a child, and then you think you know what children are like. Who yours resemble. How it is, being a parent. Everything has changed, and will never be the same. There can be no enormous surprises left.

But then maybe you have another child. And it turns out you didn't really know what babies were like after all. You knew only that first baby. This second one is all new, something totally different. He teaches you about himself, and also—by his differences—about his sibling. That face she made (that you thought all babies make) turns out to be hers alone. Your children are not necessarily dark-haired and dark-skinned after all. (They can also be blond and fair.) As for being a parent: You knew all about raising one child. But all the rules change, raising two.

And then there is that other joy that comes when there is more than one, and that is seeing your two children together. Providing them with the gift of each other.

Audrey had been an only child for four years and a month when her brother Charlie was born. For four years she had been the central—only—star in our small galaxy, and certainly my life revolved powerfully around hers. Every morning she'd bound into our bed, asking us what we were going to do today. Sew doll clothes, make valentines, bake pies? Drive to the children's museum, play Old Maid all afternoon? We had tea parties with my grandmother's china. We sewed dollhouse curtains and embroidered hankies. I read her stacks of books at a sitting, and when we were done she'd turn to me to ask, "What do we do next?"

Even the desire for another child came, in part, anyway, out of my endless attempts to give the one I already had everything (including a sibling). I was eager for another child too, and hoping for a boy. But in my heart of hearts, I don't think I ever believed I would love another child as much as I loved the one I already had: my dark-eyed, dark-skinned, dark-haired daughter, the little girl who looked like me and gave me a chance to relive and (sometimes) rewrite my own childhood. I never had a brother, myself. But Audrey would have one.

It was a good and easy second pregnancy, filled not only with Steve's and my anticipation, but this time with Audrey's too. She and I used to carry on conversations with her sibling before he was born: Audrey, lifting up my maternity top, whispering gently into my belly button, and me, in a squeaky, muffled voice, providing the baby's response. She asked the baby questions about life in utero, but more than that, he would ask her about the outside world, and then she'd hold forth, sweetly and patiently explaining Christmas, or popcorn, or telling him about our house, our dog, the room that would be his. She sang him songs, taught him the numbers up to ten, told him, above all, not to worry about being born. She'd take care of him. Every couple of weeks I'd cook a ham—usually a seven- or eight-pounder—and whenever I got one, I'd let Audrey carry it around the kitchen for a while, before it went in the oven, so she'd get used to the weight of a baby. Pretty soon she was calling our unborn baby Hamhead, and Steve and I did too.

Eventually Hamhead—Charlie—was born. But where my daughter had been instantly familiar to me, my son showed up like a wonderful, lovable stranger. A boy, for one thing. And a big, ten-pound, blue-eyed blond. A child over whom people still express surprise when they hear he's mine (and the brother of Audrey). They're that different.

I liked him right away, of course, but where the heart gives over blindly to a first child, this time I held back some. No question about it, my first loyalties were to the child who'd been with us four years already. If he was crying, and she needed me, he was the one who had to wait. Partly that was an instinctive strategy, I think (I never wanted her to see him as having taken her mother away. Better a little motherly neglect, I figured, than sisterly resentment). But it's also true, the choice wasn't hard, in those early days. Charlie would have to win my love, earn his place in my heart. And faster than I had anticipated, he did.

He was a sunny, cheerful baby. Almost from the first I let Audrey carry him around—our real-life hamhead—and though wherever we went I'd see people looking shocked to observe a four-year-old toting an infant, I knew she'd be as unlikely to drop him as I was, she was so proud. As for him, he'd never known a life in which he wasn't carried by his sister, and was accustomed to the somewhat bumpy ride she gave him. Maybe out of self-preservation, he held his head up on his own faster than any other baby I've known.

In the first weeks and months after Charlie's birth, people who knew us, and knew of my deep and single-minded devotion to my daughter, used to ask us how Audrey was taking the arrival of the new baby. Their faces would look worried when they made their inquiries, their tones were hushed, as if what they were speaking of was not the birth of a baby, but an attack of some terrible disease or the discovery of head lice. Over and over they would ask Audrey herself, "How do you like your baby brother?" And almost as often, they would anticipate, and plant the suggestion of, trouble. "I bet he screams all the time," they'd say. "I bet sometimes you wish he'd move away."

I understand it's modern, progressive thinking to talk this way. We are all of us more in touch with our feelings these days, as they say. And once in touch with them, we're all anxious to express them, get them out in the open. Children's books about new baby brothers and sisters are filled, now, with older siblings' feelings of displacement, declarations of hatred, and examples of acting out. (*Validating.* I think that's what they call it.) But sometimes I wonder whether being allowed to say repeatedly, "I hate my brother," doesn't simply reinforce the idea for a child. She hears the words so often they begin to sound familiar, and true.

As for me, I had started out this business of having a second child with my heart and mind still centered on my first (and worried, lest he become a rival for my affections). But it came to Steve and me, after Charlie's birth, that the only real danger was not of one child becoming more loved than the other, only of the consequences if the two failed to love and support each other. I saw how Audrey rejoiced over her brother's arrival, and how little she seemed threatened by it. One more person to love her, and one more person to love, that's what he was to her.

I didn't want that to change. So, to preserve that feeling, we handed over to Audrey large measures of responsibility (real, not invented) and tried to make sure that he associated her only with good things and that she saw him as taking nothing from her, only adding to her life. When there were cookies to be handed out, she gave them. When she fell down, he was dispatched (first crawling, later staggering with his first steps) to kiss her. Inevitably, of course, his presence in our lives sometimes meant I had less time for her. But more often he served as playmate, companion, comforter. In the interest of reinforcing those things, I allowed some things I mightn't otherwise. She dressed him like a doll, put him on a leash and took him for walks, sat him down, for an hour at a time, to learn the ABCs or the names of colors. For his part, he has always been so happy and grateful for her attention he almost never complained. As soon as he graduated from his crib, he began sleeping beside her in the single bed they still share, and when he cried in the night it was (and is still) usually Audrey who calmed him and sang him back to sleep.

Sometimes I'll be on a tirade (the children will have left their room a mess, or failed, again, to pick up the dirty clothes, or spilled orange juice over the kitchen floor), and the two of them band together like sailors on a storm-tossed boat. And in a way I've never really minded. Let me be the villain, sometimes, if it solidifies their alliance.

Naturally, they get fed up with each other sometimes. Charlie breaks the leg off Audrey's doll. Audrey remarks bitterly that she wishes she had a sister. They stalk off to one room or another. Slam the door. Cry. And then someone must always apologize, look the other in the eye, give a hug. If they can't do that, it's back to the room again. Sometimes, then, I might ask the child who's having trouble: How many sisters do you have? How many brothers? (Even two is not so many that a person can afford to let one get away.)

Charlie knows his sister's name is Audrey, but that's not what he calls her. He calls her Sis, or Sissy. I never tire of hearing him speak of her that way, or of hearing her speak proudly of "my brother." The words have a power unto themselves, I sometimes think. Just as words of hatred or resentment can reinforce the feelings they name, words that speak of attachment and connection can strengthen family ties. "I want to die the same day you do," Charlie (who's going through a slightly morbid stage) told Audrey the other day. He simply can't imagine a life without her.

□

Sometimes I can hardly bear to look at pictures of Steve and me taken back when our marriage, as well as parenthood, was new. One portrait we had taken at a discount store shows the two of us, holding a five-day-old Audrey, standing in front of a Technicolor backdrop. (We had a choice: ocean, desert, or mountains. We chose mountains.) In the picture both of us look a little stunned, still reeling from Audrey's birth and the realization that we, and no one else, were the ones responsible for her. Steve and I had about twenty-five dollars to our names the day we had that picture taken, and still I spent four of them on a pair of pink baby shoes that wouldn't fit for months. We had come to this discount store specifically because they'd advertised portraits for eighty-eight cents. And when I learned that meant eighty-eight cents for each person in the portrait (and Audrey counted) I was actually upset.

No baby shakes its parents to the core the way the first one does. But if our daughter was all thrilling and overwhelming to us, our son was much the same to our daughter. When she came downstairs that first morning to find his head sticking out from under the covers in our bed, where he'd been born a few hours earlier, she said "My dream came true," and she hasn't altered her position much since then. The two of them are firmly a pair, and because they are, Charlie (who has never known life without a sibling) will never need Audrey the way she needed him.

What was new to us about our second child was not only his being a boy but, just as much, the fact that this time around we were settled and in control of things. There was a leisurely four-year space between children, a washer and dryer installed, money in the bank for Lacoste sleeper suits. The sound of my baby crying no longer brought tears to my eyes. From the first, I loved Charlie with a measure of ease and detachment I had never known and cannot manage even now for my firstborn, whose pain I still suffer as my own. It was two years after Audrey's birth before I retrieved the capacity to think about, talk about, something other than her, to walk out the door and leave her with someone else without feeling a stab. After Charlie, life seemed good and manageable. I lost the extra weight I'd gained easily, found a babysitter I liked, and didn't mind it that she didn't sing and play with him all morning. I joined the Y, started running, went away for a weekend alone with Steve. During which time, it turns out, our third child was conceived.

But where the news of my first pregnancy had been met with joy from all quarters, and news of the second just as much so, when I told people I was pregnant again, they'd tend to look baffled. "Was this planned?" they would say.

"Are you happy about it?" One woman simply asked me, "Why?"

The third time around, there were no new maternity clothes and no nursery redecoration projects. I no longer read books about labor and delivery or infant care. The months, which had crawled by when I was waiting for Audrey to be born, passed without notice, until suddenly it was January and I realized we had just six weeks left until the baby would be born and we hadn't even talked about his name.

I went to a baby shower for my friend Kathleen, who was expecting her first child right around the time our third was due. My friend Laurie, who gave the party, had asked me if I'd like a shower too. I said of course I didn't need a shower. We had plenty of baby clothes already, I said, packed away in old Luvs boxes in our attic crawl space.

And then sitting there in Laurie's streamer-decorated living room, eating a cake decorated with little plastic rattles and watching Kathleen untie pink and blue ribbons, seeing her hold up the stuffed animals and little dresses and the tiny shoes (that, I now know, never stay on), I felt foolishly close to crying. That the arrival of this third child of ours had been so little anticipated or feted. That not once in all the months of my pregnancy had Steve and I sat on the couch together (his hand on my belly), waiting for a kick.

Another friend—a mother of two who manages, as mothers of two children still can, just barely (while mothers of three and more are seldom heard from) to carry on with her career—wrote me a letter about this same point, asking me if there was still some excitement left, the third time around. A third child herself, she said, she was fishing for a reply in the affirmative. After all these years, she still wanted to believe her parents had been able to rejoice just as much at the birth of their third daughter as they had at the birth of the first.

Well, I wrote back, this baby hasn't even been born yet, and already I think I know some things about third children. (My husband, it suddenly occurred to me, was one.) Third children seldom put on clothes someone else hasn't worn first. They won't get held or sung to as much as first and second children. They must learn early (maybe even before they're born) to make do. If I had to guess, I said (and as it turned out, I was right), this new baby of ours will grow up very fast, always trying to keep up with the others.

I never got around to hanging our old Beatrix Potter mobile over the crib, the third time around, in part because the music box no longer played "Here Comes Peter Cottontail" and I was sick of the tune anyway. I never reviewed my Lamaze breathing. I never got to spend one day lying in bed reading magazines.

But when the moment came, that I felt the old familiar, unmistakable symptoms of labor, my heart raced, the same as it did for Audrey and for Charlie. This time I didn't care if we got a boy or a girl, blond- or brown-haired, handsome or pretty or neither. And I think now that it will be the total inconvenience of his timing, and the very fact that we didn't exactly need another baby around here, that I will someday offer to Willy as testimony to the way we felt about his arrival. This time around, all the essential roles had been filled. And of course we loved him anyway.

□

The day Willy took his first step our whole life changed. Now he climbs stairs and teeters at the top with one foot poised in midair. Now when his older brother and sister play Candyland, he can stand in the middle of the game board, throwing cards in the air. He pulls ingredients off shelves, he makes Cheerios mountains and pours olive oil on his head. He wakes up, shouting, at half past five—ready to start his endless investigation of our decimated house. ("What shall I break?" were the first words he uttered one morning.) He goes to bed at eight-thirty, and Steve and I follow as soon after that as possible. We drop into bed every night with heavy sighs. "Three children is a lot," says Steve.

I wanted three children, and maybe more. Of course I can't imagine doing without any one of them. It's just that right now, life around here is so grueling I have to make advance arrangements just to step into the bathroom.

I lie awake, projecting into our future. In two years, Willy will be the age that Charlie is now—almost three (an age that seems thrillingly mature and independent by comparison). Someday, I murmur to Steve, we will have a three-year-old, a five-year-old, and a nine-year-old. Someday they will be five, seven, and eleven. Six, eight, and twelve . . . I spin the different combinations in my head like a gambler, dreaming of the perfect hand.

I call up a friend who has a child a few months older than Willy (I dial twice, because the first time my son pulls my glasses off. As we talk, he sings into the receiver, which is wet where he licked it. He grabs for my coffee. Points at the record player, demanding music. Gets himself tangled up in my extra-long telephone cord). "How long does this stage last?" I ask her. "When does it get easier?"

"Search me," she says. "I'm still waiting."

Our older two children are taking the new Willy surprisingly well, considering. They're devoted to him, even though (in the last two days) he has destroyed three pop-up books, the right paw of a Gremlin puzzle, and one of Mr. T's ears. Where once my children used to beg me to play cards or blocks, now all they can hope for, often, is that I'll get their brother out of their hair. "Mo-om!" they call out, at least thirty times a day. "Come get Will."

But he doesn't want me, of course. He's a wriggler, not a cuddler, and what he really wants are the other kids. He's a third child: the one I had no time to nurse after the fourth month. The one who got his milk unheated, straight from the refrigerator.

Willy's the one we were always calling by his brother's name (it had been so recently that we'd had that other blonde-haired baby boy under our roof). He's the one we never got around to sending out announcements about, never took pictures of. He grew, like one of those weeds that somehow manage to push up through the cracks in a side-walk, without a whole lot of close tending. Of course he walked at ten months: He could see this was no house to be a baby in. Not this year, anyway. Better to get moving, to grow up fast. So he did, and he has.

Our third child is a wonderful, cheerful baby, who smiles when his brother bops him on the head with a stuffed animal. Once when he was a few months old I heard a loud noise upstairs, where he was napping, followed by a small peep. I couldn't go check it out right away because Charlie had just got stuck in the sofa, while Audrey was trying to fold up the hideaway bed with him inside, and somebody had turned on the hot-air popcorn popper without putting a bowl underneath to catch the popcorn. When I finally managed to investigate upstairs, I discovered the bottom had fallen out of Willy's crib (which is, like everything else he uses, pretty beat up, from the two previous occupants). He was lying on the floor with his mattress on his head, cooing. This is a baby who does not expect life to be a bed of roses.

I tell these stories to friends, smiling ruefully, but they're sad stories too. I love babies, love sitting in a chair, just rocking them, smelling the tops of their heads, studying their toes, and I haven't gotten to do those things much this time around. Not that Willy's suffering: he has a brother who (in spite of the occasional bop) almost never races through a room without stopping to pat his head, and a sister who likes to hold him by the armpits and waltz him around the room to our Cyndi Lauper record.

Mostly I'm sad for Steve and me, that we're seldom able to relish this time and take it slow, that all we can do right now is grit our teeth and count the months until it's over and we don't have a baby around here anymore. And then—oh, will we ever miss it.

□

The hardest thing for me about having three children is finding a way to be with them one at a time. Used to be, with two, Steve could take one and I'd take the other. Now even when both of us are on duty, we come up short. The books I read to Willy don't interest Audrey ("If I hear 'Scat, scat, go away, little cat' one more time, I think I'll lose my mind," she says). Charlie wants to do puzzles. Willy wants to eat them. Audrey draws with markers. Willy scribbles on her picture. Willy wants to go out. Charlie wants to stay in. Charlie and Willy want to watch *Sesame Street*. Audrey is trying to play the piano. Audrey and Charlie want to see a movie. Willy insists on staying in the lobby, swinging karate chops at a life-sized cardboard image of Rambo. That's how it goes around here these days.

Being with one of our children—any one, alone—is a dream for me now. I'll sometimes corral one of them to come along with me on a trip to the dump, just for the few minutes we'll have in the car together. Every now and then the naps work out right, and I can fit in a game of Cootie with Charlie while Willy's asleep, or Charlie and Willy will go to bed early and Audrey and I can race off to her room and read a couple of chapters of a book with no illustrations that she loves and Charlie hates. I have caught myself, during those times, with an edge of tension in my voice that comes from knowing how rare this time is, and how much I want to do in it. "Let's not waste time setting up the Cootie legs in the holder," I say to Charlie. "Willy's going to wake soon." "Hush!" I snap at Audrey. "You'll wake your brothers."

Then I try to remember what the point of all this is— namely, just being together and giving whichever child I'm with the gift of my undivided attention. And then I think about the night I spent last winter with my son Charlie, snowed in at the Ramada Inn.

I was supposed to fly to New York City and interview a famous child-development expert who had a new book out. It was going to be a brief trip, but even so, my trips are always hard on my husband and children. So I invited Charlie, the one who had seemed in greatest danger of getting lost in the shuffle, to come along. I extracted the promise from him that he'd be good during my interview, which would take no more than a couple of hours, and packed a satchel full of all his favorite books, plus crayons, paper, and fruit roll-ups, to keep him occupied while I worked. After that, we would see the dinosaurs at the Museum of Natural History, have dinner with friends, sleep over, and fly home the next morning.

That was the plan. The day of our trip dawned cold and cloudy, with light snow flurries, but still we set out around lunchtime for the small, mostly commuter airport thirty miles from where we live to catch our flight to the big city. By the time we reached the airport, though, the snow had turned to ice and the runway was coated. No planes flying out all day, and no way I could make the thirty-mile drive back home. So I crawled at ten miles an hour, stopping three times to de-ice the windshield, to a Ramada Inn a few miles down the highway from the airport and checked in with my son. "Is this New York City?" he asked, looking dubious. (Maybe he'd slept through the plane ride? Maybe the inter-

view was over, before he'd even got to eat his fruit roll-up?)
No, I explained. This is Keene, New Hampshire. There's
the supermarket where we sometimes shop, and there's the
car wash Dad takes you to. We're sleeping here tonight.

Of course the first thing I did was make a call to the city,
postponing the interview until the following week. Then I
called Steve, back at the house, and told him not to worry. I
was so cold from being out in the storm that I unpacked my
flannel nightgown and Charlie's sleeper suit and, even
though it wasn't yet four o'clock in the afternoon, put them
on. Then we made a pile of books next to our bed, climbed
under the covers, and read every one.

We played tic-tac-toe. We did dot-to-dots. We colored. We
took a bath. We sang "I've Been Working on the Railroad."
The motel had an indoor pool, and I, miraculously, had
packed a body suit that could pass for a bathing suit, so I
went for a swim while Charlie jogged around the pool, calling and waving to me and hiding behind the artificial potted
palms. Back in the room, I got into my warm clothes again
and ordered a chicken dinner from room service. We set up
our food cart in front of the big color TV and watched a
couple of shows before drifting off to sleep as the snow piled
higher and higher outside our window. Out on the highway,
hardly a car passed by. It felt as if the world had stopped.

The next morning I woke early to Charlie bouncing on the
king-sized bed. Pulling back the curtains. I could see our car
out in the parking lot, completely buried in snow and ice.
But the sun was shining. Plows were moving. We'd be out in
an hour or two.

We turned on the *Today* show and saw the child-development expert I was supposed to interview the day before,
talking about the problems of working parents. We got
dressed and headed for the motel restaurant, where we ate
French toast and picked up our paper placemats as souvenirs

of our trip. We packed our bags, stuffing in a couple of those individually wrapped soaps for Audrey and a postcard of Keene. We paid our bill and headed out to shovel the snow off the car. We were home in time for lunch.

———

UPWARD
MOBILITY

In my years of parenthood I've given a good deal of thought to the issue of children and money. I'm not speaking, here, of those depressing figures one encounters, periodically, that tell what it costs to raise a child these days—figures that (if I'm to take them seriously) leave Steve and me, with our three kids, about a million dollars short. And that's not even counting where we'll stand if even one of them turns out to have an overbite.

What I'm speaking of is how a parent goes about teaching her children (as our Depression-educated parents used to put it) the value of a dollar. About money in general—what it is and where it comes from, where it goes, and most of all, the appropriate attitude with which to regard it. That you shouldn't love it, can't hate it. Have to respect it, mustn't worship it. Not to squander or hoard it. And really, this money-explaining business makes communicating the facts about sex or religion or the electoral college system seem pretty elementary.

A child's earliest relationship with money is oral. Around the age of twelve months (but of course mine were precocious) they start putting coins in their mouths. Now Willy likes to put pennies in his big sister's bank, counting as he goes (one, four, seven, two, nine . . .). He has been known to tap me on the head at three in the morning with the sweetly voiced request, "Penny please, Mom." And in his rowdier moments, to tear through the house yelling at top volume, "Five dollars. Five dollars. Five dollars." It doesn't take long, clearly, for a child to grasp the idea that these are powerful words.

But where Charlie and Willy remain happy with any coin, Audrey has learned about the deceptive value (given their relative size) of a dime over a nickel. Her greatest reverence she reserves for paper currency. And when, once, she observed me bent over a stack of bills, in tears, she hustled off to her room and came back a few minutes later to shower me with a pile of hand-colored tens, twenties, and fifties, all bearing presidential-looking profiles. If money can't buy happiness, she's learned, it can at least cheer a person up.

I won't attempt, here, to fully dissect the bizarre anatomy of this particular family's finances. Steve and I—who haven't had a single employer or a weekly paycheck in our seven years of marriage—collect our dollars pretty haphazardly. Every now and then they rain down on us, and (never sure how long they'll have to last us) we may buy three lobsters or a car, or fly off to the Bahamas. And then there comes a drought, and the next thing you know I'm setting up a tableful of our possessions at the town flea market. Whatever the current state of our affairs, however, they are not typical or stable. Watching a local news segment, we can only laugh nervously as the money expert offers advice on a family's life and health coverage (and pronounces them, with only a hundred thousand dollars' worth, underinsured). We work very hard at providing our children with a happy and stable home, at being parents they can rely on. But as for owning a piece of the rock—well, the best we can offer is shifting sands.

Of course our own hard times have no real similarity to the poverty of, for instance, a babysitter we had once, who—at age twenty-two—got all her teeth pulled because she couldn't afford fillings. For us there has always been an end in sight, the promise of a check in the mail, no fear of being cold or hungry. We don't let our children entertain the notion that doing without new shoes or this months *Sesame Street Magazine* has anything to do with hardship. Still, it certainly hasn't hurt them to get the sense, during our leaner times, that my wallet isn't bottomless, that the bank is not some magical place whose windows one can drive up to anytime (in a car whose gas tank is perpetually full), with a cash drawer forever open and a fat envelope of bills always inside.

Partly because of the intermittent instability of our situation (and also, I think, because this is a universal fascination), Audrey is close to being obsessed with the theme of rich people and poor ones. When Audrey plays with her Barbies, the rich girl, in the evening gown and fur stole, is usually mean and speaks in a vain, cruel voice, while the poor one is sweet and humble. To Audrey, rich means having a house with several bathrooms. And having grasped the meaning of wealth, she's wasting no time in passing on the news to Charlie. A recent lesson at the school she periodically runs, which he has little choice but to attend, was titled "How to Draw a Rich Girl." (With lots of frills on her skirt, and smiling broadly, that's how.)

Like parents everywhere, we hold forth regularly (when Audrey's making faces over her asparagus and requesting that the crusts be cut off her toast, when she pours the left-over milk from her cereal down the drain) on the hungry children who would give anything for that milk and those crusts. Audrey's comprehension seems to come and go: I have found her feeding steak to our dog Ron, but also, as she stands at the edge of the giant sand pit that serves as our town dump, throwing away school worksheets and musing on how lucky it is that she did them in pencil, because some poor little girl who can't afford to go to school could pick them out and erase the answers and do the work all over again.

What else are my children learning about money? The concept of inflation seemed to come naturally: At a recent art show held in her bedroom, Audrey's pictures started out with price tags of one and two cents, but when (with her father, brothers, and me as customers) they started going like hotcakes, she began crossing out prices, upping them to ten cents, even thirty, as fast as we could hand over our coins.

Audrey is, at least, getting the idea that spending involves making choices and sacrifices, that if I buy her a new blouse, she won't be getting a turtleneck. We've tried to teach her about doing jobs to earn money and about saving it, too. (Like me, Audrey has frequently sold one possession to get the money for a different one, and like me, she maintains a strong appreciation for thrift shops and Salvation Army stores. Her most beloved outfit is a very fancy white organdy communion dress, only a couple of sizes too large, that we found at a yard sale—although she wears it seldom, for fear of appearing rich.)

I try, all the time, but pretty lamely, to make sense of the world for our children: Explaining the nightly news to Audrey as best I can during the commercials. Reducing to a six-year-old's terms the idea of money for defense versus a nuclear freeze. Playing a car game: Which costs more, a house or a hundred Barbies? a visit to the dentist or a trip to

McDonald's? But I know that, as much information as my husband and I give our kids, the world of finance and economy makes little sense—must seem more than a little surreal, even. We have a two-year-old son who, at the mention of Jesse Jackson, starts dancing wildly around the room and singing "Beat It" or "Thriller." We have a daughter who believed, after my wallet was stolen in New York last fall, that now we'd be poor. And here am I, trying to untangle things for them, while our checking account stands mysteriously overdrawn again, with our projected monthly budget looking good until the realization hits that we've forgotten to allocate money for food.

□

One of the biggest discount stores in our area was going out of business—every item marked down 50 percent. Now I bet I've made about five hundred trips to this particular store over the last ten years—handed over a couple of thousand dollars, for probably a ton of bobby pins, curtain rods, beach balls, and jumper cables. So it seemed necessary to pay (literally) my last respects.

The place had been pretty well stripped by the time I got there, with half of what was left broken or dirty, and heaped on the floor. The snack bar, where I had hoped to purchase Charlie's tranquility with a bag of popcorn, was closed down, looking like Pompeii at the moment the volcano erupted, with grape soda still percolating in a cooler and coffee cups on the counter. No time for coffee anyway. Shoppers were racing ahead of us, cleaning out all the most popular bra sizes, stripping the shelves of shampoo and vacuum-cleaner bags and batteries. The speakers that used to pipe gentle organ music in my ears were transmitting urgent messages, meanwhile—like an emergency broadcast system during a wartime air raid, notifying shoppers of additional markdowns ("hurry, hurry!") and reminding us that soon the doors would close forever. I picked up my pace and flung a pair of crew socks into my cart for my husband, hitting Charlie on the head by mistake. We were off and running.

There is a danger, at an event like this one, of confusing the end of this particular store with the end of civilization in general. You begin to feel as if this were your last chance ever to buy anything. So you get four lipsticks, and enough photograph albums to see your infant son through high school graduation. I bought sneakers for my three children's next three sizes, and, for Steve, five packages of underwear and (an impulse from somewhere out in left field) a set of car seat covers.

Charlie was pretty quick to pick up the tone of the event. Having rejected the seat in my shopping cart designed for children in favor of the deep basket section of the cart, he stood, as if at the prow of the ship, facing out to survey the ocean of merchandise before him. Sometimes he'd reel in a string of Christmas lights or grab a stuffed animal by the tail. In the shoe department he hauled in a whole clump of tangled together fuzzy bedroom slippers. His diaper had come undone and was hanging down one pant leg; he had appropriated a hat, and he was waving to people as if he were running for office. I had never seen the particular crazed look that appeared on his face when, after I let him down from the cart for a moment, he clutched a bag of sponges and began to spin in circles, singing "Beat It." Even after I picked him up and was walking briskly down the aisle with my son under my arm like a rolled-up newspaper, to regain my cart, he still kept reaching out hopefully for kitchen spatulas and panty hose. And of course I know where he acquired the tendency. As I loaded my bags into the trunk of our car, I couldn't even remember, anymore, what it was I'd bought.

The morning after our excursion to the going-out-of-business sale I spread my purchases out on the bed to show Steve. The crew socks were terrific, he said, but they were women's socks. The top of the blender was great, and so was the bottom. They did not, unfortunately, go together. Boxer shorts, when taken out of the package, turned out to be the kind of underwear that certain very corny comedians are discovered to wear when their pants fall down on stage. Steve informed me that he does not wear this type of shorts, but if he ever decides to join the circus he's all set, with nine pair. By the time I brought out the car seat covers we were both expecting the worst. The covers were intended, of course, for bucket seats. But who knows, someday we may buy a car like that.

Though the store had announced a policy of Positively No Returns or Exchanges (and did not seem at all touched to hear of what a devoted longtime customer I had been), a few days later I was able, after making the thirty-mile trip once more, to replace my two half-blenders with a fancy reel for Steve's fishing rod. When I got home, he looked at it with interest and said he has been meaning to learn how to fly cast, and maybe in a few years he'd get the hang of it.

This morning Steve stopped at our local clothing store—just for a minute—and bought a complete wardrobe of underwear. He said he would've looked for a sale, but he didn't think we could afford one.

□

The ice show was in town. Not in our town, of course (we had a circus with a couple of performing dogs one time, and that's been about it), but in the nearest big city, a hundred miles south of where we live. We thought we'd take the children.

Steve took Audrey to see this particular ice show several years ago, a couple of weeks before the birth of Charlie. Audrey was four then. Tickets cost a lot, but she'd never seen an extravaganza like that—all that glitter, those feathers, the sparkling lights, the twirling skaters in their ruffled skirts—and we knew she'd love it.

Audrey and Steve got home late that evening, after the long drive home, but she wouldn't go to bed until we'd studied every page of her souvenir program. She explained to me—with only the faintest wistfulness—that some kids got these special flashlights, with Mickey Mouse ears, and when the house lights were turned out for the show to begin, all those kids turned their flashlights on and spun them around. But if you got the light, you didn't get the program, and the program was better.

We read and reread that souvenir program all year. First, just Audrey and me; then three of us, Audrey with one arm wrapped around her newborn baby brother; and then (when he got older, and wilder) we did our reading during his naps, when we could be sure he wouldn't lunge for the pages and rip them (as he frequently did when we were reading). By the time the next February rolled around, I knew the names of all the stars of the ice show, and how old they were the first time they put on skates. I could tell you the name of the choreographer, the assistant choreographer, and the lighting designer.

So when commercials started appearing on TV for that year's all-new ice spectacular, Audrey would shoot me a longing look. Money was tight that winter. I remember bringing a few boxloads of china and antique lace to the secondhand store in town to come up with money for three tickets.

That year we left one-year-old Charlie at home with a babysitter and set out with a backpack full of homemade snacks and a thermos of juice. Once again Audrey came home from the ice show with a souvenir program—and a new ambition: to be a figure skater. Every pond I'd drive past that winter, I'd study the ice conditions, looking for a spot where we could work on our skating.

The next winter we were broke again, and once again I was pregnant. As it turned out, Willy was born the day before Audrey's sixth birthday party was supposed to take place. Because the party had to be canceled, Steve took Audrey and Charlie into the city instead, to see the ice show—the first time for Charlie. He came home clutching his program and talking about those Mickey Mouse flashlights we couldn't get. I sat on the bed, nursing newborn Willy and feeling a thousand miles away from ever again dancing on the ice.

This year when they started advertising the ice show on TV, I made no promises to the kids. With Willy walking, every outing is complicated—putting three children into snowsuits, buckling three children in the car. Steve and I tried taking them all skating one afternoon last week (pulling Willy in a sled), and gave up before Audrey had her second skate on, when for the second time in ten minutes, and bundled into layers of snow pants, Charlie announced he needed to go to the bathroom.

Then last Sunday morning, while we all had breakfast, I started thinking about the ice show again. Not wanting to raise the children's hopes, I passed a note to Steve, suggesting it, and he nodded. I called up Boston Garden: good seats still available. We found a babysitter for Willy and headed for the city.

Our seats were high above the ice ("Is this heaven?" I heard one woman ask in the only row behind us) and Audrey was disgruntled about that. The show had not even begun before the barkers were upon us, offering hot dogs, sno-cones, Cokes, balloons, popcorn, and of course those flash-lights. Our children knew the one-treat rule, but still they looked enviously at the children around us, wearing their Donald Duck beanies or hats with blinking lights on the brim, licking ice creams, sipping drinks.

The show began. All our favorite Disney characters were there, and the beautiful blonde star, in a costume even more dazzling than the one I remembered from the pictures in last year's program. The clown was funny. The villains were mean. The chorus was in perfect step. One of our favorites was a daredevil skater who bounded out, jumped through a flaming hoop, somersaulted backward, and landed standing up.

Now I want to say clearly that our children didn't behave badly at the ice show. Charlie mostly concentrated on his sno-cone, but he didn't whine for more, once it was gone, or beg for a glow-in-the-dark sword. Audrey sighed when a woman skated out wearing a gauzy blue fairy dress and wings. After the show was over, both children even thanked us for taking them.

But driving home, with the children asleep in the back, the Happy Meal boxes strewn on the floor of our car, the souvenir program lying between the car seats, I felt an odd sadness come over me.

The day had cost us—with meals, gas, parking, and babysitter—seventy dollars. This year we could manage it better than before. But along with that easing up of my wor-ries has come something else: We have begun taking too much for granted. That naturally, when the ice show comes to town, we'll go. Naturally, the costumes will be dazzling. The skaters could fly, and—accustomed as we have become to marvels—it might not astonish us.

Crossing the state line back into New Hampshire, we passed a moonlit pond, with no snow on it, and a perfectly glassy surface. I looked at Steve. We were both thinking the same thing. Next year, we'll just take the children skating on a pond.

□

The invitation, addressed to Steve and me, said we were part of a select group chosen to visit Outdoor World, a new concept in vacationing. And just for listening to the no-obligation introductory tour and lecture, we'd have our choice of three exciting gifts: a gas-fired barbecue, a portable telephone–clock radio, or a grandfather clock.

I had just been thinking it was about time Steve and I took off without the children for a day at a beach that happened to be right down the highway from Outdoor World. I had also been thinking we could use a barbecue. We are the only people I know who grill their hamburgers in a birdbath.

Plus, friends of ours recently took one of these no-obligation tours, and not only did they come home with a movie camera, they had a good time too. "While you're listening to the lecture, you sort of make believe that you might really buy the time share, or a condo, or whatever it is they're selling," my friend Kem said. "It was a nice fantasy."

So I called for our appointment, assuring the voice at the other end of the line that I was indeed over twenty-three, that Steve and I are employed and earning more than an amount so modest I figured this couldn't be the most select vacation concept in the world. A person could qualify for Outdoor World and food stamps at the same time.

Saturday morning we headed for the beach. We had a good five hours in the sun before it was time for our appointment but still it was hard to rouse Steve, who was in the middle of a good book. "How long does this tour take anyway?" he asked, and shaving a half hour off what I'd heard over the phone, I told him an hour and a half.

We found Outdoor World easily: a broad expanse of scrub

and dirt, right off the highway, with a faintly incongrous lookout tower plunked down in the middle. As we drove in a guard who looked about eighteen, with bad skin and a uniform way too big for him, stopped to check that we were on the visitors list. As we sailed through the checkpoint we smelled smoke and saw that a woman who appeared to be the Outdoor World recreation leader had started a barbecue, using a couple of cinder blocks and some old metal racks that looked like refrigerator shelves salvaged from the dump. That made us feel right at home.

Most of the other couples waiting for their tours were already lined up in the reception area—a pretty motley-looking crew, for the most part. A lot of them were discussing the relative merits of the grandfather clock over the portable telephone. One man put in a request that the tour leader talk fast and get the whole spiel over with in an hour.

It turned out we would each have our own personal tour leader. Ours was Tammy, newly transferred to this particular Outdoor World from another one out west. I had meant to ask no questions and discourage small talk, to keep things moving, but both Steve and I found ourselves liking this woman, asking about her drive cross country and how she liked New England. It was fifteen minutes before we got going on the tour.

The "concept," as they like to call it at Outdoor World, was this: For a basic membership fee, plus annual dues, we'd be entitled to stay for free at any Outdoor World campground across the country. (At this point, Tammy was flipping through a colored brochure, showing us campgrounds that looked a lot more luxurious than this one, which was, she assured us, new and not yet completed. "Use your imagination," she said, gesturing with a flourish in the direction of the scrub.)

Free campsites might be all very well, I said, but we don't own a camper. No problem, it turned out. For just fifteen dollars a night, we could rent a pop-up camper at any Outdoor World. Nineteen dollars could get us a little trailer with kitchenette. For around thirty dollars we could live like kings in a two-bedroom camper. For thirty-nine dollars there was the deluxe model, with TV, microwave, separate master bedroom, and wall-to-wall carpeting.

Now, I have to tell you, it was these campers that got to me. We live in an old house: hardwood floors, exposed beams, three fireplaces, dutch ovens, the works. We have privacy, birds, woods, wildflowers. But sometimes I feel I spend my whole life—every waking hour—taking care of this home of ours.

I suddenly pictured the streamlined life we could lead if we belonged to Outdoor World. Zapping up our dinners in the microwave or outdoors, at the campground, on our new barbecue. Eating off paper plates. No toilet-paper-roll collections stashed under the children's beds. No year-and-a-half-old plaster cast, from a child's broken arm, collecting dust in the closet, along with about three hundred similar souvenirs. No lawn mowing and garden weeding and house repairs and septic trouble. And in all that extra time we could be exploring our country, spending time with each other and the kids. Gypsies, with not a care in the world besides which Outdoor World to stop at next.

Of course I didn't quite imagine dropping everything and moving into a camper. But I have to admit that by the end of our tour (getting the lowdown on campgrounds on the French Riviera, the Alps, Italy, Greece, the British Isles) I was pretty curious as to how much the whole thing cost.

Six thousand four hundred dollars. That was for the basic membership, in one campground, for life. But then there was the Master Membership, with full privileges in all five hundred campgrounds worldwide, lasting not just for one lifetime but for three. The thought of our grandchildren, and their children, hooking up their propane tanks on their camper sometime in the twenty-first century was a little overwhelming.

"What do you think the Master Plan costs?" Tammy asked us. Twenty thousand dollars, said Steve. Twenty-five, I suggested.

"Just a thousand dollars more than the basic membership," said Tammy, beaming. But only if we signed up this very day. Even as she spoke, the loudspeaker was announcing names of new members and reminding us that there were only a few places left.

It's hard (now that I'm back in my messy, cluttered, inefficient, unstreamlined house that I love more than any other place on earth) to reconstruct my thinking processes that afternoon at Outdoor World. It's embarrassing, too, knowing how close I came to becoming one of those faces in the Polaroids on the walls at the Outdoor World reception area: New Members, still working on their first lifetime. Now the whole thing seems, obviously, like a racket. But right then, thinking about those campsites waiting for us, those built-in beds, that no-wax linoleum, that endless coast-to-coast expanse of swimming pools, recreation directors, and hibachis, the idea of having our family vacations all figured out for the next three lifetimes sounded very tempting.

It was Steve who took my arm and steered me out the door (picking up our gas-fired barbecue along the way). Five minutes later, back on the beach, watching the sunset, I had got my senses back, and I heaved a sigh of relief. Easily taken in as I am, I told Steve, I don't know how I managed to make such a smart choice in a husband.

□

We were going camping, but first we had to buy a new tent. We had one, but it wasn't big enough to hold all five of us. So Steve said he'd just run over to the sporting goods store and pick up a two-man model he'd seen on sale there the week before. I announced that the children and I would come along.

"There's no need for both of us to go," said Steve. He knew exactly which one he wanted. He'd be back in an hour.

But the children were up for an excursion. (Audrey was already arranging pillows in the back of our van. Charlie and Willy were gathering up their stuffed animals in preparation for the half-hour drive. Even a visit to the supermarket is a major production for us these days.)

"All right," Steve said, twenty minutes later, after Audrey returned from one last trip to the house for her new Chinese parasol, with Charlie close behind carrying an additional half-dozen books. And we all took off.

In the entry of the store there was a deluxe four-man tent set up, complete with sleeping bags inside and even a circle of rocks and a hibachi in the front, artificial hot dogs resting on the grill. There was a lantern, and four camp stools surrounding the artificial campfire. A bag of marshmallows, even. Steve walked briskly past the display, heading to the ninety-nine-dollar model at the back of the store, which he had picked out the week before. "Here it is," he said, pointing happily to a small green tent, low to the ground, with no sleeping bags inside and no marshmallows.

Charlie climbed right in. He lay down in the tent, put his thumb in his mouth, sucked for a moment, and announced that he liked it. Audrey wriggled in beside him, looking thoughtful.

By the time the saleswoman approached us, Steve was already reaching for his wallet. "This is the one we want," he said—not one to linger in stores any longer than is absolutely necessary.

"Now we do have another model of this tent for just twenty dollars more, with a double reinforced zipper and a sturdier rain shield and pockets for things like car keys," said the saleswoman, pointing to a nearly identical model, in blue, across the aisle. Right away, Audrey perked up.

So we inspected the hundred-nineteen-dollar tent—zipping and unzipping, trying out the rain flaps, the window, his thumb. Charlie liked this one too, but Steve looked dubious. "I had the other tent all picked out," he said. "It'll do the job just fine."

"Since we're getting a second tent, and we'll be going to all the trouble of carrying it and setting it up, maybe it would make sense to get one of a little better quality," I suggested. Steve, a more experienced camper, said the ninety-nine-dollar model had everything we needed.

"Blue is Charlie's favorite color," said Audrey, helpfully. "And what if a hurricane came, and water got in the green tent? My dolls would get wet."

"Dolls?" said Steve.

The two of them were still debating that one as I wandered over to a hundred-and-eighty-dollar tent with a screened porch attached. Charlie was wriggling into a model called the marmot, a mummylike construction just big enough for one person. The saleswoman was explaining that bikers use that kind of tent on cross-country trips. She was beginning to look a little edgy.

Audrey, meanwhile, had discovered the dehydrated meals, in their little foil packets. "We can have ice cream," she said, calling out flavor possibilities to Charlie. Steve was still standing back at the ninety-nine-dollar green tent, like a man on the deck of a sinking ship.

"The great thing about this tent," he was saying, stroking the green one, "is that it's light enough to put on your back. When you get out into the wilderness you don't want to be carrying any extra baggage."

I don't think anybody was listening, though. Audrey was testing back rests. Charlie was inspecting compasses. And I—always a comparison shopper—found myself drifting over to the deluxe four-man tent in the display (the one with the marshmallows). "I thought I'd see how much this one costs," I said. "Just out of curiosity."

The deluxe model—on sale that week—cost a hundred ninety-nine dollars. Just a hundred dollars more than the little green tent (that's how I put it). Or twice as much (if you were talking to Steve).

Audrey, seeing me glance at the price tag, rushed right over. "Wouldn't it be great if we bought this one?" she said dreamily. Charlie was playing with the pretend campfire. "I like the rocks," he said.

We got inside. (With this tent, you didn't even need to crawl—it was that roomy.) We lay down—Audrey, Charlie and I—on the sleeping bags and stared up at the roof of the tent. Which had a skylight.

"Cozy," said Audrey.

"Awesome," said Charlie.

Out in the store, meanwhile, I could hear Steve asking the saleswoman if she'd seen his wife anywhere. "Do you have a little boy who was trying out butterfly nets?" she asked him. "Probably," said Steve."Well," she said, "last time I saw him he was over by the hunting knives."

It wasn't easy, but we tore ourselves away from the big tent. I went over to Steve. Told him maybe this one made sense for us. "The green tent is fine now," I said, "but think of what it will be like when our kids are teenagers." And then I mentioned an issue of occasional debate: the possibility that someday we might have another child.

"My sister!" Audrey cried out. "We have to leave room for her."

"I don't think so," said Steve—and I decided not to ask whether he was referring to deluxe tents or additions to our family.

Well, from then on things got dicey. Suddenly Audrey didn't even like the green tent. Steve said the one she liked was way too big. Charlie pointed out that it would have lots of room for stuffed animals. And camp stools. And pillows. And some books, and a few puzzles.

"Hold on," said Steve. "If you want all of that stuff, why bother going camping?"

I had been the original advocate of the big tent, of course, but suddenly I felt a wave of indecision. Actually, the little green one would be cozier. It did get hard, lugging stuff to our campsite. And then there was the issue of money. "For the amount we'd save by getting the green tent," I pointed out to Audrey, "we could buy you a winter jacket and ski pants." (She had been studying some earlier, over in the other half of the store.)

"You mean you're going to get me some?" she asked.

"No," I said. "You're missing the point."

We went back and forth for almost an hour. Just when I'd become totally convinced that we should get the smaller tent, Steve would say maybe we did need the big one after all. I'd lie down under that skylight and think, yes, it would be nice to see the stars overhead. And then Steve would stick his head in and say, "A hundred dollars more is nothing to sneeze at." "Right," I'd say. "Let's get the green one." And then Audrey would look disappointed, and Steve, observing her, would look unsure. And meanwhile, it was becoming increasingly clear that another half hour of debate could mean the total destruction, by Charlie, of the marmot tent. So it was decided.

"We'll take the big blue tent," said Steve, taking a deep breath while he wrote out the check.

"Right," I said. "Good choice."

But out in the car, buckling up our seat belts, I could see he wasn't happy. "That's an awful lot of tent we got," said Steve, pulling onto the highway for home. "I hope we didn't make the wrong decision."

"Fine," I said. "Let's turn back right now."

"It was going to be so simple," he sighed, another mile down the road. "I was going to walk into the store, pick up the green tent, and go home. How did I get off course?"

"Turn back," I said.

He drove another ten miles, looking miserable.

"Turn back," Audrey begged. "I don't care which tent we get, I just want to be happy."

We drove back to the store. We sat in the parking lot debating tent sizes for another five minutes. In the end we decided—without even getting out of the car again—to keep the big tent and go home. Not so much because it seemed better, anymore. Only that we couldn't stand one more complication.

"Are you going to be mad every time we look at this big, expensive tent?" I asked Steve.

"No," he said. "I'm just going to let it be a reminder. To keep things simple."

Which is, of course, the whole reason why we go camping in the first place.

———

TALK OF THE TOWN

□ *Softball Season* □ *Ursula Leaves Town*
□ *Marlon Brando's Phone Number*
□ *The Norton Fund*
□ *School Play* □ *Travelers Pass Through*
□ *More Babysitter Problems*

Every spring Steve debates whether or not to join up with the softball team again. (Two games a week, plus occasional umpire duty, take up a lot of time. Then there is the risk of injuries—something he never thought of seven summers back, when both of us were younger and felt invulnerable.)

In the end, Steve always signs up again for his old spot, center field, and though time was I would have welcomed the end to his summer softball career, the truth is now I'd miss watching him from the bleachers nearly as much as he'd miss playing. It's six years now that he's been on the team— six years I've been packing up children, juice, cold chicken, diapers, nerf balls, and Goldfish and heading out to games.

It has become as much a part of the rhythm of summer as tending my zinnias or picking blueberries.

We were less than two years married, new to this town and to small-town ways, the summer Steve first joined the team. Of course the softball league had been around forever, but his was a new team, just starting up—a team of men who had little in common but the fact that they had not grown up here. That, and the love of softball (although for nearly every one of them it had been more than a few years since his last time at bat). The local paper sponsored the team, which meant that its editor (also an outsider and a would-be ballplayer) bought a dozen regulation balls and black T-shirts with THE MESSENGER printed on the front. We were assured of press coverage, if nothing else.

It was a motley crew of players then (and still). It happens that Steve is a good ballplayer, with a long Little League history behind him and plenty of all-around athletic gift, but in fact he would have been urged to play even if he'd never before put his hand in a glove. I had simply gone into our local bookstore one afternoon, and the owner asked me if my husband might like to play ball. I said I thought he might. The bookstore operator said, well, that's two people on the team, anyway. He—a (predictably) bookish fellow named Jake—had never played the game himself, but he was open to learning. He was even reading up on the sport. And of course there would be other players.

And there were. There was Mark, a young lawyer, new to town, recently separated from his wife. A smart, sophisticated, highly articulate man—gourmet cook, music lover, wine connoisseur—whose fondest childhood memories were of sandlot Little League. Fred, a big, bearded carpenter who lived in a cabin in the woods. Phil, a private-school administrator, Princeton graduate—a fellow who knew every obscure rule in the playbooks, and the batting average of every

Red Sox player from 1955 on. Douglas, a friendly, easygoing local boy who worked at the lumberyard. Pete, a shy, gangly naturalist who hitchhiked fifteen miles to games (and then home again) because he didn't own a car. Gus, who'd left a job at Procter & Gamble to live, without electricity or running water, on a piece of old family land he was farming at the farthest end of town. Ray and Jim and Marty, three bachelor brothers, house painters, who rode to games on motorcycles, with different girlfriends on the back every time. Sam, the hearty, beer-bellied manager of a local plant, an unexpectedly erudite man who quoted Camus and made his own Polish sausage. Ernie, the newspaper editor, and David, his one and only reporter-photographer, a red-bearded former high-school track star. Steve, my artist-and-house painter husband. Jake, the bookstore owner, son of a former Russian ballerina and a Harvard classics professor, who'd never swung a bat in his life. And a few others, who dropped in and out, over that first summer.

They weren't exactly cheered into the leagues, those Messengers. Even then (seven years ago), the players were mostly older than those on any other team, and a pretty alien-looking lot, with their beards and their leftward-leaning bumper stickers, Gus's multicolored old pickup, Mark's Peugeot. Not everyone on the team fit the label, but the Messengers swiftly acquired the reputation for being non-conformists, a little weird. Different, mainly. That was enough.

But it turned out that those Messengers could play ball. The team had a few stars. Hot-tempered Fred, a power hitter who might strike out twice in a row, then come up with a crucial home run when the bases were loaded. David, a smooth, effortless-looking pitcher. Mark, the cool, analytical shortstop. Big Sam, in his catcher's mask, more agile and graceful than his shape would have suggested. Six-foot-four-inch Phil, at first base, with arms and legs so long he seemed able to span the distance between first base and second. Steve, known for his speed as a runner, and for making occasional impossible catches in the field.

Behind the bench, the glory of the husbands belonged to the wives. The women—I among them—lined the single row of bleachers, sipping beer and catching up on town news, but always when it was our own particular favorite coming up to bat, each of us would focus on him. Some, like Fred's wife Maria, liked to call out encouragement just before her man went up to bat (and later, when he made it to home). My way was always to go suddenly tense and quiet.

Of course it was only a game (I used to say, especially in the early days). I used to make fun of them all, and how seriously they took their playing: the way Fred would sometimes come close to striking the umpire on an unfair call, the gloom that would overtake the players on the bench when they lagged by half a dozen runs. Then, gradually, I saw the thrill of a good play: Ray to Marty. Marty to Mark. Mark to David. I'd feel, for myself, the euphoria that came when (to the jeers of a particularly hostile opposing team) Fred would hit a home run and the Messengers would rally. I saw the men embracing on the field, as if they were brothers, and wished I could play ball too, wondered if I could ever make a hit out there.

In fact, there was one woman on the team (the only woman in the league. Naturally she belonged to us). Doris was a mother of two, well into her thirties: a small, tight-muscled woman who showed up for every game, even though she seldom played more than an inning. She made hits, she caught the ball. She could run. She simply wasn't as good as most of the men, and so, like Jake from the bookstore and Ernie from the newspaper, she warmed the bench a lot. She was the source of some fierce debate too. Some players felt that everyone deserved equal time on the field (the point was simply having fun out there). Some players had the killer instinct, their eye on the league pennant, and because of them, Doris sat out a lot of games.

There were plenty of bitter moments that summer and every one after it. Fights with other teams, fights among our own (brothers when they won, hotheads when they lost). Back on the bleachers, the women arbitrated battles among the children (just a couple of kids, that first summer, and then new babies every season after). We followed the progress of a dozen pregnancies over those half-dozen summers (kidded each other, every year, about whose turn it would be next June to wear the maternity tops that went the rounds). Many of us saw each other only in the summer, and so the children seemed to shoot up, mysteriously, from the September playoffs to the first practice the following May. Audrey went from diapers and eating dirt, that first year, to riding a baseball bat as if it were a hobby horse, to organizing softball games of her own on the sidelines with the children of other players. She and Fred's daughter, Chloe, were the senior children, presiding over a growing band of babies and toddlers. Every year the two old-timers would lead the young ones off, instructing them in the peculiarities of each playing field. Poison ivy growing here. A good cemetery to play in over there. In one favorite playing field, a swingset and teeter-totter and a water fountain.

The passage of years showed in other ways, too. In the final game of the Messenger's second season, Steve collided with Ernie in the outfield, both of them running to catch the ball on a crucial play. Steve broke his leg, and after that the wives always looked worried when they saw two players running for the same ball, and someone always yelled, "Call it!" The next season a carpenter named Bill broke his shin, slamming into a second baseman, and developed complications. The next summer he came back, but only to watch, not to play. When he told us he'd had to give up carpentry, and was studying for his real estate license, a kind of chill went through the group. Nearly everyone had kids by now, mortgage payments, doctor bills. The Messengers didn't take so many chances anymore.

Somewhere around the fourth season, David, the red-bearded pitcher (sports editor for a bigger newspaper now), had to sit the summer out on account of having broken his arm in a winter basketball game. Steve broke his arm too, skiing. The wife of one star player left him ("He's always loved ballplaying more than me," she said before leaving town for good). Doris gave up benchwarming in favor of amateur theatricals. Douglas got married and switched to bowling and volleyball. Gus got a telephone. Ricky, the team hellion, became a cop. Phil got a job near Boston as headmaster of a large private school. Sam turned forty and turned in his catcher's mask.

Steve still played, and so did a handful of others from that first summer's team—most of them even improved their playing, one way or another—but none was so quick to slide into home plate anymore or to try to steal a base. The players no longer went out for beers after the game (the kids had to get to bed, and besides, they'd be up early the next morning).

Of course, the roster changed considerably over those six seasons. The team changed its name when *The Messenger* stopped sponsoring. For one season, the players all wore T-shirts proclaiming "This shirt not paid for by The Messenger." Then they became Homestead Builders, with a whole group of young and unfamiliar faces on the bench. And though they have yet to win the league championship, summer after summer they come close.

One odd turn of events is the surprising alliance the old Messenger players have built up over the years with the once-hostile adversaries on other local teams. Rivals on the field, still, they meet in the streets or at a wintry town meeting and shake hands, comparing summer plans and team rosters. They call each other Stevie, Freddie, Davey, Boomer.

There is something that happens to men who have played ball together. They may not have dinner at one another's houses, may not even know where the other fellow works (certainly almost none of my husband's teammates has ever laid eyes on his paintings). And still the bond is tight, and deep.

They haven't gotten around to taking a team portrait these past few seasons. We keep Steve's from that first summer framed and hanging on our bedroom wall. The familiar faces in their black T-shirts catch my eye often, through the year: sober-looking young men, with babies and toddlers on their knees who are second-graders now. Younger, slimmer, with longer hair, and more of it. They are smiling, most of them, even though they'd lost a game moments before the picture was taken. It was summer, after all. There was still beer in the cooler. There would be other games, more victories.

I remember a night (we were in the sixth inning of a game against J and J Auto Parts) when an unexpected rain began to fall, just as the sun was setting, and a rainbow stretched clear across the field, from third base to first. Even the youngest children looked up from their hot dogs and squirt guns to watch. There was another night, when a giant purple hot-air balloon landed smack in the middle of the outfield during the seventh inning of a game against Contoocook Furniture. And then there was the night we played Profile Seafoods (this goes back to that first season, the only one in which Jake, the bookstore owner, ever played). It was August, and though the team always let Jake go in for an inning or two, as long as the score wasn't close, he had yet to make a hit or catch a ball in the field. That night someone hit a pop fly, right in his direction, and he reached up his arm (more of a wave than a catching attempt) and caught the ball. He was so dazzled and amazed that he began jumping up and down, right there in the outfield, doing a little dance, screaming, "I caught it. I actually caught it." The other Messengers joined in, yelling and calling out his name. Everyone was so happy that not one of us even noticed the runner from the other team, sliding into home plate to score. That night, nobody even minded.

□

I first met my friend Ursula more than ten years ago. We had just moved to town and knew no one.

Ursula and her husband Andy were outsiders too—though they had lived here close to thirty years. In their early sixties then, their children grown and gone, they didn't belong to the big white church on Main Street, or the Moose lodge, or the local American Legion post. Andy was a long-time leftist who still reminisced fondly about the presidential campaign of Henry Wallace. He was a printer by trade, and briefly (until local sentiment forced him out) editor of the town paper, *The Messenger*. Ursula was a retired elementary-school teacher, the daughter of Finnish immigrants, raised on a nearby dairy farm where her sisters and various nieces and nephews still lived. From the first I could see in her a melancholy streak I always imagined as having something to do with Finland and those long sunless months among the fjords—even though she was born in Massachusetts.

A neighbor introduced us, and Ursula invited me into her kitchen for tea and a slice of pie (blueberry) that day. In all my years of visits, all the hours I've spent in that kitchen, sipping tea and talking to Ursula, there was seldom a time when one kind of pie or another wasn't just coming out of the oven. I'm not sure what we spoke about then: her garden (from which she gave me cuttings), the birds she fed daily, who flitted around her garden in such numbers that it could have been an Audubon sanctuary. Sewing maybe—she did that, too. I do know she took me on a tour of her wonderful old house: the basement filled with canned goods, and

Andy's enormous, hundred-year-old printing presses; her sunny sewing room, with fabric scraps all around, and boxes containing the pieces from every pattern she'd ever sewn; the collection of rocks and minerals she and Andy had gathered on their expeditions around New England, Ursula's blue and white china, her wallful of cookbooks, and every issue of *Family Circle* and *Woman's Day* from the last twenty years, filed for recipes; the big old upright piano in her living room, painted salmon pink. The garden, filled not just with the usual perennials, but with wildflowers Ursula had dug up and transplanted, including a jack-in-the-pulpit whose single annual bloom she'd call me every year to announce.

I guess a person could call it woman's talk, all this discussion of pressure cookers and pie crust and flowers, crochet stitches and scarlet tanagers. But the truth is, we were always talking about more than those things, Ursula and I (or any of the dozens of mostly young people who passed through her kitchen constantly), over the years I visited there. What it came down to, really, was a way of looking at the world, a set of values, which acknowledged not just the importance of using old-fashioned cake yeast for making bread or of never cutting thread with your teeth, but also fairness and generosity and—always—a respect for the natural world.

A short woman (especially beside her tall, rangy husband), Ursula always despaired of her weight, and dressed mostly in loose homemade blouses and pants a little like pajama bottoms. My children always loved her embrace, in part, I'm sure, for the roundness and softness of her. Even for me, a grown-up, it felt good to get a hug from Ursula, and more than once, over the years, I turned up on her doorstep in need of one.

Even when I first met him, Andy wasn't entirely well. He was an infinitely gentle, slow-moving, vague sort of man, and a few years after I met him we learned he'd been diagnosed as having Parkinson's disease. He must've had it for years, but because he'd always been a little fuzzy, a little slow-moving, nobody noticed that much. I remember a visit Andy and Ursula made (to our kitchen, this time) just after the birth of Audrey: Audrey in Ursula's arms, wrapped in a patchwork blanket Ursula had just finished making for her, all of us eating slices of a pie Ursula had brought. Andy sat, by the woodstove, in a rocking chair, silently munching on his pie, and then, slowly, he spoke up. "Isn't it something," he said, "that a man actually walked on the moon."

Partly because of his completely unhurried, quietly thoughtful ways, he was a wonderful, natural companion to young children. When Audrey was little, I used to bring her to Andy and Ursula's house whenever I'd try to sew a dress or to do a little canning. Ursula and I would be bustling about in the kitchen and there would be Audrey and Andy, in the living room, sitting together in Andy's La-Z-Boy rocker, watching *Sesame Street*. "Are you sure Andy doesn't mind?" I'd ask—as the hours went by. "Oh no," said Ursula. "He likes watching that show anyway, but I don't usually let him."

The summer Audrey was three Andy began saying, quietly, that his heart was giving him trouble. Several times Andy and Ursula's daughter, Alison (who came to visit every summer), rushed him to the emergency room at a hospital thirty miles away. Every time, some doctor or other would take Ursula and Alison aside and tell them there was nothing really wrong and offer lectures on hypochondria. The Parkinson's was just affecting his mind, that was all.

All that summer, though, Andy was depressed. He stopped taking his afternoon swims down the road at Gleason Falls. He was too tired to take Ursula blueberry picking and looking for rocks. He told her she should learn how to drive. He sold his old horse, Duke, who had been living in the barn for years even though nobody could ride him.

Then one morning, very early, I got a call from Ursula, who was practically screaming. Andy had collapsed on the kitchen floor. The rescue squad was on its way. Come over, come over right away.

He was dead by the time they reached the hospital. Alison came; when she had to leave, Audrey and I drove back over with our suitcase and spent the night in an upstairs bedroom so Ursula wouldn't be alone. We woke early, but of course Ursula, who in the best of times was always up by five, had been up for hours. With breakfast ready.

Ursula lived alone in the big house four more years. We came by more often after Andy's death, but still she complained that there was no one to cook for anymore. Pies went bad, cookies went stale. The house was cold in winter. The garden was too much to keep up with. Ursula took in boarders a few times, as much for the company as for the money, but there was always a problem. They would turn out to be vegetarians, or they'd be on a diet, or they didn't believe in white sugar. Or they simply didn't stop enough, at the kitchen table, for tea and conversation.

So finally, last fall, Ursula packed up and moved to an apartment in Massachusetts, near her sisters and the family farm. She put her house on the market; and all winter, driving by (explaining to Charlie, for the hundredth time, why we weren't stopping at Ursula's for pie), I'd fantasize about buying it.

But somebody else bought the house, and the closing is today. Hearing that Ursula planned simply to abandon Andy's big old printing press in the basement, Steve and some friends spent all last weekend dismantling the press and hauling it to a neighbor's barn. I noticed, as I watched them carry the last pieces out to the truck, that (though she had left her irises and lilies in the garden, and the special late-blooming lilac Andy had planted for her), Ursula had dug up and moved her jack-in-the-pulpit. As for the pink piano, it's in our living room now, and I am working away at scales nightly. As Ursula says, no home should be without a piano, and no piano without a home.

□

My friend Jessica is, like me, a married woman, mother of three children, living in rural New Hampshire. She wears old clothes a lot and cleans out sheep stalls and buys groceries at Cricenti's. She's also a former Miss North Carolina, a fact which amuses her but isn't central to her existence these days. But because Jessica and her husband are innkeepers, she frequently comes in contact with a pretty unlikely sort of person for these parts—the kind who flies in to New Hampshire for the weekend with his girlfriend, who brings with her three suitcases, none of which contain mud boots. Some of these visitors are kind and considerate people—friends— and some are virtual strangers who stop in for a quick dose of the country and a few sets of tennis and the novelty of a venison steak before heading back to the airport.

Now the truth is, Jessica is a beautiful woman—with the kind of natural glamour that doesn't require klieg lights or makeup. She's an artist by training, but for the last twenty years it's been her children and her home to which she's mostly turned her talent. Now her youngest son has his driver's license and there are no more rooms left to redecorate, and she's finally able to get back to her studio. But that twenty years' interruption (as much as she chose it and, mostly, loved it) has had its cost. "Back in North Carolina," she recently told one of these weekend visitors from the city, "a young woman was either talented or pretty, but never both."

"Oh," said the visitor (an actress, an ingenue). "And which one did you used to be?"

Well, one day when I was over at Jessica's I asked her for a phone number I needed, and she handed me her address book to copy it down. And there on the same page with bug sprayer and bike repairs was the phone number of Marlon Brando.

Naturally I had to get to the bottom of this. It turned out that Jessica didn't really know Marlon Brando. But one of these weekend visitors had the number in her book, which she kept leaving around open, next to Jessica's kitchen phone (from which this weekend visitor was making frequent long-distance phone calls to "the coast"). And somewhere near the end of the weekend, after about the fourteenth of these phone calls—emptying out this woman's ashtray again—Jessica found herself copying down Marlon Brando's number. Also Jackie Onassis's number, and Ryan O'Neal's and Warren Beatty's, and a few others besides. Not that she ever intended to call these people up. She just liked flipping through her address book and seeing their names now and then.

It was her own private joke, having Omar Sharif in there with her veterinarian. Then, too, every now and then someone like me would spot one of those names, and sometimes, like me, they would comment; but frequently they would simply be silent, and forever after they'd be wondering, every time they called Jessica and got a busy signal, whether maybe she was on the phone with Marlon.

I was getting so much enjoyment out of the idea that Jessica asked me if I'd like to put a few of those numbers in my address book. What woman couldn't use the odd movie star in her life? So I said sure, and for the last couple of years now I've had Marlon Brando in there, right above "bus station," and below "barbershop." I never flaunt it, but every six months or so someone will notice the name there, at which point I either explain or (depending on the circumstances) simply act mysterious. The whole thing has worked so well I have come to feel that everyone ought to put a famous name or two into his or her address book, beside whatever number she chooses to make up. (The area code for Los Angeles, incidentally, is 213.) Not to put the neighbors in their place, or so the babysitter will see. Just as a reminder: There are all kinds of beautiful people.

☐

Because this is such a small town, the newspaper comes out only once a week here, and when it does the news is likely to be who won a milking contest and whose aunt has been visiting from Maine. For controversy we consider questions like whether or not to rename Dump Road after a beloved and recently deceased town fireman. Photographs on the front page feature unusually large trout, high-school athletes, and good-looking woodpiles. Then a month or so back, on the top of page one, came the headline "Two in Family Have Cancer," accompanied by a large photograph of Mr. and Mrs. Norton and their three children, all of them stiffly facing the camera and looking understandably grim.

The story below the picture went on to tell the Nortons' story, based on the reporter's visit to their home and the afternoon he spent there. Eighteen months ago, the family's middle son, Billy, was diagnosed as suffering from leukemia and put on a program of chemotherapy. Then, a couple of months back, on the very day Billy was found to be in remission, his father was discovered to be suffering from another form of cancer. The paper didn't say it outright, but for the father, especially, things don't sound too hopeful.

He can't work now, of course, the paper informed us, and neither can his wife, because she's so busy driving back and forth to the city, bringing her husband and son for treatments. The family has no medical insurance, no relatives in the area, no savings. Already they have had to give away their beloved family dogs. They don't know what they'll have to do next.

Reading news like this, of course, leaves a person reeling. (Also, filled with the knowledge of his own relative good fortune: Thank God it's not me.) I kept looking back at the faces of Mr. and Mrs. Norton (just a few years older than Steve and I, I figured). Mr. Norton very gaunt now, of course, but bearing the look of a man who used to be well built and muscular. Mrs. Norton, a good-looking woman, with dark circles under her eyes, her mouth forming a perfectly straight line. The little boy with cancer, his hair just beginning to grow back in tufts, like a baby's. Almost saddest of all were the older brother and younger sister, who don't have cancer. I wonder if they ever feel guilty about their good health.

At the end of the story about the Nortons there was a plea for contributions. "We're proud people," said Mrs. Norton. "We hate asking for help. We just don't know where else to turn."

Well, this is, as I said, a small town, and people here believe in taking care of their own. Even though the Nortons hadn't lived here all that long—didn't work in town, or belong to a church, or appear to have a lot of friends here—people began organizing the minute that story came out. Audrey came home from school a day or so later to report that every classroom was decorating a coffee can for local businesses to put out for contributions to the Norton Fund. Then the third grade announced a car wash. The school nurse approached me about donating the proceeds from a school play I was directing. There were posters for a dance on behalf of the fund, and then a concert.

It's come to the point where now you can't buy a cup of coffee or pick up a newspaper in this town without seeing one of those Norton Fund coffee cans and that photograph of the family taped to the cash register. A couple of days ago Audrey came home from school with a letter from the principal, informing us that the elementary school would be putting together a bunch of food baskets for the Nortons, to be delivered on the last day of school, and asking that every child in the school (about five hundred) bring a canned food item for the Norton family. When I forgot to send in a can, that first day, Audrey delivered an impassioned retelling of the Nortons' plight for me, and then marched off to survey our pantry shelves for good items. "I think one is enough," I said, as she reached for a whole stack of tuna cans. *"Mom,"* she said sternly, "they're desperate. Everybody has to give as much as they possibly can."

Well, I have become increasingly uneasy about all of this and about why I haven't opened my heart to the Nortons. All the more so because the family's situation is so unequivocally terrible. (Cancer. It's the nightmare that haunts us all. Multiplied by two.) Why don't I feel better about the way our community has rallied for these people—by doing precisely what my husband and I try to teach our kids? Namely, to always lend a hand.

It's just that I'm picking up these troubling undercurrents—hidden strings attached to all of our community's love and charity. It is almost as if, with the contents of our coffee cans, we have purchased the right to scrutinize every aspect of the Nortons' lives, and not surprisingly, they come up short in a few departments. There's the story told me by a friend about a mutual acquaintance of ours who lives near the Nortons. One of the gentlest, most sweet-natured women I know, she showed up on my friend's doorstep in tears, a couple of years back. Mrs. Norton had just chased after her, screaming, because—backing her car out of her own driveway—she had almost hit one of the Nortons' fifteen tied-up dogs.

Then there is another woman in our town, who tells my friend she drove past the Nortons' house the other day (drove out there specifically to check things out, actually), and what she saw were half a dozen dogs, still tied to trees, three ten-speed bikes, a new addition, and a moped.

"Why doesn't Mrs. Norton get a job?" I have begun hearing some people ask. Someone else will point out, then, that she has to drive her husband and son to treatments. "What about nights?" they ask then. "And what about the sixteen-year-old son? He could get work after school. He could help out."

We have all of us become experts on the Norton case. Our quarters and our canned tuna entitle us to speculate, debate, and finally, to judge. It's possible that Mrs. Norton isn't a very nice woman, I think to myself. But is her trouble any less real, for the way she screams at her neighbor? Do we only help people who don't tie up their dogs? Is what we want to see—driving past the houses of people we help out—signs of unabated misery? Does a person holding his hand out forfeit the right to a ten-speed bicycle? How about a five-speed, then? How about a one-speed?

Last night as we were clearing the table after dinner, I made a few remarks to Steve about some things I'd been hearing around town concerning the Nortons, and Audrey overheard. "How would *you* feel if you were them?" she pointed out. "You wouldn't act so nice either." And of course she's right.

So I sent a can of tuna in to school today, along with a can of baked beans, and some cream of mushroom soup that nobody in our family ever seems to want. I pictured what dinners at the Nortons' will be like this summer, as they make their way through five hundred cans of baked beans, sardines, and maybe the odd Spam. I thought again of the haunted face of that father—who is suffering (all of us here now know) from cancer of the left testicle. And the boy, reading in the paper that his chances for survival are "pretty good." And the healthy brother and sister—maybe stopping in Weber's News now and then for a pack of gum. Standing at the cash register, studying that construction-paper-covered coffee can with their family's name on it and knowing it's headed their way.

□

In September of the year Audrey turned six, a meeting of concerned parents who might like to raise money for an elementary-school field trip was called at her school. That seemed like a good idea. I had been a parent of a child in this school system exactly two weeks at this point, and hadn't burnt out yet. Audrey's new purple sneakers were still purple and not, as they would be come November, gray. She still had the top to her thermos. Life seemed filled with possibilities. So I went to this meeting, along with seven other mothers, six of them, like me, the parents of first graders.

We started talking about ways to earn money, and all the usual suggestions came up. A bake sale, a yard sale, a raffle. Then I said, "Why don't we put on a play?"

Even then I knew there were easier ways to earn money. (I think Steve, for one, would have written out a check to the school, on the spot, exceeding by a dollar whatever profits this play might conceivably bring in, if he'd known what this play would do to our life.)

But money isn't everything. I acted in plays all through my own school years (though never in elementary school. Nobody ever wanted to put elementary-school children in a play, and I had always wondered why. Stay tuned.)

Anyway, those old plays represent my happiest school memories. I wanted that for my daughter, and for the many children in this town who have never seen a play, never been applauded for anything they've ever done. I knew a few like

that, back when I was growing up—kids who could barely
read, kids who wore the same clothes every day and de-
voured their hot lunch as if they hadn't seen food for twenty-
four hours, which they probably hadn't. Goofy kids with
hardly any friends, oddballs who got on stage and suddenly
were stars. Children so shy they could hardly open their
mouths—but oh, could they ever dance. For them, especially, being in plays was a lifeline.

Everybody at the meeting agreed that a play sounded
great. Before I knew it, I was given the job of director, and it
was decided that we'd put the show on near the end of May.

End of May, I said. That's blackfly season around here. So
we made it a play about a little town like this one that's overtaken by blackflies. Of course the blackflies would be first
graders (typecasting). I would write the play. And every
child who wanted to could have a part.

Ninety-seven children wanted a part. "Don't worry," said
the teachers. "A lot of them will drop out." And before I
knew it the cast was down to ninety-four.

Every one of those children got a line. Every character got
a name. "Mrs. Apple, Mrs. Yogurt, Mr. Telephone, Mr. Paperclip, . . ." I would call out, at the beginning of Townspeople Scene Number 16. For the last dozen or so parts, I started
naming characters after whatever I saw on my desk.

They did get to know their lines, most of them—which is
not to say they knew when to recite them. There were times,
during rehearsals, when I thought I might have to stand
onstage throughout the performance, holding a yardstick
and tapping heads, like the player of an enormous human
xylophone. At every rehearsal, about thirty chilren lost their
script pages. About forty children would ask if they could go
to the bathroom. Ten needed change for the soda machine.
Five wanted to know when they'd be getting their costume.

We found a choreographer, but because she gave birth by

Caesarean section just six weeks before rehearsals began, there were a few problems. First, we needed a babysitter. Then, because she was nursing, we needed a breast pump. Then, when the breast pump didn't work, we needed formula. "Whatever you do, don't give Patrick formula with iron," were my last words to my choreographer, the day Patrick started taking formula. (Iron constipates.)

Wednesday the choreographer called me up to tell me Patrick was constipated. I told her how to carve miniature infant suppositories out of Ivory soap chips.

Thursday we were still waiting for the soap chips to take effect, and meanwhile, I was tap dancing.

I haven't told you yet about my friend Erica—another first-grade mother—whose job it was at rehearsals to keep certain fifth-grade boys from beating up or kissing certain first-grade blackflies. She called one morning to tell me she thinks she's getting ulcers. "I'm tired of being the heavy," she said—understandably. So that day her job was passing out Oreos.

I have not told you about Scott, who decided, after six rehearsals, that he didn't want his leading role anymore and dropped out. Or my closet, which by the last week of rehearsals was piled waist high with every item of clothing I had worn, but had not had time to hang up, in the last four weeks. Or the fact that I was spending about three hours on the phone every day, rounding up breast pumps and top hats.

But in the other column was a boy named Ben who's stayed back twice and still can't read much, who knew every one of his four lines perfectly. A boy named Jimmy who practically lives in the principal's office, who turned out to be one of the best actors in the school. A girl named Susan who was always the first one to arrive at every rehearsal, so she'd be sure not to miss anything. A couple of townspeople who danced their hearts out, and some who knew not only their own line but everybody else's too, which they would recite softly, under their breath.

When I told Jimmy's mother how good her son was in the play, she looked at me incredulously. "Jimmy?" she said. *"Jimmy?"*

The thing about a play is that when he's onstage Jimmy doesn't have to be Jimmy. He gets a fresh start. He's Mr. Paperclip. And people will clap for him.

□

We grow five kinds of tomato plants in our garden, and lots of basil. In August, when everything comes ripe, I cook batch after batch of tomato sauce from scratch. I can my sauce in quart jars—rows and rows of them, enough so our family can have spaghetti once a week for a year. I make an extremely thick, rich-smelling sauce, and I'm very proud of it. Every few months I go down the steps to the cellar, where I store my jars of sauce, and count how many containers are left, to make sure the supply will last us through to next year's tomato harvest. And while it's true that I love the taste of this sauce of mine, served up on a plateful of pasta, what I love even more is the sight of those jars, still unopened on my shelves.

Last year a happy miscalculation left us with more sauce than we needed. So one night, just days before I was due to can my new batch, we decided to give a spaghetti party and serve up what was left from the season before. I made a big salad, baked a couple of pies, rented a couple of Charlie Chaplin movies, and called up some friends. This being a small town, with not a whole lot else happening on a Tuesday night, most of them said they'd come, and one friend asked if she and her husband could bring along a pair of travelers they'd just met. We had plenty of food, so of course I said yes.

Here in New Hampshire, where new diversions are few and our social circle small enough that most of us run into each other at least half a dozen times in any given week, the kitchen is as good a place as any to create a little drama. Some of my methods could seem a little corny to sophisticates. (Piña colada, served in a coconut shell. Homemade potato chips. Tempura, served by a cook—me—in a kimono and accompanied by a scratchy record of koto music.) I stick sparklers in my cakes and fortunes in my cookies. I guess my theory has been, if you can't go to Peking, you might at least try Peking duck. And so our palates know a good deal of variety. Even if the rest of our lives does seem a little mundane.

On the night of the spaghetti party Steve and I fell into a routine of preparations so familiar we don't need to discuss them anymore. He scrubbed the bathroom. I waded through the grass to pick a bouquet of flowers. This being the first cool night of the season, he laid a fire, while I spread a tablecloth and chose my twelve favorite unmatched flea-market dishes. I stuck the garlic bread in the oven, he rinsed wine glasses. I fed the children early, Steve lit the fire. I put on a record and my best apron. And then we waited for the guests to arrive.

I love this moment: after the preparations are done, sitting by the fire, admiring my clean house, smelling dinner on the stove, listening for the sound of cars in the drive. On this particular evening, our guests were all old friends who come here a lot. All except for the travelers passing through: a couple named Jo and Martin, probably in their early thirties like Steve and me.

Before she even got out of the car, I knew Jo was going to be beautiful, with the kind of looks I most envy, because they have nothing to do with makeup or rollers, or days of trying on clothes in Bloomingdale's. She was tall and slim, but not skinny, tanned, with long straight hair held back by a tortoise-shell clip. She wore jeans that fit perfectly and a belt she had probably owned for fifteen years, and a white cotton blouse with mother of pearl buttons, and she carried an ancient-looking leather backpack, which, I later learned, contained all her wordly goods. Reaching out my hand to shake hers, I realized my other went—automatically—to stroke Willy's blond head. Because who I become, at a moment like that, is my children's mother. Who Jo was, was simply Jo.

She turned out to have an accent: exotic, unplaceable. I asked where she was from and she thought for a second. "New Zealand, sort of. But nowhere anymore, really." She and Martin, a lean, dark, remote-seeming man, were on the road—had been for over three years. They had spent last winter in Nepal, last week in London. Tomorrow they would set out for the west coast of Canada. But tonight they were in this little town of ours in New Hampshire, where spaghetti sauce was bubbling on the stove and an applewood fire was burning.

I've never been much of a traveler myself. I spent the first eighteen years of my life in one small New Hampshire town. When—during a brief stint in New York—I met Steve, we thought we'd get a van and just travel around for a year or so, picking up odd jobs on the road. Our friends took us at our word and showered us with sleeping bags, outdoor cooking sets, and road atlases for wedding presents. And they kept asking (a sore point) just when it was that we were planning to leave.

Our scheduled departure date was always being put off. I would find myself poring over seed catalogues. Steve began talking about how nice it would be, after our trip was over, to build a studio here. Intellectually, we knew that this was the time in our lives to be footloose and free. But we acquired a dog. And I kept thinking about what to name a baby.

We never precisely canceled our travel plans; they just got less and less ambitious. In the end, we spent a long-delayed honeymoon weekend at a beach a hundred miles from home, remarking frequently to each other on how good it was to have a change of scenery. Then we came back to this place in New Hampshire and had Audrey. Followed four years later by her brother Charlie. And two years after that by Willy. Now here he was in my arms, resting one sauce-orange hand in a proprietary manner on my shoulder, while Steve got Martin a beer and Jo examined my flowerbeds. Our dog Ron was licking her foot. Charlie was demonstrating his breakdancing.

Jo and Martin had no children. Neither did they own pets, a garden in need of weeding, a mortgage, a mailbox to which bills are delivered daily, or a pantry full of spaghetti sauce and preserves. Sitting by the fire, seeming instantly at home the way perpetual travelers often do, they told us the story of how they'd met. Jo had just come from India, Martin from France, when they ran into each other in a Moroccan cafe. From there they went to Scandinavia, working on a fishing boat, and then to Poland. "Never go to Poland in January," said Jo.

During dinner Jo told us about climbing the Himalayas, about an ashram she visited in India, how she'd sold liquor and cassette players on the black market and how much better it was to get dollars than rupees. She told us about a meal of hallucinogenic mushrooms they'd been served in Nepal. A fabulous dinner, she said. Adding that my spaghetti sauce was also very good.

But on this particular evening being a good cook seemed not to matter very much, and my stocked pantry seemed more like an anchor than a treasure chest. I asked Jo if she didn't find it hard, in her travels, to avoid the temptation of picking up possessions. (Knowing that, for me, part of the pleasure of a trip would be the acquisition of things to fill our house with when I got back.) No, she said. Things only tie you down.

After we had our pie and got the kids into bed, I asked Martin whether they saw many people with young children on the road.

"Oh, sure," he said. "They have a great time. Who wants to see their children get stuck in a rut?" But domestically minded as I am, I was wondering what those babies' parents did about naps and diapers, and thinking that our children have known too much of rootedness already to move easily into a nomad's life. Like me, our children are attached to familiar objects and rituals: Audrey lines up her dolls and animals in a particular order on her bed every night. Charlie maintains a corner of his room he calls his Keeping Area, where he arranges his two favorite Astrosniks, a postcard of Pinocchio he got two years ago, a cardboard teepee we made, and a plastic Happy Meal bucket from McDonald's. Even Willy likes to drink out of a particular cup, while sitting in a certain chair and watching his beloved *Pokey Little Puppy* video. I guess Martin would say my children are stuck in a rut.

This particular evening, what we were watching was Charlie Chaplin, in *The Gold Rush*, playing a lone vagabond who strikes it rich. When the movie was over, one of our friends took out his guitar and we sang a few songs. Sometime around midnight, the party broke up.

The next morning, eating breakfast, Steve and I talked about the travelers. What struck him about Jo and Martin, Steve said, was how you couldn't quite place them. Sort of like television characters who inhabit one of those towns with no climate or dialect, that could be anywhere. "They seemed weightless," he said—not really critically, just bemused. "I kept on thinking Martin was walking on air."

Feeling, myself, weighed down by about three thousand pounds of excess baggage, I said walking on air sounded fine to me. I looked at the sinkful of plates waiting to be washed, and the cat, licking scrambled eggs off Audrey's plate, and my two sons, fighting over a water gun, and said there were days when I wouldn't mind locking the door and walking away, standing on a highway, and sticking out my thumb.

Where I went that morning, instead, was into town on our weekly excursion to the dump, with a carload of trash. We ran into Jo and Martin on the way, just as they were setting out on their travels again.

"You know," I told Martin. "I dreamed last night that I was traveling. I woke up envying you."

He said that was funny; he'd dreamed he had a house like ours. I asked him if he thought of how he and Jo lived as just a stage in their lives, or if this was how their lives would always be.

"I don't believe anything lasts forever," said Martin. I thought at first he meant the traveling. But, studying the unsentimental face of this man who has got used to saying good-byes daily, I guessed that might apply to Jo, too, and wondered if she felt the same.

We are differently constructed, all right, those travelers and I. When I hear a song I love, I want to buy the record; when I spend a really pleasant evening somewhere, I want to spend another; when I met a man I loved, I wanted to set up housekeeping with him. When I encounter people who interest me, I write down their address and telephone number.

Martin and Jo, on the other hand, moved on that day, writing down nothing. I don't think they got our last name, or that in a month or two Martin, at least, will remember in which New England state they spent a night, eating spaghetti and blueberry pie. I got the sense, that night, looking across our living room, that Steve and I, and our children and our guests, were a few more characters in the epic drama of his travels. People he might tell about, in passing, some night in Nepal.

For a couple of days it depressed me, thinking of the adventures that they were having and we were missing. Wincing over what Jo must have thought about my stacks of women's magazine back issues, with recipes cut out, and the sentimental songs we sang that night. "Country Roads." "Red River Valley."

But I also thought of Charlie Chaplin, walking down that dirt road as the thatch-roofed farmhouse faded from view, twirling his cane with that brave jauntiness. And I know that though I may take some trips and wander down some roads in my time, it's life under the thatched roof for me.

Sometimes I find myself thinking of the night the travelers passed through, as we lie in our bed under our patchwork quilt, listening to the slow, sighing respiration of our dog, or our children murmuring in their sleep; sometimes an image of them flashes before me, just as I'm reaching for a jar of this year's batch of spaghetti sauce on my pantry shelves. Like Martin, I am never sure that anything can last forever. Still, I like having a few tomatoes growing in my garden and knowing I'll be here to harvest them.

□

Our babysitter Vicky, who'd been living with us for a year and a half and to whom our children were devoted, had moved on. Unable to face the prospect of replacing her with a stranger right away, I took the summer off, but by late August I knew I'd better get to work, so I started running my ad. I had been interviewing job candidates for several days when Lydia called, and we had a number of pretty good prospects lined up. But I could see, with many of them, that like all the babysitters who have come and gone before, they would move on sooner or later (probably sooner) to children of their own, or better jobs, new places. And where other applicants needed to be sure they'd be home by four, or specified (wisely enough) that their evenings and weekends were always reserved for their own families, Lydia burst into our lives to say that she would always be there for us. She had almost no family of her own anymore, and no home. (She'd been a live-in housekeeper, for the last year or so, for a man who owned a weekend place in the next town but almost never used the place, who paid her no salary, just kept the refrigerator stocked and attended to her bills. She was starved for companionship and activity. And I knew we could provide it.) "Whatever you can manage to pay me, that'll be fine," she said when I apologized for not being able to offer a handsomer wage. "I just want to work for you."

She was fifty-seven years old, but looked younger. She wore a T-shirt that said "I gave my soul to rock and roll" and big purple earrings, and she promised to show Audrey her entire costume-jewelry collection (a quick route to an eight-year-old girl's heart). She happened to have a spare pair of earrings on her, in fact. She put those on Charlie's bear— filling him with awe as well. Also in her purse: a harmonica ("you never know when you might need one of these"), a couple of coupons she thought I could use, and some interesting shells. She was full of cleaning tips, plans, recipes, good ideas of adventures to go on with the children. "Your kids will never be bored with Lydia around," one of her references told me, when I called the next day. Or as Lydia put it (hearing of our struggle to get Charlie to stop sucking his thumb), "he won't have time for that, I'll keep him so busy."

None of Lydia's references was a former employer, precisely, but they all knew her from way back and attested to her boundless energy and enthusiasm, her wonderful cooking, her efficiency around a house, and above all, her love of children. Ours were fascinated with her: She told them about meeting an Indian chief in Nova Scotia who made her a feather headdress. She told them about the meteor that landed on her cousins' Indiana farm, where they grew corn for corncob pipes, and how that meteor burned right through one side of the farmhouse and came out the other. She told me I should throw cucumber peels into our woodstove, to guard against chimney fires, and (hearing me start up the engine on our old Plymouth Valiant) warned me that the starter motor was about to give out. "Nonsense," laughed Steve. "I just gave the car a tune-up."

I hadn't officially hired her yet, but in the week or so while I was tracking down her references, Lydia called daily, sometimes twice a day. "I've been thinking about your kitchen floor," she would begin (cutting right through the small talk). "I know just the kind of oil to put on it. I'll get that floor so shiny you'll see yourself." One time she called to say she wanted to let me know she'd be out for a few hours. Just in case I called.

The truth was, I felt as eager to have her working here as she felt to work for us. Our lives (in the absence of Vicky) had already become so frazzled and hectic that I couldn't wait for her to start. Steve—always the cautious, moderate one—suggested we take some time before making a decision. But he was so busy, too, that it was usually ten o'clock before I'd get around to raising the babysitter issue, and by then we were both too tired to discuss it.

So finally I called Lydia and told her she had the job. She came right over, in a borrowed car (having none of her own), and began moving boxes in: Her crown of thorns plant. Her record collection: Jim Nabors. The Grateful Dead. Beethoven. Shoeboxes full of jewelry, stuffed animals, more plants, a Mr. Coffee she'd found at a yard sale, hardly broken at all. A wine carafe in the shape of a geisha girl. Her Indian headdress.

She spent the next few days moving in. Sometimes, when

she'd come with another carload, I'd be working at my desk in the downstairs of the little house where she'd be living, and once I was under such a tight deadline I had to tell her, as she bustled in and out, that this wasn't a very good time for me. "I'll be quiet as a mouse," she said, hauling her spider plant up the stairs. But she wanted to show me a recipe she'd been saving, and a painting someone had given her, and a necklace, and a stained-glass plant hanger. One time she just wanted to come over to the desk and give me a hug. "I love your family," she said. "You know, you'll never get rid of me."

She came over one night around dinnertime, a few days before she was due to start working for us, and mentioned how much she loved hamburgers, so naturally we asked her to join us. She began telling us stories about her former employer—how he cursed at her, that he knew jujitsu and could kill you with his little finger. She told about a woman whose children she cared for once, out in Ohio, who drank too much, and (when the children were out of earshot) a man she knew who sexually abused his stepdaughter. During dinner, I noticed, Charlie kept trying to say something, but he couldn't get a word in edgewise. Same with Willy. There was something about Lydia that simply filled up every inch of space in the room. After she left, no one said anything except Audrey, who remarked, "Boy, it's really going to be different around here."

Later, once we had the children asleep and the kitchen cleaned up, Steve and I lay silent in bed for a long time: both of us staring at the ceiling, both (I knew) thinking the same thing. "We've made a mistake," I told Steve. "Let's not do anything hasty," he said. "We'll talk in the morning."

But in the morning, he had to go off to work early, and then Lydia was on the phone to me again. She'd seen an ad in the paper for a jungle gym someone in a town just forty miles south of us was giving away to the first person who'd claim it. Maybe we should drive over there and get it? Meanwhile, she had another carload of stuff to bring over. Her former employer's girlfriend was moving into her old room, at her present house, and it was really uncomfortable being there. The employer was cursing at Lydia. The girlfriend didn't like Lydia's corned beef and cabbage. "She's not a very nice woman," Lydia whispered into the phone. "And I think the two of them are in trouble with the IRS."

A friend of mine had been over, visiting, when Lydia called. After I hung up, I told her what was going on. How I had begun to feel as though Lydia was not simply moving into our house, she was taking over our lives. That instead of freeing up my energy and concentration for my family, Lydia had me more frazzled and preoccupied than before. My privacy was gone. My home no longer felt entirely my own.

"I'll watch the children for you," said my friend. "Drive over and tell her it won't work, before you weaken."

So that's what I did. And Lydia, to her credit, was neither angry nor hostile. Only very very sad—and so, of course, was I. By the time I got home again, the phone was already ringing: Lydia again, holding the receiver up, so I could hear her former employer's girlfriend yelling in the background: "Don't you bring your damn junk back here. You're not sleeping here tonight."

We spent the next three days moving Lydia's funny, lovable, sad accumulation of possessions out, to the home of a friend who said he'd take her in until she found another job. And while, a week and a half before, it had been all I could do to manage my own household and my problems, now I lay awake, trying to think of where Lydia might go, how we might help her find another job. In the end she called to say she'd found one, housekeeping again, for an old lady in another state. She came by yesterday to pick up the last of her stuff. We hired a new babysitter—a lovely young woman named Joanie, who will not live here with us and can't start for a few weeks because she's getting married. And will probably leave us before very long, as good babysitters nearly always do, to start a family of her own.

One other thing: The day after I told Lydia she didn't have the job after all, the starter motor on our Plymouth Valiant died, just as she'd predicted it would. Of course, she'd also predicted—joking—that we'd never get rid of her. And I guess it was the fear that she might be right about that one too that led us both (two women, almost equally needy, in very different ways) to where we both are now.

———

CELEBRATIONS

I love holidays, and Christmas most of all. I am always reminding Steve of that. Usually I'm in tears as I tell him.
It's December 23. Two A.M. I am standing in the middle
of our kitchen, surrounded by bits of wrapping paper and
three-quarters-finished doll clothes. I am forming marzipan
fruits. I have my fifth batch of cookies in the oven. I have
been writing notes inside Christmas cards featuring a cheerful family group photo. I have just exploded: That Steve
doesn't help me enough. That the children never pick up
their messes. That I haven't sat down all day. Steve (who has
been sleeping, and got up to suggest that I call it a night)
says, "Next year, promise me we'll have a simple Christmas.
Maybe we should just take off to some warm island. You
know how you get about the holidays." But I love holidays, I
wail. And Christmas most of all.

It's just that Christmas encourages excess, and even in an
off month like March or August, I am prone to excess. I

want so much for the holiday to be perfect (same goes for my children's birthdays, and to a lesser degree, Valentine's Day, Halloween, Easter). And the strain of pulling off that much happiness, on schedule, sometimes drives me right over the brink.

So, though we have had some wonderful holidays around here, we have also had some awful nights before and days after. Fights, tears, accusations, recriminations. I am determined to bake not only a pumpkin pie but also apple and pecan, and also a Buche de Noel. I drive a hundred miles to buy Steve the gift of a Caribbean steel drum. Then come home tired, angry because he hasn't emptied the dishwasher.

I learned my tendency toward Christmas hysteria early: from my Jewish mother (who, having been deprived of Christmas for twenty-five years, celebrated with a secular frenzy) and from my lapsed Protestant father, who chose the month of December to sink into an annual melancholy over his childhood, his vanished religion, and the mockery that we were making of that religion under our roof. Then as now the tree became the focus of our unease. Never able to find one quite perfect enough for our living room, our perfect Christmases, my father and I used to gather branches discarded from other trees and graft them onto ours to fill in gaps no one else would have noticed. The first Christmas after my parents' divorce, when for the first time in my eighteen years I bought our family tree alone, I ended up coming home not with a single tree but with four. "We'll make a Christmas forest," I told my sister. Hours later—the trees mounted at last, and filling most of our living room—we stood there and surveyed the interior landscape that was meant to elevate us from our gloom (and of course didn't). "A Christmas hedge," said my sister dourly. And naturally, once again I cried.

When our parents divorced and my mother gave up Christmas, I was the one who inherited the family's huge collection of ornaments. (My sister lived too far away to transport them, but also, I think, she wanted no part of the tradition they represented.) So now, every December, with a family of my own, I unpack the familiar balls and angels, elves and Santas and birds with spun-glass tails, and I try to see them in part as reminders of seasonal hazards. The children get excited, of course, but the one most apt to lose control over the holidays is not any of them.

These days, I cry less over Christmas, my birthday, and the four-week period, from the end of February to the end of March, when all three children celebrate their birthdays. I think I realized a while back that during all holidays I'm in danger of being like the runner who wins the race but expires at the finish line. I can't say that I have my holiday madness under control, but I'm learning.

The first crisis of our holiday season occurs the day we get our tree. Steve wants to go out on our land and cut one down. In principle, so do I. I love the thought of our expedition into the woods. Steve carrying the hatchet, and our snowsuited offspring trailing alongside. I believe in the lessons such an expedition teaches them—about self-sufficiency, the value of things money can't buy, cultivating a watchful eye in the woods, appreciating the infinite variety of ways an evergreen can grow. . . . I even like the difficulty, after the tree is cut, of carrying it back up the long hill to our house, and the way that walk reminds our children that some of the best things in life are not easily come by. In fact, there is just one thing I don't like about procuring our Christmas tree by what Audrey calls the olden-days method. And that's the tree itself.

As anyone who's ever cut uncultivated trees in a forest can tell you, they tend to be scrawny, and the grafting operation necessary to remedy the situation would involve so much drilling into the trunk as to leave very little trunk at all. Even the best of olden-days trees, when viewed in a stand in the living room, generally end up looking pretty forlorn. Also (with their fewer branches and numerous gaps), they never hold enough ornaments or lights. There's no concealing the wires, and no opportunity to hide a single mysterious blue blinker deep within the greenery, because the greenery just isn't there to hide it with. I speak from experience: Our household has gone the natural route for six of the last seven Christmases.

Here's how it goes. The day (usually a Saturday) dawns bright and full of promise. The sun is shining. There is a cover of snow on the ground—enough to put us all in the holiday mood, but not so much as to become a downright nuisance. By now the children have probably been clamoring to get a tree (everyone else has theirs) for so long that when Steve announces today's the day no one even complains about missing cartoons.

Steve sharpens his hatchet, I stuff my pockets with emergency animal crackers and set out the popcorn and cocoa for our return. After first determining that everyone has indeed paid a visit to the bathroom, we dress our two younger children in long johns, flannel shirts, sweaters, and snowpants, leaving Audrey to get suited up on her own. Steve is likely, then, to put a hand on my shoulder or stroke the tense muscles at the back of my neck and ask (in the calming voice of a yogi) whether I'm ready for this. "It's only a tree," I recite. "Right," he says. "Only a tree. Only a tree." And then we venture forth.

Of course, it always ends up that halfway down the path to our woods someone announces that he or she needs to go to the bathroom. But I have taught myself the trick of pretending, at moments like these, that Dr. Spock is standing directly behind me, judging entrants for the Mother of the Year Award. So I simply smile, reach for whatever small person is now dancing wildly in the snow beside me, and carry him (usually the person is male) back up the hill and into the house. We peel off the layers, pay a visit to the toilet, and begin our odyssey all over again. Still smiling, and maybe singing Christmas carols. But underneath my own layers of wool and flannel, my nerves, and my calm resolve, have already begun the irreversible process of first fraying and then unraveling altogether.

We reach the woods. Charlie (who has refused to put on his mittens because if he did he couldn't suck his thumb) is now complaining of cold hands. Willy is hungry—but I'm ready for that one. He doesn't like hippopotamus animal crackers, he tells me, and when I am finally able (on the fourth try) to produce a tiger, it turns out that one of the legs has broken off. We have a brief showdown. (I threaten to toss out the entire stock of cookies. Audrey and Charlie plead with their brother to take the broken cookie. Steve wisely disappears down the path.) Willy accepts his cookie. Charlie puts on his mitten. Dr. Spock gives me a silent, admiring pat on the back (asking me if I'd like to help him with the chapter on two-year-olds, for his next edition).

Steve calls to us, "I think I've found one." We hurry to look. It's a thicker tree than the usual forest-grown variety, to be sure, but short. I shake my head firmly. "But this one would be perfect for my room," says Audrey, who promises to carry the tree back to the house, all by herself, if we'll just let her have it. Steve chops it down for her. "Look, Char," says Audrey to her brothers, "I get my very own tree." It's not hard to guess what happens next. We have two small trees cut now (Willy and Charlie having been persuaded to share theirs). But the big tree, the tree of my dreams, is still hidden somewhere within these fifty snowy acres, if only we knew where.

We trudge around a good deal, looking. Steve nominates half a dozen candidates. As gently as possible, I veto every one. Now the edge is in Steve's voice. Pointing to a thirty-foot-high pine, with a beautiful thick top, he asks me whether I'd like him to cut that one down for us. After a moment's consideration, I say yes, I think that one might just do. It turns out Steve was kidding.

Meanwhile the children are getting cold. They have made their snow angels. They've examined deer footprints. They've polished off the animal crackers, and a few icicles to boot. "Where's our house?" demands Willy—and I know that question means things are about to go downhill fast.

So I allow myself to believe that the next pine Steve nominates for this year's tree is a reasonably good one. As he's chopping it down, he mutters something about turning this side toward the wall. But we're all singing, Audrey's making plans for our gingerbread house, Charlie's giving Willy his refresher course on Santa and the elves, and I am feeling—despite the temperature outside—warm and good, and something else. Mature. Able to put childish things behind me. In touch, at last, with the true meaning of Christmas.

We haul the tree, and our children's trees, and our children, up the long hill to our house. We lean the tree outside for a few hours, to shake off the snow, while the children and I carry the boxes of ornaments (many of them ones I can remember from when I was Audrey's age) down from our attic. Steve saws a few inches off the bottom and snips some branches. He carries the tree inside and stands it up in the customary place. We step back to admire it. (Willy, too young to remember much of this from last year, is simply dumbfounded to see a tree in our house. The vision seems to bring on a general questioning of all the rules he had, up till now, imagined were unbreakable. Suddenly he's jumping off the sofa, throwing popcorn in the air. Announcing he'd like to bring in some dirt, too. Charlie has fallen asleep, meanwhile. And Audrey just wants to start putting on the tinsel.)

As for me, I am not proud of this, but I'd better confess it.

I lean over to my husband (who has chopped down this tree, and carried it half a mile, and pruned it, and stood it up and secured it with extra wires, even), and I tell him, "You know, it's kind of skimpy. Maybe we should give this one to the birds and buy a tree."

That much of the scenario never changes much; it's what comes after that varies: Steve, calmly, evenly, reminding me of my promise to stop trying for a perfect Christmas. Audrey, veteran of enough of these discussions to know they can get dicey, urging me to sit down, put my feet up, have a cup of tea. Charlie (always the one who tries hardest to bring cheer) comments happily that the nice thing about this tree is that if someone's standing on the other side, it doesn't block your view of them. That one's enough to send me right over the edge. "We have a scrawny tree," I moan, sending Dr. Spock running from the room, with his head in his hands. He's right—this morning it's hard to know who in this room is the mother and who's the child.

I am trying to grow up about Christmas. Most winters I come round, on the subject of our home-grown tree, and even end up conceding that—with presents underneath and, preferably, my glasses off so as to blur the outlines some—it looks pretty good. And not only am I getting better about scraggly trees. These days I'm also allowing our children to decorate the gingerbread house the way they want it (instead of neat rows of alternating colored gumdrops and M&M's), and baking only two or three varieties of Christmas cookies instead of the customary eight or ten. Three years have passed since the Christmas when I woke Steve up (around three A.M.) to express my sudden panicked fear that we hadn't got as many toys for Audrey as for Charlie. (Neither one of us could get back to sleep afterward. Our children woke, at seven, to find us bleary-eyed and exhausted. And needless to say, there was no real toy shortage.)

It's not that hard, from the calm distance of September or

early October, to know which route is the right one to choose. (Trying to match some calendar or magazine's images of what a Christmas tree, or a Christmas, is supposed to look like. Or inventing one's own.) Beauty comes from within, I teach my children. "Tis a Gift to Be Simple," we sing every night, for our grace. And then they start piping all those songs into the supermarket ("Chestnuts roasting on an open fire, Jack Frost nipping at your nose . . ."), and before you know it, I'm heading for the aisle where the chestnuts are and longingly eyeing a perfectly symmetrical twenty-five-dollar blue spruce as I pull out of the parking lot.

□

I had been trying to get out and do some Christmas shopping for weeks, and every time it looked as if I'd found the time for the sixty-mile round trip to the nearest city, something went wrong. I thought I had things set up last Sunday, but ten miles from home our car broke down (clutch problems, $250 plus towing). So home I went, empty-handed again.

Because it's so hard for me to get to stores, I delegate a lot of my shopping to friends or to our babysitter, Joanie. I read the sale circulars every week, circling the things I'd get if I could ever make it to those stores. Sometimes I'll hear that my friend Laurie or Sheri or Randy is heading to the city, and I'll ask her, could she pick up those sale pantyhose, or the Barbie Bubbling Spa, or mittens for Charlie. I trace my children's feet and send off the outline, with a request for winter boots or jelly shoes. About half the time something goes wrong: The shoes are fluorescent green, the boots don't have felt liners. My panty hose are baggy, or too short. My beach towel says "Surf's Up," Charlie's mittens are pink, with pictures of Rainbow Brite on them. Still, we're all used to this around here. My family seldom complains. Only, lately I've been feeling as if my inability to shop for my family is some kind of indication that I've lost control of my life. A couple of weeks ago I even had to ask a friend to pick up a bra for me. Not surprisingly, it didn't fit.

So this month, when one of the biggest discount stores announced it would be open round the clock through Christmas Eve, I figured I'd found my answer. I'd get the children to bed, pack the lunches for the next day, put away the laundry, make myself a strong cup of coffee and head out to go shopping. I could even stop at the all-night supermarket in the same city and pick up the sort of fruits and vegetables I can never find at my local grocer's. Persimmons. Leeks. Fresh bagels. A bunch of carnations, maybe.

It was midday when I hatched my plan, and the sun was shining. At eleven-thirty, when I had finally got myself ready to go, it was harder to get moving: There was a fire in the fireplace. Our children were murmuring softly in their sleep. Steve was just brushing his teeth, getting ready for bed. And the night outside was bitter cold, the wind howling. I made myself a second cup of coffee, then grimly headed out into the night, with a shopping list in my pocket and a bag full of items to return, bought the last time I asked someone to do my shopping for me.

Ten minutes later, the car had begun to warm up. I turned on the radio, but all I got was static, so I drove in silence, slapping my cheeks to stay awake. I studied my shopping list as if it were a battle plan: Masters of the Universe figures or Sectaurs? Construx or Legos? Walkie-talkies or the Fisher-Price sing-along radio with microphone?

In good weather it takes about half an hour to get from our house to the city where I was headed. That night, of course, the roads were nearly deserted, except for truckers, night-shift workers, and maybe (I liked to imagine) some hopeful young couple just heading off to the hospital to have a baby. So I made good time, exited onto Main Street just before midnight. Drove past the big plaster nativity grouping, an all-night convenience store, a bank (temperature reading, eighteen degrees). Not a whole lot of night life in this city.

Then I reached the discount store, with maybe fifteen cars parked outside and the lights blazing. I got myself a shopping cart and skimmed my list again.

If I came to this store at this time of year on a Saturday afternoon there would be shoppers everywhere; the merry jingle of cash registers, and carols piped in over the loudspeakers. There might be a Santa Claus outside ringing a pair of handbells, and announcements for shoppers to hurry over to this department or that one for a special lasting fifteen minutes only. Traffic would be so thick I'd have to keep both hands on my shopping cart to steer. I'd hear children's voices, asking for candy, asking for GoBots, Cabbage Patch Kids, My Little Ponys. My own children would be with me, hopping in and out of the cart, wanting me to come look at some treasure they'd just spotted.

In the middle of the night, it's different. There's no music. No voice announcing, "Shoppers, hurry over to the small appliance department." No Santa. No children leaning out of carts, grabbing for toys. Only one register open, and the cashier at that one just standing there, reading *Soap Opera Digest*.

I had been having trouble keeping my eyes open as I drove to the store, but once I started shopping I wasn't tired anymore. For the first time in years, I was alone in a department store, with no child in my shopping cart. I went up and down every aisle.

What I bought: toys, of course. I spent ten minutes studying the various superpowers of an array of Masters of the Universe figures, trying to decide between Spikor, with telescopic arm, and Stinkor, with gas mask. I stood in front of the Barbies for a good quarter of an hour, comparing the evening-gown selections as if I were shopping for myself for a dinner at the White House. This could be my last Christ-mas of doll-related purchases. The choices were hard.

Money was an issue, of course, but I had a charge plate in my wallet, and the dangerous, illusory sense of limitlessness that comes with it. What really held me back (as I looked at the motorized, child-sized three-wheeler, knowing how Charlie would love tooling around on that thing, and the Cabbage Patch Twins, and the thirty-five-dollar Voltron fig-ure, and the hundred-dollar GI Joe aircraft carrier) was a different sort of restriction: the internal kind. Like most mothers, I want to give my children everything. But I also know that part of what I need to give them is the under-standing that Christmas is something more than a toy festi-val. Not having enough money to buy everything is only one reason not to buy everything.

I reached the checkout counter (no line) a little before three A.M., stocked up with not only Christmas purchases but also shampoo, paperclips, a garlic press, pantyhose in my size. Handing over my charge card, I asked the sales-woman if it was always this quiet during the nighttime shop-ping hours. "Things usually pick up around five A.M.," she said.

On my way home I stopped for groceries and then for gas at a self-service pump manned by a young boy in a glass booth. I was wide awake by now, could've kept on going, even, if there'd been any other stores open. Driving home I sang Christmas carols and watched the moon—so large in the sky, and low to the horizon, that at first I thought it was a UFO. Passing through the streets of our town I saw the lights on in one or two houses (hard to tell if those people were getting up or just going to bed). It was four o'clock in the morning.

I pulled into our driveway. I carried in my bags quietly, so I wouldn't wake anyone, and put my groceries away. I put on my nightgown, crawled into bed beside my husband.

"Mission accomplished?" he asked. "We're all set now until the birthday season starts," I answered, starting to reel off a list of my purchases. But he was fast asleep again before I was halfway through.

☐

All three of our children have had good and simple births. All three were born at home, on our bed, within a few hours of the first labor pains.

But something happens to me between the births and the birthday parties. It seems that all the worry I don't put into the original event gets spent on every subsequent celebration of the date. For the whole month before, I am thinking about the presents, the games, the cake. I debate the designs on ten different plates at three different party stores. I try (unsuccessfully) to engage Steve in debates over Fisher-Price versus Tonka. The morning of the party, if the sky looks overcast, I picture a blizzard and no one showing up.

For seven years now I have been trying to put together the perfect birthday party—where everybody wins a prize and gets the color of balloon they wanted, and no one cries, and when it's over the birthday child is gracious, thoughtful, and happy, instead of overwhelmed, overtired, overwrought. For seven years now, the perfect birthday party has eluded us. And still, every year, I knock myself out again.

It was Audrey's seventh birthday and of course I wanted it to be perfect. Weeks before, I had reserved the swimming pool at the Y for an hour, and rented a VCR and two movies for afterward. I hunted in half a dozen stores for a certain kind of bracelet Audrey loved, that I figured the other girls would appreciate too, for favors. We studied a dozen styles of invitations before arriving at the design we liked best (a jazzy-looking sneaker, sealed with a bow-shaped sticker, that opened to reveal party details). We bought an ice cream cake, with Audrey's name in purple, edged in roses. We hung streamers, and I stayed up late, writing the clues to a treasure hunt and then planting the treasures: miniature Cabbage Patch Kid figurines, all different. I had driven fifty miles to find a store that carried them.

The morning of the party, one mother (of twin guests) called to say her girls were sick and couldn't make it. I managed to say something about hoping they'd feel better soon, but I got off the phone with my stomach in knots. I presented the facts to Audrey with attempted casualness. "Megan and Erica can't make it, Aud," I said. "We'll have them over another time soon."

She looked sad, a little troubled maybe, but not devastated certainly, or even (as I was) worried. The girls' absence would bring the guest list down to four.

I mentioned to Audrey the names of a couple of friends from last year's school, whose mothers I could call to see if they were free, but Audrey shook her head. "No, thanks," said my daughter (who proved herself, once again, to be a good deal more rational than I). Then she went back to playing with her new birthday present from us—an elaborately outfitted model of the Love Boat, with dolls, swimming pool, and shuffleboard.

The guests arrived, with much giggling and many purple accessories. They all brought purses, and carried them throughout the treasure hunt. Then they made their way into our living room to watch Audrey open her gifts.

The one she saved until the last was from Charlie. She could tell it was a Barbie doll, she said, from the shape of the box. Not just any Barbie, as it turned out: This was a Crystal Barbie, in an iridescent gown, with diamond earrings and a ruffled stole. But the thing she loved best were the shoes: see-through, and slightly iridescent, dainty as Cinderella's glass slippers.

"Why don't you wait till later to study them?" I suggested as she slipped them off the doll's feet. "Yup," her friend Kate concurred sadly. "I have a Crystal Barbie too, only I lost the shoes and now she doesn't seem special."

After we'd all had cake, we headed out to the Y and then home again for pizza and a double feature of *Splash* and *Charlotte's Web*. Got everybody into sleeping bags around ten-thirty listened to the giggles die down. Woke a little after midnight, to find Audrey's friend Tammy—a girl who had seemed fearless, only hours before, on the diving board—trembling beside our bed, wanting to know if she could get into bed beside me.

The next morning I made blueberry pancakes. The girls played for a couple of hours before I drove them home, with balloons and streamers blowing out the car windows and everyone calling out, "Hip, hip, hooray for Audrey!" Sitting in the back seat, and with a bow off a package stuck on top of her head, she was a little quiet (she had been waiting for this birthday, as she put it, a whole year, and now it was over), but I knew she'd had a happy time.

And then, home once more, with the house finally tidy again and quiet, I noticed my new seven-year-old on her stomach, peering under chairs in the living room and reaching under sofa cushions with attempted casualness.

"You lost something, didn't you?" I said.

She nodded miserably. "One of Crystal Barbie's shoes."

I didn't have to say I told her so. I pushed back all the furniture and took every pillow off the couch. I lifted the rug, and I emptied the wastebasket full of wrapping paper. Something had taken possession of me—I was irritated, upset, even a little frantic at the mess I was making in the room I'd just finished cleaning a half hour before, but I couldn't stop looking for that shoe.

"It's okay, Mom," Audrey said finally—more upset by this time, I think, by the vision of me going crazy than she had been by the lost shoe. I would be embarrassed to say how many wastebaskets I went through before I finally gave up.

It was a few hours later that the memory came to me of something eerily similar that my own mother had done, one spring twenty years before. I had just got a new Skipper doll—to cheer me up, because my father had been in the hospital. I'd taken the doll outside and lost her shoe. My mother had spent an hour on her hands and knees, helping me search for that shoe in the thick grass. My mother—who, I always believed, could do anything—found it.

I always tell that story with affection, but I have always made fun of my mother a little for that too. What a lot of fuss to make over something so small, I have thought to myself.

Only the fuss was about something besides a doll's shoe, of course. It was about loss and pain. Small pain, minor loss, in the scale of things. The kind of pain a mother can still control, can still prevent, maybe. Knowing, all the while, how many other sorrows there will be that she can't do anything about: Little girls who don't come to her party. Children on the playground who make fun of her overalls. Boys who ask someone else to the dance instead. Colleges she won't get into. A lover who leaves.

The next day we went for a walk. It was a sunny, springlike day. Maple sap was dripping into our buckets. Up ahead Charlie splashed happily in a muddy puddle. Willy, in the backpack, grabbed for branches overhead.

"You know what I wished for when I blew out the candles?" Audrey asked me. (She could tell me, because she hadn't got them all out in one breath anyway and knew that meant her wish wouldn't come true.) "I wished I'd never have to die, and you wouldn't either, and neither would Dad and the boys."

As I said, I wanted that birthday to be perfect, and I

wanted to shield my child from loss and pain. And I actually thought that if I could only find that Barbie shoe, I could do it.

□

Charlie's birthday comes a month and two days after Audrey's. And because hers has always required such elaborate preparation, his tends to catch us short. Of cash, and of energy. The year Charlie turned two there was also the birth of Willy—two days after Audrey's birthday. Followed two days later by the broken arm Audrey sustained on the Smurfette roller skates she got for her birthday, and two weeks after that by the broken arm Steve sustained at the end of an afternoon of skiing that was designed as a celebration of our having apparently survived the other calamities. (An excursion he made, incidentally, out of a desire to escape our house, and my high anxiety, on the eve of Audrey's postponed party for twenty-two of her classmates.)

So on March 24, the second anniversary of Charlie's amazing birth, all I could do was whisper the news to Audrey and tell her to keep it from her brother. Charlie had been primed for the event by Audrey's two cakes and innumerable presents, and would (I thought) expect more hoopla than either Steve in his full-arm cast or I, nursing newborn Willy, felt able to orchestrate just then. We postponed his party until things got more normal.

Time passed, and I stopped knowing anymore what normal was supposed to be. Willy proved (by necessity) to be what's known as a good baby. Dinners at our house, that spring, featured hot dogs with ever greater frequency. The aquarium started smelling pretty strongly of fish, and the plastic scuba diver had tipped over and was now buried, up to his goggles, in blue gravel, but no one had time to do anything about it. Steve found a mouse nest (but no socks) in his sock drawer. And Charlie took to asking every few days, "Where'd Charby's birthday go?"

It was April by this time—and the longer I'd put off the birthday, the greater my anxiety and the more elaborate, it seemed, the party had to be. I made lists of things to buy, while Charlie checked the closet from which his sister's presents had emerged back in February, asking "Birthday cake now? Candles for Charby?"

Then one afternoon Audrey came home from school and instead of turning on *Love Boat* or going upstairs to play, she asked if she could bake. I was nursing Willy and trying, at the same time, to do a puzzle with Charlie. With his good arm, Steve was working on the car, which had been running erratically again. When I told her I couldn't bake with her, she asked if I could just put out some ingredients and she'd do the whole thing herself. And though the house was a terrible mess, and I was pretty frayed (but maybe because of those things too) I said okay.

I gave her a couple of eggs, a little pitcher with some milk in it, a few nuts, a few sesame seeds, some cocoa powder, and lifted canisters off the high shelf. I suggested an oven temperature of 350 degrees, but beyond that I left everything to Audrey, who did a lot of rushing back and forth to the mixer, mashing in a banana, tossing in a spoonful of mayonnaise. She cracked the eggs herself and chose a pan shaped like a star, which she greased, and into which she poured her batter. She cleaned up most of her mess. I turned on the oven light so she could look in and watch her cake as it baked. I told her not to expect too much. A cake is a pretty delicate thing, I said. She wasn't worried.

After about a half hour of cooking I lifted the pan out of the oven and the cake tester came out clean. The cake, turned upside down on a gold plate, slid out of its pan perfectly star-shaped. Audrey ran to get two candles (not little birthday candles, but a pair of half-burned tapers) and stuck them in the center. "Charlie," she said. "It's your birthday now."

For presents all we had was a dollar-twenty-nine cowboy hat we'd picked up a couple of days before, still in its brown paper bag, tied with a ribbon. I lit the candles, and we all gathered around. We sang "Happy Birthday," Charlie extinguished the flames, and Audrey served up the cake— which probably wouldn't win a bake off, but tasted okay. One might even say tasty.

Then Charlie opened his present, put it on his head, and began to gallop around the living room, whooping, "Cowboy, cowboy." Audrey, without a moment's hesitation, stuck her fingers in the remains of her cake, smearing brown crumbs on her cheeks. "I'm an Indian," she said. She tied the ribbon around her head for a headband, handed Charlie his hobby horse, and the two of them ran around and around chasing each other until bedtime.

There is a lesson in all of this. I hope I have learned it.

———

YEARNINGS

The first call came around nine o'clock one night, more than a dozen years ago. I was living alone in the country—unmarried, twenty years old. Watching whatever happened to be on TV, finishing my second bowl of ice cream, when the phone rang. The man talked like a cowboy, said he lived in Oklahoma and his name was Lloyd. He'd read and liked a book I wrote. The name of my town had been mentioned somewhere, and my phone number was listed with information. He wanted, he said, to be my friend.

I thought it was a joke, someone I knew from college (I'd dropped out after my freshman year), one of my old acting friends trying out an accent for some play he was in. That's what I figured. But there was also the odd way this call had come at a moment (not by any means a rare one, in those days) when what I needed badly was someone to call me up and say he'd be my friend. There were things he said that made me feel he really knew who I was. A Hank Williams record that I owned too was playing in the background while we talked. He'd held a lot of different kinds of jobs, worked at a Campbell's Soup factory one time just because he wanted to see the tomato soup he loved. He talked about books he read, promising to send me about a dozen he mentioned: American history, obscure short-story collections, movie-star biographies. He was a birdwatcher, and said I had to have a copy of Roger Tory Peterson's field guide. Hank Williams was singing all this time: "Jambalaya," "Your Cheating Heart," "I'm So Lonesome I Could Cry."

"Come on," I said, as we were finally about to ring off. "Who is this really?" Your friend Lloyd, he said. From Oklahoma. I said all right then, what's the Oklahoma state bird? "Scissortail Flycatcher." That sounded like a joke for sure.

The next day I looked up the answer to my question in an almanac, and of course he'd been right. A week later came a package containing the only picture I ever saw of him (cut from his high-school yearbook) showing a very handsome dark-eyed boy, the center forward, plus the books he'd promised, each one elaborately inscribed with my name in oversized capital letters on the first page. "Property of . . . Hands OFF. KEEP OUT!!!" Now and then, reading along or flipping through the pages, I'd come across a few words that were underlined, with a comment in the margin. In a biography of Vivien Leigh, her birthday (the same as mine) circled in red, with exclamation points all around it. Something about birds, or country music, and sometimes a subject I didn't even think I'd mentioned (a food I liked, a movie I'd seen four times). If a character in a novel wore her hair the way I did on the cover of my book, there'd be a comment. And over and over again there the words, "Don't forget, you can always count on me."

I know what all this sounds like (psychopath twisting the phone cord; unhappy young woman alone in the woods). My mother, hearing about Lloyd, made no comment, then called back a day later to say, "I can't stop thinking about that man in Oklahoma. I'm scared for you." I told her, told myself (and the many people I entertained with the story of his increasingly frequent phone calls) that I was getting into this because it was such a good story.

And though he called me, by now, twice a week (very often after the old *Mary Tyler Moore Show*, that he and I—hard to say *we*—both loved) and though I seldom cut the calls short, I never phoned him. At some point, though, I realized that if he disappeared, I'd miss him. He sent packages weekly: books, newspaper clippings, tapes—but I never (though I copied down his address) mailed him anything. Even his strange form of communication—forming an attachment based on a photograph from a book jacket, talking only by phone and exchanging precious little information about the basic facts of either person's daily life, work, family—made an odd kind of sense to me. Never mind that he was thirty-eight and I was twenty, that his passion was the Oklahoma Sooners football team and I built dollhouse furniture. The very fact that our two lives held so little in common seemed to me, now and then, to suggest the presence of some much deeper form of kinship. Of course it seemed crazy that I was sitting in my house in the middle of a New Hampshire winter (and then another one), on a Saturday night, talking for an hour with a man I'd never met, who lived two thousand miles away, someone who had just got home from his office Christmas party, where a divorcee from the secretarial pool had stuck his cowboy hat on her head and invited him to be her date at a rodeo next weekend, a man who said no, because he wanted instead to stay home, watch Mary Tyler Moore, and call me. But every now and then I'd go to a party too or visit friends at college, where I'd find myself face to face with some young Ivy League type, and I'd ask him what his major was, and he'd tell me about applying to medical school—and all the social rites and customs we'd go through, on the way to absolutely nothing more than the cheese-and-crackers platter, seemed just as crazy to me as what was going on with Lloyd. Maybe more so.

He sent me strange, wonderful presents. A deluxe two-key harmonica (with the request that I learn how to play "Red River Valley" in time to perform it, over the telephone, for his birthday in May). A pair of blue cowboy boots and an Oklahoma football jersey. A four-record set of bird calls. A pair of apple-head dolls made by Oklahoma Indians. An antique green-velvet doll-sized chaise longue. A hand-inlaid veneer table that played "Lara's Theme" from *Doctor Zhivago* when you lifted the top. One of the first American Cuisinarts, with a gold plaque attached to the side inscribed with my name and the words "HANDS OFF!!!" He sent so many books that I had to buy two new sets of shelves. For my part, I sent nothing, but any time an article I'd written showed up in the *Ladies' Home Journal* or *Seventeen*, he'd know about it. He was keeping a scrapbook about me, he said.

Once in a while he'd make some remark about paying me a visit in New Hampshire. There were one or two times, real low points in my life, when I felt I had to go away somewhere, and Oklahoma (more than some other place where old friends and family lived) came to mind. But it was easier to be brave on the telephone than in real life. In real life, I left my house in New Hampshire and got a job in New York. Had a few appropriate-seeming boyfriends who weren't nearly as interesting or funny, as good company or as devoted to me as Lloyd, and whose names and faces I can't now recall. Lloyd still called on Saturday nights—though sometimes I'd be out and I'd come home to find his message on my new answering machine. He never got the hang of waiting for the beep.

Then I met Steve (whose family, on his father's side, were Oklahomans), and within a month I'd quit my job, given notice on my apartment, and made plans to move with him back to New Hampshire and get married. And even though over the four years since Lloyd had started calling, not one word of love or commitment had been spoken, still, with Steve there in the room, I felt guilty and two-timing the next time Lloyd called me. I meant to tell Lloyd about Steve that night, and then the next time he called; but he was full of the story of a cheese dish that he was sending me he'd seen in a store window in Oklahoma City, and a toy bird in a cage that sang just like a real one. He'd made a tape for me of the last episode of the *Mary Tyler Moore Show* that he was sending enclosed in a five-pound can of macadamia nuts.

I wrote Lloyd a letter (easiest of all to be brave on paper) telling him that I was getting married. He wrote back to say he'd always be my friend, but that he probably shouldn't call me anymore. If he were in Steve's place, he wouldn't like it.

I heard from him, after that, only on Vivien Leigh's and my birthday every year, and at Christmas, when he'd send Audrey a red and white Oklahoma Sooners jersey in her current size and some hugely extravagant toy. (An enormous stuffed elephant. A deluxe baby doll with thirty-piece layette, packed in a wicker suitcase. That one came on a Christmas we had so little money we gave her balloons and bubble-blowing solution. Steve wrote to Lloyd after that to say please, no more presents.)

Over the years, in various periods of hard times, we've sold most of Lloyd's presents to me, though I still have the bird-call records and the personalized Cuisinart. I still think of him now and then (when I'm grating carrots, and some-times, rereading an old book, when I come upon a reference to Tammy Wynette or red-winged blackbirds, underlined in red). And sometimes, when I'm feeling fed up with my real-life, nine-year-old marriage to a man I love who gives me meat thermometers and dish towels on my birthday—a man who loves me, but is not about to keep a scrapbook documenting my life—I think about how much easier it is to carry on a romance with someone if you've never met him.

□

A few years back, over a period of several months, I used to visit a woman in the state mental hospital. Sometimes I drive past that hospital on my way to buy groceries or to take one of my children to the doctor. I feel almost like an escapee, the relief is so great, still, that I'm on the outside.

I first read about Linda in the newspaper. Years before, her father had killed her mother and was found not guilty by reason of insanity. When later he was released from the state hospital, and within the year, found dead of a gunshot wound, his death was ruled a suicide. For months Linda had waged a protest with the authorities until finally they agreed to exhume the body. Sure enough, there was a bullet wound in him that proved it was a murder, and the one who shot him was the daughter who'd insisted they investigate. They found Linda not guilty by reason of insanity and sentenced her to the state hospital. Which is where I sent her the letter saying I'd like to meet her and write a book about her story. She said sure, come.

I was living, then as now, in this house in the country, with Steve and Audrey, who was just a baby. It was a couple of years since I'd lived in the city, working as a newspaper reporter—but I still liked to talk about my old days as if I were a character on *Hill Street Blues*. Never having quite as many stories as I would have liked.

But now I was spending my days picking strawberries and

making jam, with a baby strapped to my back and no shoes on. There were, in fact, rough edges in my life: the constant eruption of little battles that mark the early days of a marriage and pass, if one survives them, into truce or much more serious warfare, greater pain or deeper intimacy, and sometimes both. And there was a difficult, often stormy father in my life then too—my own beloved, infuriating, alcoholic parent whose calls I avoided and didn't return. That woman locked inside the state hospital was nothing like me, and the father she killed—a burly, violent, gun-loving small-time businessman—was nothing like mine, who liked, when drinking, to sit in the living room late into the night, conducting Mozart horn concertos played on a scratched record. Still, reading this other woman's story, I drew comparisons between Linda and me, imagined her story addressed mine and held larger implications about fathers and daughters, madness and sanity. I don't remember what else I said about her case, but it seemed to make sense at the time—enough that a publisher was going to pay me a sum out of which (there was always an uneasiness surrounding this) I would pay a percentage required by Linda.

So I used to visit her. Unlike most people in state mental hospitals, she looked good. She was about ten years older than I: mid-thirties. She'd known her share of successes in the world: achievement in sports, excellent grades, and a few semesters at a medical school. She had good teeth, good skin, a good figure.

Because she was, at the time, the only woman in the state to be committed on criminal charges, there was no women's forensic ward to place her on. So Linda, with her books and Johnny Cash cassettes and her calligraphy pens, inhabited a world of women who never got out of their bathrobes and didn't always make it to the toilet on time. Tapes I made with her are hard to make out, chiefly because there was always so much yelling going on around us. Some of the women on that ward had been there twenty years and just sat in chairs all day, staring straight ahead. Signs along the hallways, decorated with some staff members' attempts at rendering Snoopy, instructed patients on subjects like "Five steps to a cheerful outlook" and listed days of the week.

Many times I was the only visitor on the floor. The first fifteen minutes of my visit were often taken up by her questions about the business aspects of our arrangement. She knew just what kind of car she wanted to buy with part of her earnings when she got out: a Pontiac Trans Am.

Then we'd settle down to her story, beginning with childhood: tap-dancing lessons and target-shooting practice, times when her father hit her mother, intimations of sexual abuse. We got along well. I never felt any particular warmth from her and I always felt she was evaluating my behavior pretty closely, but of course that's precisely what I did with her. When you're having a conversation with a person in a mental hospital you measure everything she says, so a remark about the orderlies having it in for her sounds paranoid, and if the person says, "I could've killed him," you can't help but think that maybe she could have.

Making the transition from inside the hospital back to Steve and Audrey was always hard. I'd break into a run when was I out the door, and often I'd cry drivng home. And often, too, I'd get into a silly argument with Steve afterward. I'd make some remark about Linda's psychiatrist, how the nurses and orderlies hated my being there. Steve said I was spending too much time at the hospital.

The big issue surrounding Linda at the time, she told me, was that everyone at the hospital suspected her of using drugs. She said she wasn't. But her doctors gave orders that she couldn't have any money in her possession.

That was a terrible blow. Linda needed to buy cigarettes, and liked, once a week or so, to order a lobster dinner delivered from a local restaurant. It got to the point where most of what we talked about when I came was the money business, and every time I'd take a dollar out of my wallet to buy groceries, I'd think of her and feel something approaching guilt. Then one day she asked me if I'd smuggle in a hundred dollars for her.

At first, and for a long time, I said no. I have always been one to obey rules. But here in the hospital, Linda used to say, resisting authority was a healthy sign of sanity. When a person stopped fighting, that was the moment you knew she'd be spending the next twenty years staring at the Snoopy posters.

What she said made sense. Also, our work together was going less and less well; we hardly ever talked now about anything besides how much money she'd get for the book and who should play her in the movie. I guess I felt that if I would just bring her the hundred dollars and be done with it, she'd trust me.

It wasn't easy, smuggling in those two fifty-dollar bills. A female attendant searched me every time I came. The day I brought the money I was in a cold sweat, and even after I'd managed to turn it over to Linda I couldn't calm down. When I got home that day Steve told me I was going crazy.

I'm not completely sure even now of all the reasons why everything fell apart after that. A few days later I was called into the office of a hospital administrator who said he'd been given reason to think Linda was using drugs again, and no one could figure out how she got the money. I said I didn't know, and he believed me.

Linda's brother called me, wanting his share of royalties from my still-unwritten book. I drove up north to the motel he ran and spent an evening dickering over figures at his kitchen table. From where I sat, the stuffed head of a huge buck deer killed by the dead father seemed to be staring me in the eye.

A couple of days later I sent Linda a letter telling her I

couldn't go through with the project. I sent back the money I'd been paid for the book, and to make up the lost income I wrote a whole lot of magazine articles about marriage and babies, sounding like an expert on both. My father, who had moved away by this time, and hardly ever called me anymore, died in his sleep, and I realized, touching his face as he lay in his casket, that of the many feelings I had for him, wanting him dead was never one.

I had told Linda, when I quit the book, that I'd still come and visit her. But I never went back.

□

My friend Beverly is a mother of two boys, ages three and ten. She's a singer and songwriter, a crackerjack seamstress, a deeply religious woman. She loves her home, she loves her husband, and she believes strongly in the importance of a home-cooked dinner on the table for her family. No one, meeting her six months ago, would have said, "Here is a person with a deep void in her life. Here is someone who needs a hobby."

But three months ago ("on a whim," she says, and because she figured it would be fun for the children) she and her good friend Jane took their boys to a place called Funspot for an afternoon of roller skating. Everybody had a good time. And you might have thought that would be that.

Only, two days later, Beverly left her three-year-old with a babysitter and returned to Funspot at ten A.M., alone. She took a private lesson with a fellow named Russ. She goes twice every week now—as much as four hours at a time. She's bought herself a skating outfit and good skates. She even dreams about skating. "It has changed my life," she says, her eyes fairly burning.

We are in her car when she tells me this. We're making the thirty-mile drive to Skate World (the new rink she's graduated to). We have each left children at home, and husbands in charge of making dinner. It's four o'clock in the afternoon—the hour I am usually chopping vegetables and putting on the potatoes—and I am (I can hardly believe it) headed for Skate World.

"Up and floating," says Beverly. "That's the essence of roller skating." I sit a up a little straighter in the seat listening to her, and ask what it was that possessed her to make this surprising change in her life.

"Well," she says, "it just makes me feel so—free."

All day long, she's taking care of children. Doing laundry, running errands, tending to all the little pieces of business that seem so unimportant by themselves but add up to a way of life.

And then she gets to the rink. Puts on her sheer-to-the-waist pantyhose and her little black skirt and her white skates, steps out on the floor, and rolls away. "It doesn't feel like you're exercising," she says. "Your wheels just keep moving, and you have to follow. You're flying."

I ask her what she thinks about while she's skating. "Nothing," she says. "Not even my children. When I'm skating, all I do is skate."

After it's over, that's when she does her thinking. "I'm learning all these things," she says. Not just about skating either. "I've come to see you don't have to be arrogant to hold your head up and keep your back straight. I feel so proud at the way I keep improving. I actually believe I'm good. And it carries over into all the rest of my life. When I'm singing, I close my eyes and say to myself, 'Just pretend you're skating.' And then my voice just opens up."

When she was a young girl, she competed as a gymnast, and she showed a lot of promise. In her junior year of high school she was chosen for intensive pre-Olympic training, but that was the year her family had to move to Belgium. On the day of her last meet before leaving, she was injured doing warmups and had to miss the competition. "I never knew whether I could've won or not," she says twenty years later. "That always bothered me."

In her adult life she continued to do a little gymnastics now and then, and sometimes she'd roll up the rug in her sewing room and do an interpretive dance, all by herself, to Ann Murray singing "You Needed Me." She danced it for her son one afternoon, and, watching her, he wept. But other than that, she says, her exercise these past few years has been pretty much confined to running up and down stairs.

We get to the rink. Inside, nearly everyone seems to know Beverly. There's an eighty-three-year-old man named Pete (he doesn't do Mohawk turns the way he used to, but he still skates). There's Mike, in his early thirties, and legally blind, who started skating five years ago (forty hours a week, after work) and does the Glide Waltz as if the wind were carrying him. Little girls with skinny legs and fancy skating skirts, who merely laugh when they fall. Gray-haired women— one, named Mary, with a flower in her hair. I am surprised, for a second there, to see a vastly overweight woman, well into her fifties, emerge from the dressing room in a short purple skating tunic. Then she puts on her skates, and she's transformed. She takes off, suddenly weightless.

There's Oliver, a sort of oddball character. "Oliver wishes he had a partner for the Mirror Waltz, and he hates being short," Beverly had told me. Sure enough, the first thing he does is ask me how tall I am. It is the first time in my life I've lied about my height. (I shave off an inch, but I'm still too tall. Plus, I can't skate.)

But watching Beverly out there working on her figures (tracing and retracing a pair of circles, trying to keep her outside wheels on the black lines, while Pete and I look on and nobody breathes), I long to try. I rent a pair of boots and stagger out onto the floor. The organ plays "Melancholy

Baby." And Beverly was right: I am not thinking about fertilizing my rose bush or what to make for dinner tomorrow, or reminding myself to get the winter clothes into mothballs. I am not worrying about how on earth I'd manage at home if I broke my arm here tonight. I'm not even thinking about how much Audrey would love it here. I suppose anyone watching me would see a thirty-two-year-old woman in a pair of old jeans, hobbling around the floor. But in my head, I'm thinking, "Up and floating. Up and floating. Up. Floating."

As for Beverly, she's in her own world here. There are more accomplished skaters, of course (a young girl in purple, who jumps and spins; a white-haired woman in a black skating outfit, who dances the Society Blues as if she were born on skates; Mike, cutting across the rink in what looks like a single move), but few float better than my friend. She's unfastened her long hair, so it trails behind her, and she moves her arms as if she were conducting a hundred-piece orchestra. It happens we're in a prefab warehouse with cinderblock walls, called Skate World, listening to a little old man play the electric organ, but this might be the stage of the Kirov Ballet, or Lincoln Center, or Paradise itself, to look at her. "It's hard to believe she just started skating this spring," says one old-timer, standing on the sidelines with me, watching.

Her husband has never seen her skate. One of these days, he'll come along with her. What she'd really love would be for him to learn also; there can't be many feelings better than doing the Mirror Waltz across the rink with someone you love. There are a half dozen really accomplished married couples out on the floor tonight, and though most are in their forties or beyond, and some are gray, it's easy, watching them, to imagine how they would have looked as teenagers.

But it's also true, Beverly sort of likes it this way: coming here all by herself, doing something that is all hers. Coming to Skate World, where, as she says, "I'm not Mrs. So-and-So. I'm just myself." She knows nothing of Oliver's life, or Mike's, or Mary's, outside the rink, and they know nothing of hers. "I think of them all as friends, but I never picture them away from the rink," she says. "I just imagine them going round and round forever. All the rest of the time, I'm so many things: a singer, a wife, a mother. But what I love is that here all I am is a skater."

□

I was in New York—a city where I once lived in a Gramercy Park penthouse, carried on a career, maintained charge accounts—for the first time in over a year. These days I give little thought to my old life in the city. Nearly all the clothes I bought and wore when I lived there have gone out of style, and the rest I have little occasion to wear. But I came back to New York to celebrate the marriage of our two good old friends Greg and Kate, a painter and a writer, like Steve and me, who met at the same time we did but chose a very different course—of freedom, work, travel, each other.

We were in our friends' downtown loft—exquisitely remodeled, white and spare—for the post-wedding party. My first thought, entering the room—and finding it filled with men in good suits and women in three-inch heels, wearing real pearls and carrying mixed drinks—was surprise at what a lot of older people had come. Then I realized they were just my age, these lawyers and psychiatrists and television executives. We went to the same schools; I even knew some of them, nearly a decade ago, when we had all just come to this city, had just gotten our first apartments and grown-up clothes.

An elegant-looking woman came over to me. We were both due to turn thirty in a matter of weeks, we discovered. Not surprising, really, that the information emerged so swiftly; the knowledge of my upcoming birthday had been much on my mind and clearly much on hers.

But she was a vice president with a large advertising agency handling the Johnson & Johnson account, a woman who flies all over the country looking at cute babies, while I at that point dealt mostly with my own, and the one on the way. (There were, at this gathering that included surely fifty women of prime childbearing age, just two—me and one other—who were pregnant, and only one child present.)

She pulled me aside, sat me down, leaned in close. "How do you do it?" she asked. "What's it like?" She might have been talking about conquering Everest or kicking heroin, but in fact what she meant was having children, being a mother.

And she wasn't talking about the elaborate balancing act pulled off by so many successful New York professional women who manage to have children and a high-powered career too. She was talking about my having made the choice of motherhood at the expense of career. Though she didn't say it quite this way, what she was also talking about were my five-dollar Chinese shoes and my self-cut hair, and how invisible—not unwelcome so much as incongrous—a "non-productive" pregnant woman was at a gathering like this one, where every conversation begins with "What do you do?" I identified myself as a mother of two young children. It's a real conversation stopper, that one.

No question, the thousands of hours Steve and I have spent reading *Goodnight Moon* and Babar to our children, zipping and unzipping their snowsuits, singing them "The Itsy Bitsy Spider" and the *Love Boat* theme song, have taken us away from work. But there's a drain on us greater even than the physical one, the hours of child care and dollars gone to ear infections and Barbies. It's the way the focus gets blurred, the concentration lost, the way every day begins (not even close to unpleasantly) in a bed faintly dampened by our son, rescued in the early morning hours from his crib and asleep now between us with his Sesame Street pillowcase wrapped around his thumb. The ritual daily listing of breakfast possibilities: Cheerios, Rice Krispies, toast, egg (white only). The question, always asked though the answer is always no: "Can I have a doughnut?" Packing the lunchbox. Braiding the hair. Pinning Charlie down to wash his face, retrieving the boot he throws, comforting his sister, on whose head it has landed. Racing out the door at ten past eight to a seventeen-year-old car whose ability to start is always up for grabs.

By nine-thirty, when I'm home again and putting groceries away, washing juice glasses and loading the dryer, the house is empty and quiet. But haunted too, by the children who inhabit it—the concrete evidence (in the form of Matchbox cars and Fisher-Price people, barrettes and an experiment Audrey has set up involving celery sticks, water balloons, dirt, and cups of water with various shades of food coloring in them), and more than that, the energy field that lingers, nearly crackles, even when they're gone.

A few years ago, when my father was slowly dying of pneumonia, I flew out west to see him for what I knew would be the last time. I was pregant then too, with Charlie. And what I remember best about that trip was the feeling I had, greater even than my grief at saying good-bye, of something close to embarrassment at my condition. My father was a man of enormous promise and ambition who saw himself as waylaid by domestic life, detoured from what had looked like a brilliant trajectory into thirty years as an assistant professor of English at a small New Hampshire university. "Children are hostages to fortune," he said regularly, not unkindly, to me, his too-well-loved younger child.

Of course there are parents who want only for their offspring to lay grandchildren at their feet, but what my father wanted from me, on his deathbed, were timeless novels and glorious reviews, and what came instead (though he didn't live to see this) was a baby boy, fair-haired and blue-eyed like him, from his own dark daughter. Another irresistible hostage, come to wreak pleasurable havoc on his parents' lives. In a half year's time, the little inheritance my father had socked away, with enormous advance pride and pleasure in the freedom it would bring me, was mostly gone to pay bills unwritten novels had left unmet. What would he have thought if he could have seen me, two years later, pregnant again, in 1978's maternity dress (my chief extravagances are babies), sipping champagne and answering the advertising executive's question: Doesn't it bother you that your children have, well, sort of messed up your career?

Of course I know well the answers one gives here—all of them well constructed by the countless numbers before me who've taken this exit off the expressway's faster lanes. All about how comparatively brief the period of total responsibility for one's children comes to seem in the "broad overview" of a life, how the experience of parenthood transforms all the rest of one's days, increases a person's humanity. That what one does is not (the old notion) to martyr one's self for the next generation, but to enrich one's own existence through parenthood. (I remember reading a comment made by Meryl Streep, a while after she'd given birth to her first child, that the experience of being a mother would make her a better actress.)

My own view is somewhat less totally assured. I joked to our just-married friends (Kate, the bride, slim and beautiful in a strapless Norma Kamali gown with five layers of organdy flounces that I will draw for Audrey later, back home, and that she will color in, pink): I told them that in ten years I'd be spending my days at my typewriter while they were walking the floor with babies. But the truth is, maybe not. One's art can also be one's only child, and one's child can be one's only true art. It may well be that I never again do anything else as wholeheartedly as I am currently engaged in being my children's mother.

The day after Greg and Kate's wedding, I stood on the corner of Lexington Avenue and 22nd Street, holding Audrey's hand. I pointed out to her the lights in the windows of the apartment that used to be mine, overlooking the park. I told her how I hung the terrace with flowers. I told her how I served dinner on the roof one night and the meal blew away while I was bringing out the candles. There were statues of knights in armor holding up the awning at my front door, I told her, and a doorman and a shiny brass elevator. You could stand on the balcony and see the Empire State Building, lit in red, white, and blue that year, for the bicentennial. I was relieved to discover how nearly painless it felt to get into our old car and head for home.

□

Back when I was eight months pregnant with our third child, broke, snowed in, with Steve out of town for two weeks, my children sick, our pipes frozen, and the engine of our eighteen-year-old car refusing to turn over, Audrey and I got into the *Love Boat* habit. At four o'clock every afternoon—the hour that used to be reserved for *Sesame Street*—we'd fix ourselves a big plate of peanut butter on crackers and (the diet version) peanut butter on celery sticks, and tune in to the daily *Love Boat* rerun. Even Charlie got into the routine.

"Love—exciting and new. Come aboard, we're expecting you. . . ." That was the theme song. Then, one by one, and sometimes two by two, the guest stars would come on board, each one presenting his or her own terrible or comic problem. By the end of the hour, they had all managed to solve their problems, or at least to live with them, and acquired a good base tan while they were at it.

"Wouldn't it be great," Audrey would murmur, with one hand on my belly and one hand on the crackers, "if *we* could go on the Love Boat." But of course, we were dry-docked. The idea of lounging in a bikini, alongside a kidney-shaped pool, sipping a drink out of a coconut shell while someone like Bert Convy rubbed suntain oil on my back—well, it couldn't have seemed more remote to me, as I folded laundry and chopped onions for soup.

But I could dream. I could do more than that, in fact. I wrote a note to the Cunard Lines, entertainment division, offering my services aboard ship as a lecturer on writing. A few weeks later I got a form letter acknowledging receipt of my note, and then nothing. The next month our seond son was born. Then came postpartum depression, mud season, blackfly season. And then one day in late May came a phone call from the entertainment coordinator of the *Queen Elizabeth II*. Could my husband and I be ready to set sail for England, first class, all expenses paid, in ten days?

We didn't agree right away. Steve is the type who feels no day is complete if he hasn't chopped some wood or hammered a few nails. A reluctant vacationer. A man who tries to keep his shaving down to once a week, and his three ties as dusty as possible. When he heard dinners on the QE2 would be black tie, he groaned.

As for me, I was still nursing Willy and hadn't spent a night without him. I was dropping into bed at eight-thirty every night. I wasn't sure I could muster the energy for a vacation, even if we could think of a way to leave the children.

But it was also, we decided, a chance we couldn't pass up. In our seven years of married life, we'd never had a vacation like that, with no children, no work (the lectures didn't really count)—and we had never needed one more. We found a good friend who was willing to take care of our boys, and another friend who agreed to see us off at the ship and then put Audrey on a plane to her grandmother's. We leaned against the rail as the ship pulled out of port, throwing streamers and watching our daughter growing smaller and smaller on shore. It was terrible to see Audrey crying and not be able to put my arms around her.

After that, though, we had an idyllic twelve days, during which I thought about my children surprisingly little. I had brought along a state-of-the-art breast pump, in the hope of being able to continue nursing my son when we got home, but otherwise we behaved like carefree, footloose types who wouldn't know Luvs from Huggies. We drank a lot of champagne. We danced every night, sometimes so late that we watched the sun come up over the ocean. We started every morning with a jog around the deck and ate caviar with every dinner—the new rituals that replaced pouring Cheerios and emptying the diaper pail. Our new shipboard friends included an opera singer, a golf pro, and an avocado grower, and on the return trip, a retired couple who had just purchased thirty-five pairs of shoes for themselves in Portugal and invited us to come visit them sometime in Boca Raton. There was a French nobleman (who, when jokingly I asked how many ancestors of his had been beheaded in the French Revolution and whether he had a castle, answered nine and then took out photographs of two castles—his, and his cousin's). Then there was a young man with five Rolls Royces in the ship's hold and a lady friend sporting $100,000 worth of jewelry, a fellow who confessed to Steve (while the two of them sweated side by side in the sauna) that his underworld connections had been making things dicey lately. We thought he was kidding until we got our pictures back and discovered that in every one where he appeared, he had succeeded in obscuring his face behind a beach umbrella or a piece of rigging.

By the second half of our trip we knew all the ship's comedian's jokes, but it didn't matter: We were cruising. Steve—who spends his life back home in jeans and a paint-spattered shirt—found that he loved putting on his tuxedo every night. I wished I'd managed to scrounge up more gowns than the four I'd brought, to avoid repeating my outfits. I began to look a little enviously at other women's pearls and diamonds.

After twelve nights aboard ship (plus one night in Southampton, England) we were home again, stepping a little unsteadily onto land. And though during that week and a half I hadn't missed the children as dreadfully as I'd feared, suddenly I was frantic to see them. All I wanted was to rub my cheek against my baby's bottom and make a pot of soup.

Sometimes, now, we still watch the *Love Boat*, and it always makes me think of that brief, unreal interlude when we inhabited neither one continent nor the other, but a world apart from everything else. Eating, drinking, dancing, drifting in the Atlantic. Every now and then at parties (my children's) I still tell one of Mickey Marvin's jokes, featuring a dollar bill folded up in the shape of a telephone receiver and a punch line that leaves the five-year-olds doubled up with laughter. And sometimes, when I tell friends about our cruise, I take out the shipboard portrait taken of us, greeting the captain: I in my borrowed silk gown, Steve in his borrowed tux. That one also gets a laugh. The truth is, we are better suited to pumpkins around here than to coaches.

□

Thursday afternoons I pick Audrey up at school and drive her to a city twenty-five miles away for gymnastics lessons.

It's a wonderful school we go to—wall-to-wall mats and equipment, uneven parallel bars, balance beams, enormous bags filled with foam rubber, and a professional-size trampoline. There's a bench at one end of the gym for the parents to sit on while they wait for their children, and a toy bin that keeps Charlie and Willy reasonably well occupied during the hour and a quarter of Audrey's lesson. I could bring a book, but I love watching, not only my child but also all the other little girls in brightly colored leotards and gym shorts, dreaming of becoming ballerinas and acrobats. For them, anything appears possible.

We've been coming here for a year now; I know the routine pretty well. I bring a stack of books for my sons to look at when they get bored, and a couple of snacks to tide us over until dinner, which we eat at McDonald's, just down the road from gymnastics class. This is our night for the big city.

Audrey loves these classes, adores her teacher and our Thursday routine. The waiting around part is hard for my boys, but the thought of the Happy Meal they'll get afterward keeps them going. As for me, I take my pleasure vicariously—relishing the thought that I am giving my child something I would have loved, and never had, myself. All through my own school days, I remained a miserable failure at sports—the last one chosen for every team, the first one replaced by a substitute. To this day, I am unable to perform a cartwheel. For Audrey, I vowed (almost the day she was born), it will be different.

The truth is, she's not a natural gymnast either. There are girls in her class who slide effortlessly into splits and flip across the room in one cartwheel after another, girls who spin round and round on the uneven bars and do somersaults in midair off the trampoline. For Audrey, every new skill they teach here is a struggle. But she's getting them—and if I have to put a thousand miles on the car to make it happen, well, that's one of the things mothers do.

Yesterday at her first class of the new school year, I found myself sitting on the bench beside the mother of a new student, a girl just Audrey's age, whose family has recently moved to our area. So I was the veteran, the one who knew the ropes—naming the pieces of apparatus, explaining dismounts and trampoline rules and the policy concerning absences. "I signed Rebecca up because she's just so gawky and awkward these days," the woman sighed to me. And then, observing my child in one of her better headstands, the woman nodded appreciatively. "Was your little girl always that graceful," she asked, "or did she pick it up here?"

Of course I beamed, and (secure in my own child's accomplishment) I assured her that her daughter's headstands looked just fine and would get even better. Audrey looked up just then, to be sure I had been watching, and waved, and I mouthed the words "Great job!" I recognized the look of pleasure that crossed her face before she turned back to the little group of girls, ready to attempt the next exercise. She was giggling about something. Her ponytail was bobbing, and she was hiking up the tights under her red leotard—making me realize she must have grown over the summer. They're too short for her now. I reminded myself to pick up new ones for her. Maybe a new leotard too.

When the class was over, she ran up to me, still bouncing. Did I see her backward somersaults? her vault over the horse? her flip on the uneven bars? I hugged her, told her how well she'd done. "You know," I said, "I was always too scared to get up on the uneven bars, even when I was a lot bigger than you. One time, when the teacher made me do a flip, I burst into tears."

She made a face of exaggerated disbelief. "You've got to be kidding, Mom. Flips are cinchy. Everybody does those."

Nope, I said. Not your mother.

In the car on the way to McDonald's, she was still flying. Maybe next session she could sign up for two classes a week instead of one? Maybe in a year or two she could be on the team? Maybe we could get a mat, so she could work on her routines at home? "We've got that old mattress up in the playroom," I said. "That would never work," she said. "It's got to be a certain kind. You never did gymnastics, so you don't understand." In her voice was a tone—not exasperation so much as mild amusement, and the very faintest, most affectionate form of condescension. But because she is basically a kind and considerate person, she also gave me a hug, and said, charitably, "That's okay, Mom. Nobody can be good at everything."

My eight-year-old can do some things I can't. She has begun a process that will be repeated with increasing frequency by all three of my children, for as many years as I live, in which the child surpasses the parent. It's what I want for all of them. It's why I drive all these miles on Thursdays, why I sit on that hard bench, why I write out all those checks I can't always afford for gymnastics classes (also piano lessons and skiing lessons and art supplies), and why there will very likely be a regulation-style gymnastics mat under the tree this Christmas.

I remember the first time the thought came to me, that part of what being a parent meant was moving one step closer to the grave. Shifting: from protected child to child protector, from the one who walks on the inside to the one who walks closest to the road. When the thought first hit me, I was pregnant with my first child—the one who is now my eight-and-a-half-year-old gymnast—and (in the style of a nine-months-pregnant woman, who is seldom very far from tears) I was in tears. My body was no longer simply my own, I wept, but totally at the service now of a small person I hadn't even met yet. I had longed for this moment. I wanted to become a mother. Still, it was a shock to realize that if I did my job right, I would have a child who was smarter, wiser, nicer, more secure, more accomplished than

I. A child who could turn cartwheels and do flips. Who would someday say to me, "You mean, you can't even do a backward somersault? Here, let me teach you."

And see, it has happened.

□

I was in New York City the other day—without my children or my husband, or any of the paraphernalia I usually carry (bags of groceries, a baby bottle sticking out of my purse) that give me away, instantly, as a married woman, a mother. Sitting on the bus, I felt a man looking at me in a way that hasn't happened often in the eight years since Audrey was born. No way he could tell I was unavailable.

I guess, truthfully, I miss being looked at not as somebody's mother, but as my own self. One pleasure I remember from my single days was the way every day dawned with possibilities looming. You never knew if this might be the train you'd board and meet the man of your dreams. There was always the chance that tomorrow you might fall in love. Given the choice, I'll opt for loving someone, being loved, to the mysteries behind door number two. But no question, one element that's absent from even blissful domestic life is mystery. Courtship. Suspense. (It's no wonder so many mothers of young children watch soap operas and read romance novels.) A husband can be many things, but one thing's for sure: he will never be a stranger in the night.

Early last winter (it was just before Christmas) Audrey flew by herself to visit her grandmother in Canada. It's a trip she's made often, ever since she reached the age at which airlines permit children to fly alone (and, in truth, a little before then too). It's a direct flight: my mother puts her on the plane, and of course either Steve or I always pick her up at the other end.

This time she'd been gone about five days, and I was missing her badly—couldn't wait to see her coming off that plane. I guess I was in a pretty keyed-up state: a combination of excitement at seeing Aud, and Christmas, which is a holiday that (I keep reminding myself) I love, even though I'm generally in tears at least once a day throughout the month of December.

This particular December day, I'd had a fight with Steve a few hours earlier. I can't even remember anymore what it was about, but I know my themes well enough that I can guess. He wasn't talking to me enough. He had fallen asleep on the couch again. He had slept through all three times Willy woke up in the night. The only compliment he'd given me in two days was for taking the trash to the dump. He was showing all the signs of being a man who's planning to give his wife a knife sharpener for Christmas. Somewhere in there I had doubtless told him (my old refrain) that he was treating me like an old shoe.

When I set out in mid-afternoon for the hundred-mile drive to the airport, we hadn't made up. I didn't really mind the drive: I had brought with me a bunch of obscure bluegrass music tapes full of tragic love stories. Playing bluegrass banjo is a long-deferred dream of mine, but for the time being, I just sing along. That's what I did that day all the way to Boston. Then, because I had a couple of hours to spare before Audrey's plane got in, I stopped at a mall a few minutes from the airport to do some Christmas shopping.

I bought a few toys for the children and three dozen bagels for the freezer. When I looked at my watch I realized I had cut things a little closer than usual, but still, I knew, there was enough time to pick up our car, drive to the airport, and retrieve Audrey. As I walked to the parking lot, I said out loud—superstitiously—how much I loved her, and how lucky I was to have a daughter.

But when I got to the car, put down the packages, and

reached into my purse for the car keys, they weren't there. I checked again, and then I checked my pockets. I checked again, checked the ground around the car. I raced back to the toy store I'd been shopping in: no keys. No keys at the bagel stand. And now Audrey's plane was just a half hour from landing. I knew the keys might be in the car (it was too dark to see) and they might be in the snow somewhere between the parking lot and the shops. But there was no more time to look. So, frantic now, I hailed a taxi and told the driver to take me to Logan Airport fast. I had only ten dollars left in my wallet. The fare came to five.

I got to Audrey's gate with just five minutes to spare. I made a call to the Boston police, who told me they couldn't get a car like mine open and started without seriously damaging the ignition, and in any case it might be a few hours before they could get around to me. I called Steve—told him what was happening, and explained that I'd be home late.

Then I caught a glimpse of Audrey, who was carrying an enormous box holding a Barbie Dream Carriage (her early Christmas present from her grandmother) and a couple of shopping bags besides. Of course I threw my arms around her first, and burst into tears. Then I explained about the car.

Neither of us had eaten dinner, but I figured we'd better use our last five dollars to get back to the car and try again to find the keys, or someone who could get the car open. It was around seven-thirty by this time, and below freezing, with a stiff wind.

To save money, I thought we'd try and share a cab. There was a friendly, kind-looking man in the taxi line, so I asked him if he might like to split a fare. The man—Ned was his name—said sure.

In the taxi, Audrey told him our story, leaving out nothing (not the bagels, or the Barbie coach, either). And it turned out that this fellow (a nice-looking man, about thirty-five) was an engineer who'd just flown in to set up a machine he'd invented at MIT. His briefcase was full of tools. "I'll come with you to the parking lot," he said. "I'll get your car open."

Well, I said, okay; and Audrey jumped up and down on the seat, announcing, "This is great! This is just great!" I suggested she could wait inside the parking-lot attendant's booth, where it was warm and there was a television set, but she didn't want to miss anything. So she sat on the hood of the car, bundled up in extra clothes she'd pulled out of her suitcase, and leaned over Ned's shoulder while he laid out his tools on the roof and analyzed the situation.

With his special miniature flashlight beamed in through the windshield, Ned found out the keys were in the ignition. Then he took a coat hanger out of his garment bag, twisted it, and attached a screwdriver to one end. Then he attached some wire so he could maneuver the screwdriver, sort of like a fishing line, from outside the window. The whole thing became pretty elaborate.

And it didn't work. An hour had passed now, and my fingers were numb. Maybe I should just leave the car and call a friend in Cambridge to pick us up, I said. Audrey and Ned protested. "I'm going to get this thing open," Ned said.

He built a second invention. Audrey told him her long-time ambition—to be an inventor. He told her about things he used to build when he was a little boy.

We talked about all sorts of things while he worked on our car. He told funny stories about taking apart people's stereos all the time, and Audrey told him about her trip to Canada. She mentioned what a good pie baker I am. He mentioned how much he loved pies.

I was aware, though, through all of this, of the fact that Steve's name hadn't come up. I had a child, and obviously she had a father, but after a couple of hours, when the fact still hadn't emerged that I had a husband back home (and two little boys), it occurred to me that maybe Ned thought I was divorced, and available.

He was a really nice man. Just the sort of person with whom—if I'd met him at the airport, before I met Steve—I would've been happy to have dinner. It was very easy and natural, talking with him. He gave me his scarf and hat when he noticed I was cold. He really paid attention to Audrey.

Now comes the part that's hard to admit: that there came a point, somewhere along the line, when I began consciously avoiding mention of Steve and my two little boys back home. Not that I planned to head off into the night with Ned (and Audrey, and the Barbie Dream Carriage). Not that I planned anything more than a handshake, and maybe a gift, in the mail, of some home-baked Christmas cookies. But the fact is, I guess I liked holding on to the image—for a few minutes anyway—of a young single mother, being cared for, and, I supposed, courted by a kind and attractive inventor who knew how to talk to children and told me I could make standing in a parking lot for two hours on a night with a windchill factor of negative ten degrees feel like fun.

Twice, while Ned worked on our car, a couple of men came up to see if they could help. One of them even appeared, for a second there, to be making some progress with the lock for a second there. And I saw, when that happened, how much Ned wanted to be the one to get our car door open.

Which he did, finally, by taking off a window, using the coathanger to lower in a towel to remove four separate interior screws, in a procedure that was (as I told him) nothing less than brilliant.

"Now," Audrey said brightly (always up for a party), "we have to take you out to dinner. To celebrate."

It was ten o'clock by now. I explained, with embarrassment, that we were out of money. "Don't be silly," Ned told us. "This is my treat." And though I protested that we really had to get home, Audrey was starved and so was I. And I needed to warm up before the long drive home in a car with one window missing.

So we went to a restaurant that served enormous hamburgers, and Audrey had a sundae, and we all talked a lot more (I was surprised at how much there was to say that had nothing to do with my marriage and my family). Ned told us this was the best evening he'd had in months. And then, just after our second cup of coffee, I got up and said I'd better call Steve and tell him why we were so late.

I think back on this today and wince, because I saw the look on Ned's face when I said that. Now it seems just about unavoidable to conclude that I was somehow leading him on—toying with his affections, giving him reason to hope that things might turn out the way they would have in certain highly romantic movies, where the man, the woman (a widow, probably), and the child (Shirley Temple) walk off hand in hand and become, instantly, a *family*. I do know that I wasn't just using him to get my car open. For a moment there I probably allowed myself a romantic fantasy or two as well. None of which is to say that I don't love my husband, and want to stay married.

Well, it was late. Ned had been very kind. There was no danger, anymore, of my being misunderstood. So I told him I'd drive him to his hotel before we set out for the long drive home. When we got into the car and I turned on the ignition, my obscure folk music tape clicked on and he shook his head. "I didn't know anybody besides me listens to this," he said. And it turned out he played the banjo.

By the time I pulled up beside Ned's hotel, Audrey was asleep. "Be sure and say good-bye for me," he said. I shook his hand and said, "If you're ever in New Hampshire . . ." He picked up his briefcase and then closed the door very carefully, so as not as not to wake Aud.

The next morning I told Steve what had happened. Later that day (setting out for the grocery store with Charlie and Willy) I found, on the floor of the car, a package belonging to Ned, and called the hotel where he was staying. It turned out to be a crucial piece for the machine he was installing at MIT. I said I'd send it Express Mail that day. He wrote to me once, after that, saying it would be nice to get together in Boston, sometime when he came into town again. He had some records he'd like to tape for me.

I didn't write back.

———

END OF ENDURANCE

- *Dressed for Snow* - *Tomato Sauce*
- *Mom's Problems* - *Flipping Out*
- *Five-Mile Road Race*

It was the morning after our first real snowfall of the year, and school had been called off. I didn't go out to work, which meant I had an extra half hour to hang around in my nightgown, refilling cereal bowls. And then everyone wanted to go outside and investigate the snow.

Since this was the first storm of the season, we didn't really have our winter routine down yet. I had to go up to the attic and dig out our collection of snowpants, to locate an old pair of Audrey's for Charlie and an old pair of Charlie's for Willy. I dumped a bag of mittens on the middle of the floor, in search of pairs, and found (what would the odds be for this to happen, I'd like to know?), among twenty-some mittens, not a single matched set. I untangled a clump of scarves and leg warmers, plus various sorts of novelty headgear: earmuffs in the shape of teddy bears, a hat with bumblebee stripes and antennae sticking up from either side, one of those total face masks, with holes cut out for the eyes, nostrils, and mouth. I found the remnants of a couple of mouse nests in there too, but I'm used to those.

Then it was time to get the children dressed. I weighed the situation for a moment and decided to start with Willy, because he's young enough not to insist on helping me much, which can be a relief.

So I stripped him of his pajamas. I'm sure I cannot be the only parent in the world who's observed the sudden and dramatic change in behavior a child undergoes the moment he's liberated from clothing. Because they love being bare, the taking-off part tends to go smoothly. The only trouble is— once bare, the child disappears (with a whoop and, very possibly, his underpants on his head). Then you spend the next five minutes catching him.

But eventually I got Willy cornered and was able to proceed. I put on his turtleneck shirt (how many thousands of times have I said the words: "Where did your head go? *There* it is!"). I kissed his belly button, reached for his socks (not a matching pair, of course). But in the split second it took me to get his shoes, the socks were flung behind the refrigerator. And because Charlie was getting impatient to go outside by now, I reached for another pair of socks instead of fishing around for the lost ones.

Overalls. And then the ritual in which I give Willy a penny for his pocket. This morning, because I was harried and rushing, I didn't (as I usually do) hunt for a shiny one, and I pushed his toes into his boots a little more roughly than I might. He looked faintly puzzled, but unshakably jovial still. I worked his thumbs into the thumb pockets of his mittens. He flung them off. I tied his hat under his chin. He shrieked, "No hat." I gave up and sent him out the door.

Then it was Charlie's turn, and we started the whole procedure again. I pulled his sock on (to hurry things up a bit) and he pulled it off and then spent five minutes lining the seams up along his toes. After hunting down a shoelace—he took one out yesterday to make a lasso for GI Joe—I laced up his boots. But he could still feel the seam of his socks against his toes. The boots had to come off. We tried again.

Meanwhile I heard Willy outside, crying. He'd fallen down in the snow, of course. His hands were frozen. As I raced outside (barefoot) to pick him up and blow on his fingers, inside I could hear Charlie wailing, "You forgot me!"

Not likely. I made sure he went to the bathroom before putting on his snow pants. Then I zipped up his jacket (only, he has to do it. I forgot). At last I pulled his hat over his ears and launched him out the door to join his brother.

Then I had, I figured, about three minutes in which to get dressed before some diaster or other left one of the children crying in a heap of snow. I raced for my own winter socks and wool pants, sweaters, jacket, mittens, hat. I was lacing up my second boot (using garbage-bag twist ties, because it appeared that someone had absconded with my shoelace too) just as the first wail started up.

Outside, my two younger children stood stiffly (too tightly bundled for any sudden movements) while I dusted off the sled and sat Willy down. He demanded his bathrobe. Charlie munched on a piece of snow with a faint yellowish tinge to it. A few feet away, our dog, Ron, began to chew on Willy's discarded mitten.

"Let's make a fort," I said cheerily.

"I think I'm ready for a little snack," said Charlie, and Audrey agreed that hot chocolate might be nice, with an island of vanilla ice cream floating on top.

It was half past nine. It had taken us just under an hour to get dressed. We had been outdoors exactly eight minutes.

So we piled back into the kitchen and reversed the whole

process, right down to the underwear, because everybody's clothes had gotten wet in spite of the snow pants, and Willy needed a change.

I lifted him onto the changing table, sighing heavily, thinking what a long winter this would be. He pulled off the hat I'd forgotten to take off and did a little dance with it. He touched the top of his head to the pad on the changing table and looked through his legs at me, grinning. I unfastened the diaper tapes—still not amused.

You always open a diaper a little cautiously, until you know how major the clean-up operation is going to be. This time, I could tell, my son was merely wet.

But there was one other thing I could see, as I started to toss the wet diaper away: a copper penny. It landed neatly in my palm, like a tip. And I decided not to be mad after all.

□

It had been a lousy season for tomatoes. Too dry at first, and then, just at the point when they're all that pale shade of orange, and in need of two or three hot days to ripen, what we got instead were cool, rainy days and downright chilly nights. The sort of weather that makes a person feel like canning tomatoes. Only there weren't any around.

So I had been calling farm stands everywhere within a twenty-mile radius, in search of canning tomatoes. Just when I was about ready to give up, I got the word that a produce market a half-hour's drive away had three bushels of tomatoes at a good price, if I could pick them up that night. Naturally I said yes.

In truth, it was the worst possible moment for three bushels of tomatoes to come my way. The next morning was Audrey's first day in second grade, the day after that was Charlie's registration at preschool. And I still had to hem up one size seven miniskirt and get Charlie's health forms filled out, along with borrowing my friend Laurie's pressure cooker and dropping off some overdue library books and getting Willy to the doctor and me to the chiropractor and somewhere in there attending to the stacks of work piled up on my desk after our week's vacation at the beach. Steve had been working on a big job that got him home late and tired every night. And on top of everything else, I had to go into the city the next morning to work on an article.

A person might ask (as Steve did) why it was so important to me to can all those tomatoes, all that spaghetti sauce. True enough, the spaghetti sauce I make is great: all fresh vegetables, and no paste, simmered on the stove all of one night and the next day. But, Steve pointed out, stopping on his way to bed around twelve-thirty to watch me still standing at the kitchen counter chopping onions, with tears streaming down my face, something has to give. A woman with a full-time job and young children simply can't do everything mothers used to do when they didn't have full-time paid jobs. (Not that we don't try.)

In fact, I think it's because I'm not always home, not always free to read books to my children and give them kisses, that this sauce of mine seems so important. I love the way my house smells when my sauce is simmering. I love the look of all those jars lined up on the pantry shelves. And on cold afternoons in December, when it's already nearly dark by the time I come in after my day's work, I love being able to take down a jar of my spaghetti sauce and feed my family a dinner just as good as anything I could have come up with if I'd been in my kitchen all day. When I see the plate of steaming spaghetti on the table, I feel (there is no way to say this without sounding corny, I guess) that I'm offering up tangible proof of love. No one in her right mind would spend all these hours making sauce from scratch just to save money—that's for sure.

Well, the night I got the tomatoes I set them on the back

porch, with the plan that I'd get to them over the next few days. Nights, actually: after the children were in bed. The next morning, at seven-thirty, I drove Audrey to her first day of school. She kissed me a little distractedly and then ran off to compare jelly bracelets with other second-grade girls. Though few children wept, many mothers looked a little teary. I didn't cry, but I found an excuse to walk past the window of her classroom to catch a fleeting glimpse.

Then I drove off to my day's work. I put in long hours. Got a bad headache. And because I knew Steve would be tired from watching the boys all day (we were between babysitters), I picked up a pizza on my way home. I walked in the porch door, vaguely noticing that the floor had been mopped and thinking how thoughtful it was for Steve to do that.

Then Audrey ran out to meet me, breathless. "Tell me all about school," I said, giving her a hug. "Oh, that," she said. "Fine. But listen. That's not what I wanted to tell you."

It seems that her younger brothers had been getting a little wild, throwing cottage cheese. So Steve put them out on the porch with orders to play outside for a while. Audrey, meanwhile, was upstairs in her room, playing with her Glamour Gals ocean liner. Steve stretched out on the sofa with the current issue of *Sports Illustrated* and, evidently, fell asleep.

Suddenly, Audrey said, she heard Charlie yelling something about potatoes, which is what he calls tomatoes. "I thought I'd better investigate," she said.

Just then Steve woke up, and the two of them opened the door to the porch. Where they found every single one of my three bushels of tomatoes spilled out on the floor, and, as Audrey tells it, "totally smushed."

There were tomatoes on the porch screens. Several tomatoes thrown against the porch door. One tomato on top of Willy's head, with the juice dripping down his face. Willy, of course, was happy as a clam.

So Steve gave Charlie a spanking and sent him to his room. He put the salvageable tomatoes back into the boxes and mopped the floor. He put Willy in the tub and gave him a shampoo. Audrey went back to playing Glamour Gals. Right about then I came home.

"Look on the bright side," said Audrey, surveying the piles of oozing tomatoes. "You have to smush 'em up to make spaghetti sauce anyway."

The only problem was, now I had the task of cooking up, at once, before rot set in, a quantity of sauce I had meant to work on gradually over the next week or so.

Still, I managed. I put the smashed tomatoes through an incredible new machine my friend Molly brought over, which sends skins and seeds out one spigot and juice out the other. I boiled down my tomato juice to the correct, meaty consistency. I chopped up about ten pounds of celery, onions, and carrots, and added them to the tomato juice.

After I cooked that, I put the whole thing—in batches—through my Cuisinart and back on the stove, where I poured in the olive oil, heated it a little more, and tasted it one more time, to confirm that this was, in fact, the most delicious tomato sauce I'd ever tasted. And then I sterilized my quart canning jars and lids, heated up a big potful of water, poured the sauce into the jars, cleaned the rims, screwed on the seals, and set them into their boiling water bath as tenderly as any mother would tuck her child into bed.

Somewhere around two A.M. a couple of days later, I put my twenty-fourth quart of spaghetti sauce on the pantry shelf—exhausted (and smelling strongly of tomato), but happy. Estimating conservative sauce consumption at the rate of a quart a week, I figured we had enough spaghetti sauce to get us through to March. A new bushel of tomatoes, awaiting the pot, sat on the porch (on a high shelf, this time, out of my sons' reach).

That's how things stood last Thursday when I got the call

from Molly—a woman who, having lived without electricity or running water at a commune in Tennessee, used to put up about five hundred quarts of vegetables every year to feed her family. At various times I have turned to Molly for sage advice on nearly every aspect of my life, canning being one.

"I have bad news about your tomato sauce," Molly began. "Remember when I told you to can it, instead of using the pressure cooker? Remember when I explained to you that tomatoes are a high-acid fruit, so there's no problem with botulism?" Yes, I said, my heart sinking.

"Well," she continued, "that's true. But last night, just as I was falling asleep, I suddenly flashed on that bowl full of chopped carrots and celery and onions I saw sitting on your counter the other day when I came over with the food mill. And it came to me: Carrots are a low-acid food. Carrots should go in the pressure cooker."

In other words, those twenty-four quarts of sauce, with their beautiful, hand-lettered labels, those two dozen jars that I stood admiring on my pantry shelves for about five minutes the night before (thinking that, come what may, my family would be well fed this winter), were not really safe after all. Not downright dangerous, just iffy. Which, in the world of canning, is maybe the worst way to be.

So I called the county extension service, and asked (like someone at the scene of an accident, calling out, "Is there a doctor in the house?") whether the home economist was in. Which one? they asked. "Canning problems," I said glumly.

She came on the line, sounding businesslike rather than motherly. "Your sauce might be all right," she said. "But then again, it might not. The only way to be sure is to take off the lids, get all new lids, and put the whole batch through a pressure cooker. Fifteen minutes, at twenty-five pounds of pressure." The only problem with that was that Laurie's pressure cooker only went up to fifteen pounds.

Of course I called her right away.

Now, Laurie is another of those friends I turn to about every kind of problem from my marriage to split ends. She was there when I thought our entire family had head lice (but we didn't). She was there when the brake pedal in our car broke off on an expressway in heavy traffic. (Laurie got down on the floor and worked the brakes manually.) She was there at the birth of our third child. As a matter of fact, talking me calmly through the pressure-cooking process while I carried out her instructions at the other end, she sounded, again, a little like an auxiliary birth coach.

She went over the part about cleaning the jar rims, measuring the water into the pot, putting on the little gadget called the petcock, with the correct pressure setting (fifteen minutes at ten pounds of pressure would be fine, she said). "Now just turn the water on to boil," she said, "and in about fifteen minutes, when the petcock starts to click, turn it down until the intervals between clicks are around fifteen seconds apart."

So I hung up and I waited. Gradually the pressure cooker began to shake. The petcock rattled. The whole thing looked like a bomb ready to go off. But there were no ticks.

Forty-five minutes later, with no sign of ticking yet, I panicked. I figured I must've missed something. I figured the water must have evaporated by now. I figured the pot must be ready to explode. So I turned it off.

I think that's when things really started to go downhill. Now I really didn't know where I stood: no ticks on my petcock, no twenty-five-pound pressure gauge. Then I ran out of new canning lids, and had to drive into town. Then I got back, and could no longer tell which jars I'd canned and which I'd pressure cooked. I also knew there were some jars on the shelf (from my most recent batch of sauce) that had been neither cooked nor pressure cooked, but it was about ten o'clock at night, and I was exhausted and discouraged, and I figured I could deal better with the whole thing next morning.

But the next morning, when I reached for a jar to put into the pressure cooker, the lid suddenly popped off, shooting spaghetti sauce clear to the ceiling. Covering me, covering my just-washed hair and my just-washed floor, splattering drips of tomato into the children's Kix and my coffee.

"Why don't you just freeze what's left?" suggested Laurie. "Then again, if it's bad, freezing might not be enough."

"Why don't you just make sauce without carrots," said Molly, telling me a comforting story about the time she made fifty quarts of pickles that all turned out mushy. Then there was the moldy apple butter. . . .

"I bet that stuff you just canned is really okay," said Laurie. "Tomatoes are acid, after all."

"True," I responded, my hopes soaring.

"Then again," she added, "there are those carrots. . . . Maybe you'd better just throw it all out."

"Try more pressure cooking," said Molly. "Maybe you just didn't give the petcock enough time to start ticking."

"Freeze it," urged Laurie. "That's probably good enough."

"Are you prepared to live with the responsibility of my entire family's death by botulism if it turns out you're wrong?" I asked her.

She considered this for a moment. "Why don't you just toss it all on the compost pile, then," she suggested, "and chalk the whole thing up to a fantastic learning experience?"

□

The day had not begun well. Willy wanted me to bake him blueberry muffins. Audrey, whose friend Melissa had come for a sleepover the night before, woke to discover that Melissa had left in the middle of the night with a sudden attack of homesickness. Charlie couldn't find his bear. Steve was dead to the world.

So I crawled out of bed, put on water for coffee, started clattering pans for muffins, and (this being Saturday) turned on the cartoons. I changed Willy's diaper, found Bear Bear, promised Audrey we'd try another sleepover soon, and removed from the kitchen counter a piece of watermelon that had been left out the night before. With about a hundred ants on it.

The telephone rang while I was sifting the flour: a collection agency, wanting to know why I hadn't been making payments on my Mastercard. ("I've been so busy fighting a nuclear dump in my town," I told the woman. She didn't seem too interested.) On top of everything else, my whole mouth was in pain from two teeth I'd had filed down for a temporary crown, my dentist was out of town, and I had poison ivy all over my left foot.

Steve came into the kitchen and gave me a kiss. I slid the muffin pan into the oven, threw my potholder to the floor, burst into tears, and told him (for probably the five hundredth time in our nine years of marriage) that I was about to have a nervous breakdown.

Steve poured himself a cup of coffee. "I thought I'd go for a jog," he said. "Could you just hold off falling apart until I get back?"

I was still crying. Audrey and Charlie came rushing in to see what was the matter. "I'm sorry, Mom," said Charlie, who no longer waits to see whose fault it was this time. He threw his arms around me. Audrey threw her arms around both of us. The weight of the two of them knocked me over—I fell backward and cracked my head against the floor.

Now, I am a little hazy about the order of things after

that, but I can tell you some of the things I said (in no particular order), because they are the things I nearly always say to my family in times like these:

"I'm just a servant around here. Nobody appreciates me."

"Of course I'm mean and no fun to be around. I could have a pleasant personality too, if I got to sleep late and hang around watching cartoons every morning, and if I could take off any time I felt like it to go jogging."

"Just once, I'd like to see one of you put your bowl in the dishwasher without being asked."

Of course there was more: about the nuclear dump, about my dentist, who had shot me full of Novocain and then stuffed my mouth with cotton, seconds before launching into his remarks on the nuclear issue. I complained about how I never get time to hang up all the clothes on my closet floor. I moaned about not having my tomatoes planted yet.

"Please don't get tears all over my bear," said Charlie.

"I have three hundred unanswered letters sitting on my desk," I said. "Vicky leaves in three weeks and we still don't have a new babysitter. Our medical insurance expires July first. How am I supposed to plant a garden when there's twenty feet of brush piled up on it? What teacher will Audrey get for third grade? I don't think calamine lotion does one bit of good for poison ivy."

Of course I burned the muffins. Steve took his run. Audrey shooed her brothers out of the kitchen, and everyone stayed out of my way for about half an hour, until Steve came home. By then I was dressed, and glumly seated at the kitchen table, contemplating all the things about my life that seemed out of control. Steve took a shower, dried himself off, and sat down next to me with a ballpoint pen and a yellow legal pad.

"Okay," he said. "Let's make a list. We'll write down all your problems, so we'll know what we're up against."

I told him to stop making fun of me. This was serious.

"Who's making fun?" he said. He picked up the pen and wrote "MOM'S PROBLEMS" at the top of the sheet.

I told him I didn't know where to begin, I had so many.

"Number one," he wrote. "Having nervous breakdown. Number two. Have to put kids' cereal bowls into the dishwasher all the time."

"I'm always the one who has to get out of bed to change Willy's diaper at six o'clock," I said.

"What about yesterday?" Steve pointed out. Then he wrote: "Number three. Have to change Willy's morning diaper—sometimes."

"The three hundred unanswered letters sitting on my desk," I said. "Cleaning the closet. Getting Audrey new sneakers." Which was followed by "toothache" and "cat using fireplace for litter box."

Number ten was poison ivy. Number fifteen was "Texas still being considered as a nuclear dump site." Eighteen was our town fire marshal, who has been unwilling to give us a permit to burn our brush pile so we can rototill our garden. I was winding down—I could feel it. However, I had to admit, I was feeling better.

Number nineteen was the imminent departure of our babysitter, Vicky. Number twenty-one was nuclear war. Even that one seemed less than overwhelming, listed as it was just beneath "third grade."

I had stopped crying by this time. I was even munching on toast, and fixing myself a third slice. The children had stopped tiptoeing around and were back to bouncing on the sofa. Steve put the list on our bulletin board with a push pin. Where it still hangs, right beside the grocery list, a pack of morning glory seeds, and a reminder about my next dental appointment.

This afternoon it rained, and we got a burning permit.

Tonight we burn the brush pile, and tomorrow we'll rototill the garden. Check off item number eighteen. One down, twenty to go.

□

I often wonder about those housewives and mothers you hear about now and then, who simply, somewhere along the line, flip out. The ones who walk out the door and never come back or break every piece of their best china, some afternoon when their husband says he's too tired to change the baby's diaper. A woman who one day just lets the washer overflow and stops bothering to wash the dishes, a woman who simply wakes up one morning and decides to stay in bed.

And of course, at the back of it all is the image of some young, hardworking, responsible-seeming wife and mother (she cooks out of the *Silver Palate*, does Jane Fonda six days a week, gives perfect holiday parties) who one day sticks her head in the gas oven and signs off for good. I suspect many of us have wondered, at one moment or another, whether we could ever reach that point. And for most of us, the answer is no. Still, who doesn't feel the urge, now and then, to just let loose?

So this is what happened last Tuesday. I had taken off work for the afternoon, deciding to spend it with my husband (also off from work) and our children. We packed a lunch and headed for the mountains. We had a wonderful afternoon. Then, on our way home (because I wanted to prolong this good time together, and everyone was in such a good mood), I suggested we stop in a nearby town for pizza.

We placed our order, careful to specify that half the pizza should have the works on top and half (the children's portion) should be plain. The man told us to come back in half an hour, and we did—in good spirits, but starving.

But when the pizza was set before us, it was covered completely with mushrooms, anchovies, and onions, and I knew the children wouldn't touch it. I sent it back, thinking maybe the pizza man could scrape off the extra stuff and replace it with a new topping, ready to go. He said it would take twenty minutes.

And—hungry, tired, frustrated at seeing our dinner out on the verge of being ruined—I exploded. I told the pizza man a few things about two-year-old boys (what they're like after sitting in a high chair for twenty minutes, waiting for dinner). I told him (the way I tell my children; it's a habit I can't break) that he should at least say he was sorry. "I'm only human," said the pizza man. "Everybody makes mistakes."

Which was fair enough, but didn't do much for the children, who were already losing their good humor. I tried taking Willy for a walk, but having once seen the pizza so close nearly within reach, he didn't want to come. Charlie wanted to work the video games. Audrey was wriggling. "Why don't you go walk around the block by yourself and let off some steam," said Steve, seeing my clenched fists and tight-lipped expression. So I did.

When I came back, the pizza was nearly ready again. But just as the pizza man (to whom I had apologized, by now) began to cut our pizza, Steve got up from the table and headed out the door with Willy. I couldn't imagine why, and he didn't stop to tell me.

The rest of us sat at the table then for a couple of minutes, waiting for Steve to come back. Three minutes. Four. I drummed my fingers on the table exaggeratedly. Charlie began sucking his thumb. Audrey wanted to know if we could just start without the others. I said no. We were going to have a happy family dinner if it killed us.

When Steve had still not returned, after precisely six and a half minutes of waiting, I ran out of the restaurant after him. He was halfway down the block with Willy, and the two of them were walking back in our direction—but slowly, taking their time, admiring cracks in the sidewalk. "Steve!" I screamed, in a voice that must have made him think the restaurant was on fire.

Of course then he came fast, scooping Willy up in his arms and running, while I returned to our table and sat stonily across from our children and the still-untouched pizza, while the pizza man stared at me curiously.

Steve came in a minute later and sat down very calmly, explaining that he had taken Willy out to give the pizza time to cool. What was the matter with that?

Now comes the part that's hard to tell: About how I stalked out of the restaurant with my beer, all appetite for pizza gone, and then sat, alone, for twenty minutes in the car (which was parked directly in front of the pizza parlor, in perfect view of my friend the pizza man), staring at a woman's magazine that had been lying on the seat. How my family came out of the restaurant at last and Steve (not really angry) said quietly, "Ready to apologize?" And how I said nothing, and just kept staring at a recipe for Coffee Macadamia Nut Torte.

Neither one of us said anything, then, for a pretty miserable ten minutes. I was sorry, by that time, but I was also in so deep I didn't know how to turn things around. I was tired, I was hungry, I was mad at myself for ruining our lovely day. I didn't talk, then, about how I'd felt abandoned, back in the restaurant, with the pizza man giving me the evil eye and Steve gone and all the rest of us just sitting there, waiting. I didn't talk about how badly I had wanted us all to have a good time. I didn't, as I should have, close my eyes and think back to that morning and the happy whoop our children had let out when they heard that I was coming along with them. I just looked at my beer and a terrible urge came over me to throw it, and because nobody else had done anything wrong (except maybe the pizza man), I raised my cup and poured its contents all over myself.

I'm here to tell you, it didn't work. Didn't make me feel better, didn't make my children happy again, didn't result in a big hug from my husband. And if what one gets from throwing crockery, pouring the Rice Krispies out the window, snipping the clothesline in two, is more of the feeling I got from having beer drip down my hair into my eyes, then I think I'll pass on future outbursts.

It's a week now since the episode my children speak of as the night Mom threw her beer, and things are back to normal. For more days than I like to remember, though, every time I'd turn around, Charlie and Willy were dumping something (cereal, orange juice, bristle blocks) over their heads, and shrieking wildly. Of course I told them again and again that what I'd done was wrong, that it only made me feel terrible. Keeping things under control is a strain, all right. But losing control is worse.

□

This morning I baked a blueberry pie for my friend Barbara, who just gave birth to a baby boy. Then I ran in a five-mile road race, finishing 248th out of about 260 runners. I picked up my free T-shirt, stood under an open fire hydrant to cool off. And then I came back home, peeled off my sweaty running clothes, pulled on a dress, and drove with Audrey to a hillside a few miles outside of town to attend a memorial service for the daughter of friends of ours who died, three days ago, at the age of twenty months.

There is more, of course, that can be said about all of these events, beginning with Lindsay Turner, who was born with a serious congenital heart defect and died on the operating table during the sixth major heart surgery of her life—a very beautiful baby girl you might have seen, in her stroller, without realizing anything was wrong, unless you went to change her diaper and saw the scars that went from the front of her chest clear around to the back.

We barely knew the Turners when we offered to take care of their older daughter, Hannah, one time when Lindsay went into the hospital last fall. After the parents came back to town Joan told me what their year had been like: Lindsay's birth was smooth and uncomplicated, but a few hours later she suddenly turned blue. An ambulance rushed her to Boston, where Joan and Donald learned that without a brand-new surgical procedure—the first of a whole series, whose oldest survivor was not yet four—their baby would be dead within hours. Of course they chose the surgery, although, describing it later, Joan told me softly that sometimes she wished they'd simply let Lindsay die. Terrible as it would have been to lose her then, it would get worse later.

By last spring, Lindsay had survived all but the final and most life-threatening stage of heart repair, and her parents dared to be optimistic—Donald boundlessly so, Joan cautiously. They'd go to her crib every morning wondering if she'd still be breathing. And still they carrried her everywhere, too weak to walk, while Willy, three months younger, raced through our house and up the stairs, tumbling down them more than once, leaving me near tears from trying to keep up with him.

The Turners had money problems, but that was the least of it. There were problems with Hannah, who had to be left with friends and neighbors every time Lindsay went to the hospital again. There were days when Joan felt so bleak she simply couldn't get out of bed. There were people who would stop her in the supermarket and, seeing Lindsay's blue lips and fingers, tell her that she should dress her child more warmly. No one wanted the responsibility of babysitting Lindsay, so Joan and Donald never went anywhere, except to the hospital. And there was also the knowledge that they would never have another baby. The risk was too great that another child would be born with the same heart defect.

I called Joan and Donald sometimes, to see how they were doing, and now and then we'd bring Hannah over to our house to play. But the truth is, I didn't ever call as much as I should have. The demands of our own three children often seemed all I could handle—more than I could handle, sometimes.

And then too, people like helping out with small, manageable problems, and this one—about which nothing cheering and hopeful could be said, for which there were no real solutions—was just so overwhelming. Sometimes I just wanted to forget about Lindsay, and of course, for me, that was possible.

So I hadn't talked to the Turners all summer, and didn't even know that Lindsay had gone into the hospital for surgery at the beginning of July and had fallen into a coma. She remained there for weeks, until finally the doctors decided they had to operate on her heart immediately, even though the prospects looked grim.

But two days ago, driving into town with Steve and the children, heading out for an afternoon at the circus, we passed Joan and Donald and Hannah, driving in the opposite direction, and saw their car turn in to the funeral home.

No questions were necessary. We went to the circus anyway; we even laughed at one particularly funny clown. We got home very late, and I called a friend who told me that yes, Lindsay had died. The memorial service would be today. She was also the one who told me that our mutual friend Barbara had had her baby. We moved on to that other happy subject with relief.

When I first heard the news that Lindsay was dead and

the service was today, the day of the five-mile race, I figured I wouldn't run. But running this race was a deferred goal of mine, and I'd been determined all summer that this was the year I'd do it. This summer—the first in four years that I was neither pregnant nor nursing a baby, recovering from one pregnancy or contemplating another. For a few years there it had felt as though I'd given up my body to my children. I had just now begun feeling I'd got it back. Running the race was a sort of milestone.

So this morning I woke before my children did and took out my biggest mixing bowl and my pastry blender. I made two pies: one for the family that gained a child, one for the family that lost theirs. Sometimes I take shortcuts with the crust: neglect to put ice cubes in the water, prick holes in the top crust randomly instead of in a flower pattern. Today I took my time. And I could tell, just by looking at them, that these were good pies.

Then I put on my shorts and chose a T-shirt, tied my hair back and laced my sneakers tight. "I hope you win," Charlie called out as I took off for the race, but (never having run five miles in my life) all I wanted was to finish.

The temperature had already reached around eighty when the race began this morning, and the course—even for experienced runners—was what they call a killer, with a mile-and-a-half-long uphill stretch halfway through the race. Around the two-mile point I felt ready to drop. Even children were passing me.

I guess all runners use little tricks to get them through the hardest parts of a race. The owner of the supermarket sponsoring this particular event, knowing how hot and tired we'd be, had posted a sign halfway up the big hill, with a picture of an overflowing beer mug on it. But as for me—feeling more pain, by then, than I had during childbirth—what I thought about were my children, and other people's children. How much children put one through, and how much their presence in one's life enlarges one's capacity to withstand it. The way children take it out of you (all those mothers, jogging a little ahead of me, who like me were getting back in shape after childbearing). And what they give you back, too, that you didn't have before.

Before I had my children, when I was in my early twenties, I was stronger, faster, with a firmer stomach and more time to exercise. But when I was younger, I would have quit in the middle of that hill, when the pain got bad, or sooner. As it was, I thought of going home and telling Audrey (who sometimes tells me she's afraid she'll never learn to ride a two-wheeler or execute a cartwheel) that I finished the race, and because of that, I think, I finished.

I guess that hill felt like a kind of penance, too, for ever allowing myself to feel anything but lucky that my children are healthy enough to sometimes drive me crazy. Of course I never stop loving and wanting them, but sometimes I focus on all the ways they've made my life harder, all the things they keep me from doing. When the truth is, of course, they also make possible everything that's best.

TERRORS

□ *Car Pool*
□ *Reported for Child Neglect*
□ *Perilous Journey*
□ *Christa*

There are five children in Charlie's preschool car pool. The school is a thirteen-mile drive from our house, and the children in the car pool all come from different directions, so getting them all together is a complicated business. Some days we drive only as far as a lunch counter/grocery called the Corner Store and then hand our passengers over to another driver. Some days we pick up a couple of children at the Corner Store and then drive four more miles, to Route 31, to meet up with another driver who takes them the rest of the way. And once a week we make all the stops and drive the full thirteen miles. Wednesday's our day for that.

Usually it's our babysitter who does the driving. I'm out there in my nightgown and felt-lined boots, standing in the snow, buckling my two sons into the car and hurrying Audrey off to her school bus when they set out in the morning, running back to the house for the odd mitten or pretzel. But then they'll disappear down the driveway, driven by Vicky or (now) Joanie, and I'll head back into my empty house to throw on my jeans and head out to work. By the time I'm turning on my typewriter, I figure they've reached the Corner Store. I sit there for a few minutes, sipping my coffee, trying to empty my head of sandwich making and sock hunting, and pour myself a second cup round about the time the children have probably reached Route 31. They're probably just getting their coats and hats off, and sitting down for circle time, as I begin to type.

That's how it is: my mind is always divided, and my concentration with it. Many mornings I wish it could be me driving in the car pool, and if Charlie has asked me particularly plaintively, sometimes I do. But then, along with the joy of that extra hour with my own children and the others (listening to their discussions of Halley's Comet or afterschool plans, theories about how frost heaves happen and whose Mad Ball is the disgustingest), there's always a part of me that ends up feeling anxious and rushed, knowing I'll be falling behind with work and more distracted than ever.

But today was one of those mornings when Charlie cried for me to drive and it seemed important to say yes. We couldn't find one of Willy's boots, and then halfway down the driveway Charlie realized he didn't have his bear. The car was very low on gas, and I'd left my wallet at home. Five miles down the road, I remembered that Audrey had forgotten to take her avocado seed for science. Willy pulled Charlie's hair. Charlie bonked Willy on the head. Willy dropped his bottle. I had to pull over to the side of the road to retrieve it. By the time we got to the Corner Store, our first stop, to wait for the two children we'd pick up there, I was irritable and jumpy. The car bringing the other kids was late, and because it was five degrees above zero, I kept my motor running.

Fifteen minutes later, the other car drove up, bearing our

first two passengers. I put on the parking brake and hopped out to help the children into my van, whose side door is a little tricky. But I must not have pushed the brake down far enough, because suddenly I saw my van, with my two sons still buckled inside, begin to roll away, headed straight for the highway.

No way to catch it, hop in, and push the brake in time. Nothing to do but scream, and of course I did. And then I realized that the car wasn't going to roll out into the highway after all. It was going to slam into another vehicle that was parked in its path. A second later, that's what happened.

I suppose the whole thing probably happened in the space of ten seconds, but that time seemed endless as I stood watching. I saw my two sons' heads, in their winter beanies, bobbing in the driverless van. Saw the other car, a blue Ford, and the left front end where mine was about to hit. The other two children I'd been about to pick up, and the mother of one of them. All of them standing there helpless, like me.

An instant later my car hit the Ford and came to a stop, and I was able, then, to fling open the door and put my arms around my children. Who were fine—laughing, even.

The damage to our van was negligible: a ripped bumper, a couple of scratches. The other car had fared a little worse, and so, still shaking, I had to walk into the Corner Store to announce the license number of the now-dented Ford and wait for the owner to come forward. He turned out to be the husband of Audrey's piano teacher, just finishing his scrambled eggs and home fries. A policeman was sitting next to him at the counter, and on his other side the owner of our local body shop. The three of them escorted me back to the two vehicles to assess the damage and write up a report.

We exchanged names of our insurance companies. I apologized again. Then I piled my two passengers in and headed (very late now) to Route 31 to pick up my final passenger and ferry the group the rest of the way to school.

In the car, driving the final stretch of highway, I played the scene over and over in my mind. I asked Charlie if he'd been scared. "No," he said. "I knew if we kept going you'd run home and get our other car and catch up with me." I tried to remember the precise moment when I'd stepped on the parking brake. Whether, in the back of my mind, there had been that uneasiness a person gets when she knows something's wrong, knows there's something she's forgotten, but thinks that—just this one time—she'll get away with it. Like the times I have laced up my son's shoe, vaguely aware of a wrinkle in the sock, or sand in the toe, but too impatient to start over. Or when I simply pour an extra couple of ounces of milk into Willy's bottle without checking to see if what's in there is still good. All those little moments when corners can—and should not—be cut.

Well, I got the children to school. I drove home. Left Willy with our babysitter. Headed out here to work, but ended up spending most of the morning on the phone to one friend and another, telling and retelling my story. Hoping, I guess, that if I told it enough, I'd finally be free of it. By the fourth or fifth telling, I had the words pretty much set. My voice no longer shook as I described the sight of my sons rolling away from me, headed for that Ford.

I felt reassured when friends told me their own parking-brake and car pool horror stories. It could've happened to anyone, they told me.

But the truth is, I was a prime candidate for trouble this morning. It was the sort of morning when, if I were an airplane pilot or a trapeze artist, I would simply know to stay on the ground for a while. The sort of day when, not for any obvious reasons, just a general distractedness, something was almost destined to go wrong. Only, motherhood—

though it's a high-risk occupation too—doesn't allow for off days or for days off. There is no vacation.

□

It was winter, the day before Audrey's fifth birthday. Charlie was not quite one. We'd been snowed in for a couple of days, and now that we were finally plowed out, I had a long list of errands to run, with less than an hour until it would be time to pick Audrey up at school. Twelve children coming for her party the next day. The cake unmade. Golden Dream Barbie heads—those disembodied oversize Barbie heads that are cut off at the neck and mounted on a base, with makeup and curlers included—half-price at Zayre and just what my daughter wanted. My son had fallen asleep in the car instead of waiting until we got home, and if I roused him, I knew, he'd be cranky for the rest of the trip, the rest of the day.

So I left him in the car while I ran into the store. This was Keene, New Hampshire, not New York City, but still the thought of child theft flashed long enough that I didn't leave the motor running (in case someone might want my car, and take Charlie along for the ride). And I made the conscious decision not to lock the doors, vaguely picturing some far-fetched catastrophe—fire, flood—that might require a person to open the car door and rescue my son. You might ask why, able as I was to envision possible disaster, I would leave him there at all. All I can say is that the distant possibility of full-scale catastrophe was unreal to me that day, compared to the difficulties—small-scale, but certain—of life with an eleven-month-old jolted from sleep and wheeled through a crowded, fluorescence-lit discount store, and then returned to his car seat for another forty-five minutes on the road.

So I left him. I parked in front of the store. I ran all the way to the toy department. I got the Barbie head and stood in the express line, with my money all counted out and a restless, uneasy feeling: the sort you get three days into a vacation when you begin to wonder whether maybe the iron's plugged in back home. All those little actions—the cashier's small talk to the woman ahead of me, her hesitation at the price of the toy, the way she paused to open a new roll of quarters—seemed to take much longer than usual, but finally my purchase was paid for and I was out the automatic doors. My car was easy to find, with a crowd gathered round and a police car beside it, siren on, blue light flashing. When I got close enough—to hear the policeman's voice: "Is this your car, young lady?" to see the women shaking their heads—I could see my son awake in his car seat (from the siren, probably) and screaming.

The first thing I did was to get Charlie out of his seat. Then there were lots of questions. What was I doing and did I have a job? Who was the child's father? I can't remember most of what the policeman asked me except "Why doesn't he even have mittens on his little hands?" And I remember— with surprise, as someone who is always polite, even obse- quious, with police officers, and is reduced to tears by a speeding ticket—asking the policeman loudly whether he had any children, and if he'd ever tried keeping mittens on a toddler? "Well, as a matter of fact, my wife had our first ten days ago," he said. "And I can tell you she'd never leave that baby alone in a car."

Eventually he let me go, and of course my son cried all the way home, and I was pretty shaky myself—the odds of us all getting killed in a car accident on our way home probably tripled. But we made it back, my daughter loved the Barbie head, I baked a cake in the shape of a little girl with brown eyes and brown hair, the party went well. A few weeks later an unfamiliar voice called on the phone, asking to speak with my husband. It was a child-welfare officer, wanting to know if Steve was aware that his wife . . . et cetera, et cetera . . .

and would he inform her that someone from the department would be paying us a home visit?

So a welfare officer came to our house and looked Charlie over while Audrey, to whom I'd explained the situation, hovered over him, saying things like, "Remember, Mom, when we took Charlie to the Children's Museum?" and "Sing us that song Mom always sings when she puts you to bed, Char." And eventually this child-welfare officer pronounced me a fit mother and said he'd take my name out of the files provided we had six months with no further problems. Before he left he told me about a man, referred to him, who had been left in charge of his four-year-old and newborn daughters one afternoon and how the man left them for a minute to go to the bathroom, and how, when he came back, the newborn was dead. What do we learn from that story, I asked him. Only that terrible things sometimes happen.

Last month a woman I knew slightly was making scalloped potatoes while her three children played beside her in the kitchen. This was in the mountains of Nepal, where, in my imagination, the dangers come from lions and tigers. But in fact what happened to this woman's three-year-old son— while she turned her back to reach for another potato—was that he put his right hand into the Cuisinart and in about one second all four fingers on that hand were gone. The parents were on a plane to the U.S. with him the next day. Within twenty-four hours they were talking with surgeons and physical therapists and psychologists, and the scale of their dreams for that particular beloved child had shifted from any possible images of him as a concert pianist or major league pitcher to the slim hope that maybe, a few years down the line, one of his toes might be successfully grafted onto what was left of his hand.

When I heard about this mother the first thing I said—the first thing everybody says, probably—was that I'd never again let my children pour ingredients into the Cuisinart for me, that you can't be too careful. And it's true, a parent must always be watching for fingers in car doors and cars backing out of parking spaces, dry-cleaning bags and thin ice and electric outlets. And it's also true that I shouldn't have left my son in the car.

But you can be Mother of the Year and still there's always a moment when you blink your eyes or turn your back. Audrey, at age three, was attacked by seagulls and nearly lost an eye while I sat on my towel, twenty feet away, making sure she went in the water no farther than her knees. And as a matter of fact, you *can* be too careful, I believe, and if I'm sometimes, to some eyes, too casual a parent (giving birth to my children at home, for starters; letting my five-year-old carry her newborn baby brother; letting him climb stairs alone) it's partly because I was raised, myself, so protected from dangers that I never broke a bone or chipped a tooth or sustained a single injury requiring stitches. As a result, I grew up with a different kind of invisible damage, with too much fearfulness. What I believe is, there's no removing all danger from the world; there's only keeping the odds down.

□

People we know in the city, seeing the main street of this small town where we live or making the five-mile drive beyond it, through woods and farmland, to our house, say what a wonderful place this must be to raise children. And of course, in many ways it is. Summers we swim daily in a waterfall down the road. This winter we built a snow fort covered with pine boughs, and we ski out our back door. More than one fundamentalist-survivalist religious group has settled in this particular valley of New Hampshire out of a conviction that we're situated in such a way as to escape the worst of a nuclear blast. There are—I reassure Audrey, after watching a scary movie on TV—no bad guys around here.

So yesterday I let her, for the first time, walk off alone down our dirt road for a quarter-mile journey through what are mostly woods, to visit neighbors, just moved in, who have a daughter her age. I bundled her up warmly for the trip (hat, mittens, snow pants) and gave her a plastic bag filled with popcorn to eat along the way. I stood at the window, watching the pom-pom on her hat bob off down the driveway. Then she dropped the popcorn and kernels scattered in all directions; she bent to pick them up with her mittens still on, which made the job difficult. Then a strong gust of wind came. She gathered up what she could that the wind hadn't blown away, set out again, dropped the bag again. She bent down a second time, picking up kernels one by one. I thought of how impatient I'd been with her, just before she left. How (with Charlie asleep, and wanting to savor the time alone) I'd complained that she was taking too long putting on her boots. The way I'd brushed her hair (not absolutely unintentionally) just rough enough that she cried out once.

I wanted, then, to run out and put my arms around her, take her hand and walk with her the rest of the way. It seemed suddenly as if the sky had darkened and there was a wolf behind every tree. Of course, what I actually did was just stand there.

Word came this morning that my friend Janet's seventeen-year-old son was killed late Friday night—one of two passengers in a car going too fast down the wrong side of the highway. The three boys hit an old pickup truck whose occupants remain in intensive care. All three boys are dead.

I didn't know Janet's son, except as a skinny figure leaning out the passenger side of another friend's truck (he never learned to drive), trying to bum a cigarette from my husband. But I knew his story from his mother. There was no way to ask Janet how she was, how things were going in her life, without getting to "How's Sam?" And he was never fine, his life was never going well, and as long as it wasn't, neither could hers, of course. Inescapable fact of parenthood: a person's destiny comes to be controlled no longer simply by her own actions, but by the lives of however many satellites she has sent into orbit.

Janet's son was known as a town bad boy. There were drugs, of course, and school suspensions. Juvenile officers were involved, and later the police. Sam's father—divorced from Janet and living in another state—had broken off communication with his son a few years back. There had been counselors and therapists and, for Janet, a parents' support group called Tough Love. A while back Janet had found a residential drug treatment program in another city—the kind of place a kid goes to when he has reached the end of the line. He agreed to try it, the town agreed to pay part of the enormous cost. I'd never seen Janet look so hopeful as she did in September, just after Sam had left for Odyssey House. Two days after Christmas he was home for good. Kicked out (and nobody has to get himself kicked out of a program like that—you can leave anytime) for plotting to break into the center's office, steal the operating cash, and go on a spree.

My friend Janet is a wise, funny, loving but unsentimental woman—marvelous-looking and beautiful-spirited. She's an artist, a lover of birds, which is how we came to meet her, a couple of Septembers back, watching for hawks on top of Pitcher Mountain. She was just nineteen when her son was born; he was five or six when she and her husband separated. I've heard her speak, full of regret, about not having handled carefully enough that hard time in her children's lives. I've heard her voice regrets over mistakes she felt she made, things she'd do differently if she had another chance. It's hard to find yourself living under the same roof with a person you'd have nothing to do with (I've heard her say) if you hadn't happened to give birth to him.

Usually my children were around us—all over us— as we talked about this. We'd be in my living room, surrounded by the tangible chaos children the ages of mine make of their parents' lives. Cars and blocks and Fisher-Price people flung in all directions, Audrey begging for another cookie or the chance to stay up a half hour later, and Charlie, naked, having successfully eluded my attempts to put on his pajamas, dancing his wild dervish dance to the *Big Chill* soundtrack, with a plastic fire chief's hat on his head and an uncapped magic marker in his fist. They are still children of an age to be picked up and put in another place when they're heading in the wrong direction. Children to whom one can still hold out the threat of no dessert, and for whom the lyric "You better watch out, better not pout, 'cause Santa Claus is coming to town" still carries a lot of power. My daughter (though of course she can also get very angry at me) will still sometimes say, "You're the best mommy in the entire universe." My son wakes in the night with my name on his lips. I try unsuccessfully to imagine my round-faced offspring being teenagers who will someday stop smiling, stop speaking to me. Go up to their rooms and close the door, blasting me out of the house with their music. And worse.

Janet was, I know, a loving mother who did everything she could to save her son, and still he didn't make it. New Year's Eve, the week before the crash, I saw Janet and the man who—if she were freer, and not bound up by attempts to make things okay for her children—she might happily have been living with. "Something terrible is going to happen," she said, powerless to change anything.

If another friend's seventeen-year-old had been killed in a crash I'd be thinking about the senseless way car accidents have of altering a seemingly cloudless horizon. With Sam's death there is a different sort of grief—of having seen this coming as clearly as if the vehicles had been toys that were wound up and set on a track and we were all watching in slow motion. Sam's feeling of emptiness—the inability of everyone who tried to give him excitement or hope or even interest in living—appeared bottomless. He seemed so bent on self-destruction that the shock at his death lay most strongly in the fact that he was a passenger in the car and not its driver.

Parents of older children, nodding in the direction of my small ones, shake their heads and tell me, "Wait until they're teenagers. They'll break your heart." Well, I don't feel the grip of terror. I have to believe that a person has some control over the way things turn out, and beyond that I have to trust my children. But I don't feel even close to immune, either, to Janet's kind of disaster, the chaos that an unhappy teenager can bring on a household. I can't believe that I control my children's universe and that I have the power to ensure their survival. And there is no such thing as a safe place to bring up children, no matter what the water tastes like or however much the landscape resembles a scene printed on a calendar. It's always a perilous journey through the woods. Not only for the child, but for the mother, back at home, who stands watching through the glass.

□

My fears, since I've had children, center mostly on the chance of their being hurt. Sometimes, if Steve is driving in bad weather, I'll stay up worrying over whether he's safe. I tend to feel invulnerable myself. The greatest injury that could befall me would be injury suffered by someone I love. I have tormented myself with the picture of me losing my children. But never of my children losing me.

And then the space shuttle *Challenger* exploded.

I spent a day with Christa McAuliffe once. It was early last fall, just a month after she had been chosen America's

First Teacher in Space. Because we live in New Hampshire, just about twenty miles from the McAuliffes, and because, like her, I know a few things about what it is to have a family, with young children, that you love more than anything, and a job you love too (and a husband named Steve, even), I had been following her story with particular interest. Most of all, I watched her, I guess, because like her I live an ordinary life, filled with trips to the post office and frantic searches for lost shoes, and like her, I sometimes dream of adventure. Only my adventures, unlike hers, happen mostly in my own familiar home, with my two feet planted firmly on the ground.

So I called her up (that was still possible then, although the line was often busy). It was Christa herself who answered. She was taking off for Houston to begin astronaut training in a couple of weeks, and already her schedule was so busy that she had managed to spend a total of one hour at the pool with her children that summer, sitting at the edge of the water counting heads. "I can't believe it," she said. "This year I don't even have a tan."

Well, she was meeting one reporter at eight and another one at eight forty-five. Someone else at nine-thirty. That's how it went, all day long, with breaks in between for her son Scott's Little League practice and picking up her daughter Caroline at day camp. But there was a hour at seven A.M., and she said I could come then.

She met me at the door with her hair still wet, in stocking feet, and I followed her through the rooms of her house as she talked, and as she looked for Scott's sleeping bag (he was going to a friend's house), took the chicken out of the freezer to defrost, and started the wash. There were lots of phone calls too: NASA one minute. The cleaners, to say her husband's shirts were ready the next.

There were piles of letters and newspaper clippings all

over the house at that point; also helium balloons and flowers and signs saying things like "Reach for the Stars" and "Out of This World." I guess some people might've said the place was a mess, but you could tell something else too: This woman was organized. In her pocket she had a two-page list of things to do, and there was another one taped to the dashboard of her car. She had NASA's phone number attached to her refrigerator with alphabet magnets, right next to her kids' drawings. In the middle of a sentence, she'd suddenly reach for her pencil and jot something down. "Black high-top sneakers for Scott." "Get more checks." She was no less concerned with the cake for Scott's approaching birthday party than she was with her appearance on the *Tonight Show*. If the phone rang when she was in the middle of a sentence, she'd come back five minutes later and finish it. That's a skill many mothers possess, but I have never met one who had it down the way she did.

I liked her. She was brisk, confident; she paid attention to things (remembered the ages of my children, asked me a question about the town where we live, knew the names of students she'd taught ten years ago). I remember thinking, too, how different we were. There didn't seem to be a shred of ambivalence or hesitaton in her, about changing in such a major way the life she and her family had been living until now (a life that everybody liked just fine), leaving the teaching job she loved and the family to which she was unmistakably devoted, for six months' training in Houston—and then leaving the planet altogether, to blast into orbit.

She met her husband when they were both fifteen; they had been together twenty years, and though he had been, for most of that time, the kind of husband who doesn't know where you keep the cleanser, he was also totally behind her when she said she wanted to go into space. They both seemed clear on that—surprised, almost, that there would be any question. What kind of love would it be, in which one partner would keep the person he loved from pursuing her dreams?

Well, our one hour was up swiftly, and there was a new batch of reporters knocking at the door, taking pictures of her cat, her car, her son's bike. I left.

But I wanted to talk to her some more. It was that business of leaving the family that puzzled me. I have met women who work twelve hours a day and see their children mostly for breakfast and a bedtime story; I have known ambitious, driving women who want to be rich, want to be famous, want to have their picture on the cover of *Time* magazine, would just as soon see as little of their husbands as possible. She wasn't one of those. I have even known a couple of husbands and fathers who are really the backbone of their family anyway: the ones whose name the children are most likely to call in the night. The ones who know who's due for a booster shot and which grocer has the freshest chicken, and remember, when someone gets a loose tooth, to have a surprise ready for the tooth fairy. But this was a family that ran on Christa's extraordinary energy and organization and attention to detail. How could she leave her husband and children? How would they ever manage without her?

So I called a couple of weeks later (it was just three days before she left for Houston), and asked if I could see her again. She had no more time to sit and talk; I knew that. I just wondered whether I could spend the day with her, riding around town, while she did the errands on her list for the next day. She said okay.

Here's what we did that day: Drove to the local TV station, where Christa taped a show with a couple of ministers and a priest about the religious implications of space travel. Stopped by the grocer's to pick up peanut butter for her daughter's babysitter. Picked up Caroline at kindergarten and took her over to the sitter's. (I took the wheel of her car, for those three blocks, so Christa could walk over there with Caroline, alone. I recognized the impulse of a busy mother to make use of every scrap of time she can find to be with her kids.)

After leaving Caroline, Christa gave another television interview and posed for pictures for a couple of magazines. She stopped by the cable TV company to let them know that her husband Steve wanted to get the Sports Network. She picked her son up at school, listened to him tell about his day.

After that, she was supposed to pick up Caroline and take both kids over to a friend's house for the rest of the afternoon. But it was easy to see Scott wanted to stay with her, so he came along: to the doctor's office to get Caroline's immunization records for kindergarten and the grocery store to order meat for a family party Christa was giving that weekend. She told me the recipe for the casserole she was making, an Armenian dish that would serve fifty. Then we stopped for an ice cream cone. She had peppermint. Scott said in a small, proud voice that maybe they'd name the flavor after her now.

After that, I went home, to my own family, my own collection of lists and phone numbers and refrigerator magnets and errands. It had been my daughter's first day of school too, and of course I wanted to hear all about that. Also, as it turned out, this was the day my sons had their tomato fight on our porch, so all in all it was a busy day.

Christa called me once, from Houston, to fill me in on how things were going. She loved it down there. I called Steve, her husband, and he told how, when he got the children home every night, they'd say, "Let's see what Mr. Microwave has for us tonight." Christa had left him with lists of neighbors to call on, phone numbers of babysitters and doctors and take-out food places. Already, he said, he had a whole new understanding of what it was she'd been doing all these years. "Wait till she gets home, though," he joked. "I plan to slip back to my old bad habits just as far as she'll let me."

Well, she won't be coming home, and I have been trying to make sense of it, or at least find something comforting to tell myself and my children when the television replays for us, for the tenth time, the one hundredth time, those terrible haunting images of that rocket lifting off, blasting higher, going to full throttle, and then exploding in midair four miles above the Atlantic Ocean. Leaving no trace of the seven crew members, including, of course, this woman NASA had placed on board specifically so that the American people would finally have someone up there we could identify with, who could make us feel (as she did) "that could be me up there."

Other images haunt me too: Steve McAuliffe, reading her Teacher in Space application and saying, "Where is this woman? I want to marry her." Scott McAuliffe, getting off the plane in Florida with his fourth-grade class, posing before the launch, holding his mother's official NASA portrait, with a look that strikes me now as proud and wistful at the same time. Caroline's room, back in Concord, filled with jelly bracelets and nail-polish bottles, just like Audrey's. Christa and the other members of the crew, taking that last, euphoric walk toward the van that would bring them to the *Challenger*. I move closer to the television set every time they run that film, to study their faces. As if maybe, if I look hard enough, I'll find some clue to the tragedy that awaited them.

Shall I, tonight, tell my children the story of Icarus, flying too close to the sun? Is the final lesson Christa McAuliffe ended up teaching that mothers are better off staying home after all? I ask myself again, "How could she have left her family?" And how will they live without her?

What I choose to remind myself, as I put on our table the

dinner that neither my husband nor my daughter nor I feel much like eating, and later, as Steve and I lie side by side in the dark and I hold him tight, is that the only home worth having is the kind that makes you strong enough to venture forth. That nothing is worth much that comes without risk. (Giving someone your heart. Having a child. They all leave us open to danger, and loss.) And still, it's for all of us to press on, not shrink back. Who can forget that final command from Mission Control moments before the sky exploded? Full throttle.

CUTTING
THE CORD

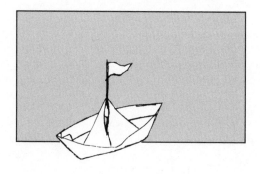

I think it's part of the pain of parenthood that however hard it is being in possession of so much responsibility, relinquishing it is even harder. Being nine months pregnant isn't nearly so difficult as going through postpartum depression. Holding a baby all day is easier than putting her in somebody else's arms and walking out the door. Though that was hard, with all three of my children, I never felt the separation so acutely as I have, at every new stage, with my eldest. Maybe because she's the girl, because she's the one who looks the most like me, the one with whom I identify. Mostly, I think, because she came first. Now I'm accustomed to the familiar, stabbing sensation (part regret, part pride) of seeing a child of mine head off without me. But I remember when it was all new. Lines from my journal, 1979:

Audrey will be one year old next week, and I am trying to decide if it seems as if she's been with us forever, or if it seems like the day before yesterday when she was born. Both are true. This year has been the longest and the shortest of my life. It's hard to remember that there ever was a time when we didn't have pretzel crumbs and ancient carrot sticks under our sofa cushions, a time when I couldn't recite the words to *Goodnight Moon*, didn't know every curve of her body and her face better even than I know my own. I have wondered often how I ever lived my life without her. But I also wonder, on occasion, where my life has gone now that she's here. It has sometimes seemed to me, over these last twelve months, as if I've gained a daughter and lost a self.

Audrey is likely to get a new stuffed animal next week, and a dress whose ruffled skirt will annoy her as she resolutely (and for the fifteenth time that day) mounts the stairs to our sleeping loft. (Where she will then stand, looking down, unsupported, causing my heart to stop, and applaud her victory over the stairs, over me.) She isn't interested in birthdays yet, of course. As for me, I feel the need for a present, a cake, a firecracker, to mark the anniversary of our parenthood. Someday I hope we'll have another baby, who will be just as dear to us as Audrey. But no one, ever again, will turn our lives upside down this way. It is easier for three people to become four than it is for two to become three.

The odd thing is: The moment when suddenly you want a baby is likely to come precisely when your life seems so good the way it is. And having a baby is the one thing that's guaranteed to change it. I was always crying, in the early days of my pregnancy. I would spend all afternoon cooking dinner, cutting radishes into roses, carrots into trees, decorating pie crusts with mermaids and swans, setting the table on our porch with candles and wine, and placing tiger lilies in the soup. And then I would sit across from Steve, watching the sun set behind his back, thinking about how it would never be this way again, and lose all appetite.

Not that I didn't long for our baby, didn't know I'd love her. It was because I knew I would that I was in mourning, I think, for my heart. When I was three months pregnant, Steve was still my one true love. When I was four months pregnant, though, and I'd heard her heart beat, felt her swimming, the baby had already begun to steal me. At six months I almost never cried anymore, and my dreams were filled not with images of Steve and me, but with visions of a washing machine and a dryer. I was on an express train to motherhood, and even though I didn't want to get off, the knowledge that I couldn't terrified me.

A few months before Audrey's birth a woman I knew came to visit with her year-old son. Her little boy was still breastfeeding—constantly, it seemed, to the point where she sometimes just kept her shirt open, for convenience. Her little boy slept in a double bed with her; her husband had a pallet on the floor nearby. She had never lost the weight she'd gained when she was pregnant, she told me, and neither would I. She was tired all the time. She complimented me on a loaf of bread that I'd just baked. "Enjoy it while you can," she said. "You won't have time for baking bread once the baby's born."

After she'd gone home I lay down on our bed and wept over the occupied territory that used to be my body, and the imminent invasion of our marriage. I was nothing but a mother. All I could think of was the baby. Now she was filling me up. Soon she would drain me dry.

Then Audrey was born. The morning after her birth it took me a few seconds to remember about her, and once or twice, for the first few days, I'd forget her name. But then my arms got so used to holding her and knowing exactly what weight to expect that when I'd pick up somebody else's baby who was lighter, my arms, expecting those other ounces, would lift him too high. I did bake bread, but with Audrey in my arms. Audrey always in my arms.

And Steve, during those first months, seemed somewhat peripheral to our tight circle. The thought came to me one morning that she was my blood relative and he wasn't, and that while there were things that he could do to make me stop loving him and stop being his wife, there was no way Audrey would ever not be my daughter.

My worst fears—that she would be too much with me— seemed to have come true. Steve was devoted to her, and she loved it when he played with her. But when she was tired or hungry, it was her mother she wanted. She didn't know, I read, that she and I were two separate people. Not for her, yet, adolescent rebellion or the devastating announcement a five-year-old I know delivered to his mother once, "I hate you, but you still love me." To Audrey, I was perfect.

At Thanksgiving we went to Steve's parents' house in Ohio and spent an evening viewing family slides. My father-in-law looking like Steve, in a T-shirt, standing outside a tiny rented house with a very pretty young woman who is now my mother-in-law and the three-week-old baby who is now their thirty-two-year-old son. More babies: getting teeth, losing them, getting them again, standing in front of a succession of larger and grander Christmas trees. Charley, Steve's father, still handsome, but losing some of his hair; Anne, Steve's mother, still pretty, but more lined. Then one by one, the children going off to college, until the slides show just the parents again, except at moments like Thanksgiving, when the children come to visit.

Now Audrey—I am both saddened and relieved to say— has already begun preparing for her departure. At the age of one, her declarations of independence are, like her, small. But when, on a day that registers five below zero, she pulls off the mittens I've put on her (three times in a row) and in spite of the cold, smiles defiantly at me, when she wriggles from my lap and heads for her own room and her xylophone, I am reminded that she is no longer what I used to call her, jokingly: my protege. And that, though Steve may never give me the looks of total adoration Audrey sometimes gives, neither is he likely ever to throw a piece of scrambled egg in my face. He was here first and will, I hope, stay longest.

Already there are parts of my daughter's life I don't know about. On weekdays, from nine to five, she goes to her babysitter Irma's house, where she plays with other children, hears Spanish spoken, listens to Irma's husband, José, play songs on the guitar that I have never heard. The top of her head, that used to smell like me, smells like Irma's kitchen now. Audrey knows some secrets. We no longer own her, if we ever did.

□

We go back and forth like dancers, my children and I. Two steps apart, one step back together. They need me utterly, they need me not at all. They want me to help, they want to do it all themselves. And luckily, they do still want me, need me, and I hope (for moments, anyway) they always will.

We were in our car, driving to the movies—my friend Ellen with her three children and me and my two older children. Steve had been away on a trip for two nights and I was finding every opportunity to be somewhere besides home. (So much so, that I was taking my seven-year-old and three-year-old to see Fred Astaire in *Top Hat*, at a theater some thirty miles away from our home.) Ellen is divorced, so for her, single parenthood is familiar and holds no new terrors. But I had been feeling lonely. Nights, especially, seemed long.

It was dark. Our older children were giggling and whispering in the back seat, recounting adventures and making future plans. Charlie (who was permitted to come along, instead of staying with Willy and the babysitter, only after taking a solemn vow that he would not cry or whine or spill his refreshments during the movie), sat very quiet and bolt upright in his car seat, sucking his thumb, listening to the others, looking out at the night. Suddenly his voice piped up from the back seat, "I want you, Mom. I want you."

I was at the wheel. The movie was due to start in fifteen minutes, and we still had a good thirteen minutes of driving to get there. "Remember your promise," I told Charlie. "You said if I let you come to the movies with us, you'd be a big boy."

"I want you," he said again. Not crying, not whining. Just a statement of fact, but delivered with some urgency, the way a child might say he needed to go to the bathroom or that he just remembered he left his science project on the kitchen counter.

"When we get to the movie you can sit on my lap," I said. "You'll get popcorn. Maybe a drink."

Audrey joined in, "You're lucky to be here, Charlie. Think of Willy. He didn't get to come at all."

"There's going to be dancing in the movie," said one of the other children helpfully. "Do you like to dance, Charlie?"

Charlie loves to dance. When I put on our Michael Jackson album for him and he starts moving to the beat, I think he forgets where he is entirely. He jumps off furniture, he twirls, he poses, he gets down on the floor and spins. When the song ends, he freezes in position, with one hand raised, and one finger pointed. His face registers something that sure looks like passion to me. And then he wants to hear the song all over again.

But right now all he wanted was me. "I want you," he said again.

"Shall I sing you a song, Charlie?" I said soothingly. "Would you like 'Hush, Little Baby' or 'Fox Went Out on a Chilly Night'?"

You. I want you.

Ellen laughed softly in the seat next to me. She's been on her own for a couple of years now. A young, attractive woman, living in a small New Hampshire town with not a whole lot of single men over age nineteen around. "I'd love to hear those words," she said. And the truth is, you don't even have to be divorced for those words to have a strong effect. Husbands and wives, married a few years, paying bills, raising children, putting up and taking down storm windows, don't always get around to saying those words to each other.

My son was saying them again. Over and over, like a chant. Like the little engine that could, going over the mountain. Like a mother comforting a child who's just fallen down the stairs ("It's okay, it's okay, it's okay"). Like a medicine man, dancing around the bonfire, pounding a drum.

"Tell me what you want, Charlie," I said.

"I want you to hold me." That simple.

Now, there are lots of ways I try to be a good mother. I tell my children every day how wonderful they are, and how much I love them. I read them lots of books, I play games, I seek out interesting, stimulating "quality time" experiences at museums and concerts. I take them to old Fred Astaire movies, at which, if the truth be told, they will be politely attentive, but a little less than enthralled. I read about child development, and I debate, with my friends, ways to approach discipline, the importance of bedtimes, whether it's a good idea to perpetuate the notion of Santa Claus.

But the truth is, there is not much that's more important, I sometimes think, than just putting your arms around your child, tight. They want me. I want them. With all of our new, heightened consciousness about child sexual abuse— all those sensible and necessary reminders for children, in between the Saturday morning cartoons, to the effect that their bodies are their own, and private, and not to be violated—I have to insert the assurance, here, that what I'm talking about here isn't incest or sex abuse. But sometimes I like my children to be in bed with me. Sometimes I can't keep my hands off them. I want to nuzzle my face in their bellies, take a bite out of their ears, kiss every one of their toes.

So on the way to the movie, with three minutes left, and the older children groaning faintly, "Come on, we'll miss the beginning." I pulled over alongside the highway, put on my parking brake and my warning lights. Got out, came around to Charlie's side of the car, opened the door and unbuckled his seat belt, picked him up and gave him the number of kisses he asked for, which was ten. Buckled him back in again. Got back in the driver's seat. Headed off to see the show. Fred Astaire got Ginger Rogers too.

□

Steve and I had been away on a trip for three days, leaving our children home with Vicky, and amazingly, everything had gone well. Then the plane touched down and the flight attendant made her announcement about checking under the seat for carry-on bags. And when I did I realized my purse was missing.

I could have left it in North Carolina, when we changed planes there. I could have left it in Savannah, at the airport waiting room where we sat for a half hour before boarding the plane. I could even have left it in the ladies' room, or in the cab we took to the airport. All I knew was, the purse was gone.

When we got off the plane I rushed, first thing, to the baggage office and had a man there call those other airports. All lines were busy, so he told me he'd take my name and let me know if anything turned up. I could tell from his expression (hearing the long list of places where the purse might be) that he didn't hold out much hope of reuniting me with my bag. I could feel an awful headache coming on as I began tallying my losses.

Naturally, my wallet and credit cards were in my purse, but that wasn't the half of it. There were my glasses. My driver's license. My checkbook. It had taken me weeks to get my account in order, and now I wouldn't have a clue where I stood.

Standing at the baggage carousel waiting for our suitcases to emerge, images of other items in that purse kept coming to mind: a pair of screw-on earrings in the shape of fruit baskets, that I'd bought at a flea market. (They always hurt, so I'd often end up taking them off and sticking them in my purse. But I loved those earrings.) A favorite toy of Charlie's. A long letter I hadn't got around to mailing.

Well, we found our suitcases, and Steve went to bring the car over to the door just outside the baggage claim. We buckled ourselves into our seats, shivering in the winter weather, still dressed for Georgia. Here in Boston it had begun to snow, and we had a hundred-mile drive ahead of us. I could tell from the way Steve held the wheel and the look on his face that the roads were very slick.

It usually takes us an hour and a half to make that drive from the airport, but that night we took twice as long. Three times we started to go into a skid, and we passed half a dozen cars that had turned around completely, or spun off the highway and landed in a ditch. I gripped the seat covers and pictured Steve and me killed in a crash, our children orphaned.

I also thought about my purse. I'm not sure whether it was the loss of the purse that made me feel more vulnerable in the storm or the storm that made me feel more vulnerable without my purse, but whatever it was I know I felt as if the ground had slipped out from under my feet. I was without my children. Our car was skidding. And my purse was in some strange southern city, where I wasn't.

About twenty miles from home I remembered my address book was in my purse, and in it were the names and addresses of everyone I knew and care about on the face of the earth, including at least thirty people I hadn't seen in years—old acquaintances I'd never be able to find without that address book. Never mind that I hadn't written or called them in years. As long as I had my address book I knew I could. And now they had all disappeared forever.

Well, we made it home safely, got the report from Vicky on how things had gone, tiptoed upstairs to take a look at the children, asleep in their beds. No disasters had taken place in our absence: the house was immaculate. There was no bad news in our four days' accumulation of mail. Still I felt unsettled, and lay awake a couple of hours, running over and over in my head the places where I might have left my purse. I pictured it hanging from the hook against a ladies' room door in Savannah. Propped on the floor next to a water fountain in North Carolina where I'd stopped to take a drink. I drifted into an uneasy sleep (dreams full of car wrecks) and woke with a gasp. I had just remembered one more thing that was in my purse.

A set of photographs (and negatives) taken one weekend in early fall. There were half a dozen shots taken on top of a mountain we'd climbed with the children: Audrey had just lost a tooth; Willy was bundled up in three layers of sweaters—the only time in his life, Audrey pointed out, when he actually looked chubby. There were pictures of a play the children had put on: Willy in a rhinestone-trimmed hat and an orange silk gown that trailed along the floor; Charlie as a cowboy; Audrey, as always, the queen. There was a really goofy bunch of pictures—my favorites—taken at a place we'd stopped at, on a Sunday drive, where they sold garden sculptures. The children loved that place, would've happily stayed there all day. We took Charlie's picture on the back of a nearly life-size ceramic deer, and Audrey's embracing a statue of a Greek goddess she'd begged to buy.

The day after we got home, when the man from the airline called back to say my purse hadn't been found, I began sorting my losses. There hadn't been much money in my wallet. Cancelling those credit cards was a nuisance, but I could bear that too. Glasses were replaceable. About the names in the address book, I told myself that at least those old acquaintances could always find me.

Losing the pictures was the worst. I understood, for the first time, what it must be like for people who get wiped out in a fire and end up (the lucky ones, who survive) with no record of their children's babyhood. Family history wiped out. All I'd lost was the record of one good weekend, and still I felt devastated.

I spent most of the next day and a half on the phone to airports—New York, Charlotte, Atlanta—trying to trace the route that plane had taken after we got off. I thought, crazily, of taking a drive up to that mountaintop again, to retake those pictures, of stopping again at the place with the garden sculptures and repositioning our children on the backs of those elves and deer. Of course I was glad to be home with my real, flesh and blood children. Still, I couldn't stop thinking about that roll of film. I imagined the stranger in whose hands my purse must have ended up—pictured him flipping through the pictures of our family, thinking about us briefly (filling in the pieces of our life), and then tossing the envelope in some trash can. I wept.

Three days after I lost my purse, I got a call from the airline, telling me the purse had turned up in Miami. When the woman who called with the news began running down the list of credit cards she'd found in my wallet I interrupted her. What about those pictures, I asked.

"They're here," she said. "I figured you'd only want to hear about the valuables. We'll send everything up to you this afternoon."

So now I have my pictures back, and today I'm sticking them in our album and thinking about what it is that makes me so compulsive about my children's photographs. (Also an envelope full of hair from Willy's first barbershop haircut. A pair of binoculars Charlie made out of two taped-together toilet-paper rolls. A pebble Audrey once gave me, with the instruction that I hold onto it forever—which I'm attempting to do.)

And here's what I think: So much of raising children is about letting go. No wonder I'm always trying to hold on to whatever I can.

□

I can still remember the struggles I went through over my hair and clothes when I was growing up. I remember what it felt like, being made to wear an outfit I hated. I remember the naked feeling of too-short bangs. Practical brown shoes, when what I wanted were red ones. Undershirts, cardigan sweaters, snowpants. I vowed I'd never make a child of mine endure those indignities.

And later, when the choice of what to wear was finally up to me, I remember the daily indecision. Changing three times, four times, five . . . laying pools of clothes on the floor of my room as I tried on one outfit after another, searching for the one that looked and felt right on that particular day. The practice of those endless changes carried on into my twenties. The tears at the mirror. The impulsive visits to beauty parlors. (Let me be a redhead. Give me curls. Take them away.)

Then I was married, and, right away, pregnant. *There's* the ultimate humbling experience, for someone who's spent twenty years examining her reflection from all angles for the least indication that she might look fat. Suddenly—no doubt about it—I was, and not just in the belly either, but round-faced and thick-ankled too. I gained fifty pounds with that first pregnancy (thinking, innocently, that I was simply eating for two). The day after giving birth to my seven-and-a-half-pound baby girl, I stepped on the scale and found I still weighed forty-two pounds more than I used to. I cried and cried and cried.

Well, I lost the weight eventually. The time came when I once again fit my jeans. But though I still get dressed up now and then, and still put on my eyeliner every morning, without fail, motherhood signaled the end, for me, of a particular sort of vanity. These days I have no time to spend agonizing over which blouse, which stockings, which pair of earrings. I step into the same pair of jeans every morning, and one of the same three tops. I, who used to spend sixty dollars on a city haircut and perm, now cut my own hair, and I don't even check a mirror when I do the back.

But the end of one kind of vanity brought with it the beginning of another sort. It began the day Audrey was born, the first time I put her in a dress. Of course I would've loved her if she'd looked like a monkey, but from the first she was beautiful, with dark skin and black eyes, lots of dark-brown hair, and eyelashes so long a woman once bent over her stroller and pulled at them to see if they were real. A friend of mine says that in the early days after the birth of her first child, she once spent twenty minutes dressing her son, then walked out of the house with him in his new outfit and herself stark naked. Heading out the door to a party, a few weeks after Audrey's birth, I once found myself saying to Steve, "I'll be right with you as soon as I put her eyeliner on." For a moment there, I had forgotten who was who.

Having a child is part birth, part death. It means stepping back, leaving the younger generation to join the older, being no longer the newest, most precious. You look in the mirror, and it tells you someone else is fairest in the land.

I never minded that. I have always revelled in my daughter's strange, exotic beauty. But it's dangerous too. I am not her. She isn't me. Brushing her hair won't make mine shiny.

In my mind I know that. But mornings, lately, getting her ready for school, I have had to keep reminding myself of our separateness, and how dangerous it is to invest one's self too deeply in one's child. In her looks, especially.

With our sons, the problem seldom arises. Very often my boys' faces are dirty or their hair's a mess, or Charlie wants to wear his red Superman cape with his maroon Oshkosh overalls, or Willy's hand-me-down socks have ruffles on them or his pant cuffs go just below his knees. None of which causes me a moment of pain.

But Audrey's another story. For years I could dress her like a doll, exactly as I pleased: in smocked dressses and A-line jumpers, overalls with turtlenecks, 1950s-style thrift-shop treasures. I styled her hair in pigtails and French braids. She owned tights in every color of the rainbow.

Then she started school, and what she wanted were shirts with pictures of Strawberry Shortcake and Cabbage Patch Kids on the front; jeans, tailored shirts, her hair held behind her ears with a plastic headband. She wanted what the other girls were wearing: conservative knee-length corduroy skirts and matching blouses. Or, the other extreme, crazy, ill-matched combinations, or some beloved but too small dress.

Some mothers with whom I conferred on this told me they simply set out their child's clothes every night; but with memories of my frustration at being told what to wear as a child, I've resisted that. As a result, the kilts and smocked dresses I've bought for Audrey—and even a lot of outfits she chose herself—hang at the back of the closet. On good mornings, when she comes down in one of the same three outfits (none of them, in my opinion, the most flattering of her clothes), I bite my tongue. But there are bad mornings, too (often the ones when I have just studied my own reflection in the mirror and been unhappy with it), when I snap at Audrey, "Can't you ever wear something different?" or simply send her upstairs to change. At my worst, I have pointed out to her how much money I spent on those unworn clothes hanging in her closet, while I say (indicating my sweat pants and T-shirt), "Look at me. *I* dress in rags!"

Our arguments make her so late that I have to drive her to the school bus—both of us close to tears. I watch her trudge across the street and mount the steps of the bus, the pom-pom on her hat bobbing, and I want to call out, "Come back." This morning, after the worst showdown yet, I ended up driving the five miles into town to meet her getting off the bus and to tell her I was sorry. Next time, I vow throughout the whole drive home, next time she comes down the stairs (as she did this morning) wearing crew socks and black patent-leather shoes, a too big skirt and a too small sweater, I will say to her only that I love her smiling face.

☐

If I were talking to a therapist about my daughter's dollhouse (and it probably wouldn't be a bad idea) the first thing I'd say is that I never had a dollhouse of my own. Variation on a theme of parents everywhere—who move through their children's youth attempting an odd mix of re-creating their own, compensating for everything their own failed to provide, and attempting to construct, for their beloved offspring, that most elusive of experiences known as a happy childhood.

In fact, it's not entirely accurate to say I never had a dollhouse: The year I turned six, my parents gave me a split-level ranch house with fireplace, doors, windows and paintings printed directly on the walls, and a set of furntiure meant to symbolize beds, chairs, bureaus. But none of the drawers opened. There was no way to tuck a doll into beds whose spreads and pillows were molded in plastic, with not a wrinkle present. The view out the windows was always the same: sun shining, red geraniums in bloom.

What I actually played with—nearly every day of my life, from age five to nearly thirteen (when self-consciousness, not lack of interest, finally led me to pack it all away)—was actually a set of bookshelves: wallpapered, carpeted, and filled with mostly homemade cardboard and balsa-wood furniture, with matchbox drawers that always had something hidden inside. I was the only one who knew that if you cut open the Play-Doh food in the dollhouse refrigerator, inside the eggs you'd find a yolk, and in the watermelon, seeds. In 1967, when I finally packed it all away, I set the contents of those shelves in boxes according to rooms, with written instructions describing how things should be arranged, for the daughter I always knew I'd have. I've gone through the years, since, still saving the paper parasols from tropical drinks at restaurants, the miniature pencils that sometimes come inside magazine subscription offers. Because as surely as I knew I'd have a daughter, I knew the two of us would someday have, not wallpapered bookshelves, but a real dollhouse.

There are children who don't make possible their parents' fantasy-childhood reenactments: daughters who want haircuts when the mother's idea is French braids, sons who greet their father's presentation of Celtics tickets with the news that they have other plans for the evening. But I have a daughter whose natural leanings, combined with a heavy dose of indoctrination, have usually tended to follow the lines of my passions. Even before she was tall enough to see into display cases without being lifted up, Audrey—breathing heavily—was fogging up the glass separating her from the museum dollhouses I took her to see, crying out in a way some might mistake for distress when she'd spot a chandelier or a mouse hole or some other particularly heartbreaking detail. And she has always set up little houses of her own—outdoors with sticks and leaves, and in her room out of cigar and shoe boxes. To Audrey every commonplace object suggests a miniature variation. Thimbles are flower pots, a burnt-out flashcube is an aquarium.

I was on the lookout for a real dollhouse for a very long time, and I considered numerous contenders. There was an exquisite, copper-roofed Victorian reproduction at a museum gift shop that was not only too expensive but too grand all around. You couldn't put a toothpaste-cap lampshade in that mansion. There was a house in a secondhand store I frequent around here, made by a middle-aged man whose dream it was to recreate his childhood home, exactly as it was in 1930, complete with Caruso recordings playing all the time, a Mary Pickford calendar on the wall, and in the basement, a furnace that really worked. No mistaking that dollhouse as anything but the product of a full-fledged obsession—but somebody else's, not mine. Though I could have bought it for $350, the house would never have belonged to anyone but him.

I saw the house I wanted to buy four years ago at a local craft show. Roy, the man who made it, used to build real houses until a bad heart forced him to retire. So now he builds little houses, but with real shingles and three coats of paint on the clapboards, polished hardwood floors and hand-turned bannisters and nine-over-six paned windows that actually open. Not fancy in their designs, but solid, homey, lived-in—the kind of house you wished your grandparents lived in, with swings on their front porches and sleds leaning against the door.

For the next few Octobers after that, Steve and I had our annual dollhouse discussion: I wanting to put in an order with Roy; Steve arguing that Audrey was too young by about twenty-five years, the house was too extravagant, and that the person who really wanted a dollhouse wasn't Audrey anyway, it was her mother. Sometimes during these sessions I would cry (my girlhood and my parents came up with surprising frequency) and Steve would make the comment that it's not until a person loses her childhood home that she seeks out a dollhouse with the kind of compulsion I displayed. Usually he'd end up saying "Go ahead, buy it," but of course I knew the objections he raised were real and accurate. I *did* want a dollhouse for the child I used to be. And in a way that's good for neither Audrey nor me, Audrey sometimes represents, for me, that childhood self.

So I held out against temptation the Christmas she was almost four, and again (more reluctantly) when she was almost five. But this fall—one of our most broke ever, at a time in our lives when I was putting off dental appointments and all but the most essential car repairs—I gave Roy my order for a $475 Christmas dollhouse, to be paid for (significantly enough) with a portion of the inheritance I had just received following the death of my father.

It's more than mildly embarrassing to admit how large the dollhouse loomed in my imagination, all this past December, as we awaited delivery: the hours I spent stitching a patchwork quilt for the brass bed, constructing a miniature Christmas tree for the living room, sewing stockings for the real stone fireplace and making doll-sized presents to stack inside it. For Charlie I ordered a yellow Tonka bulldozer from the Sears catalogue. For Audrey (not better loved, just differently so) I made a heart-shaped, doily-covered, doll-sized chocolate box filled with individually formed chocolates, the size of seed pearls. Near midnight on Christmas Eve, setting up the dollhouse in a corner of our living room, arranging the furnishings I'd been accumulating for years, plugging in the chandelier, putting the note from Santa into the mailbox beside the front door, I felt as excited as I had, twenty-five years earlier, when I lay in my bed, listening for reindeer.

When Audrey came into the living room next morning she didn't let out any screams, didn't even seem to register the dollhouse for several minutes as she painstakingly unwrapped the colored pencils and stickers and barrettes inside her stocking. Then, very slowly, she approached the house, ran her fingers over the smooth floors, opened the drawers in the bureau, picked up the baby in the cradle, looked inside the mailbox. She didn't make a sound for a long time. Finally she said, "I can't believe it's really mine."

What I felt, watching her, was not only simple parental pleasure at having found a really nice present for my child, but also relief: The whole dollhouse question had been re-solved, the only way it could've been—by getting one. I also knew that, much as Audrey liked the dollhouse, she would have liked a plastic Barbie Townhouse just as much and maybe (for the moment) more. Now sometimes I walk through her room and see dollhouse furniture and the patch-work quilt strewn on the floor. Days go by that the house stands idle. Now and then I'll suggest it might be fun to sew curtains for the nine-over-six windows, and Audrey, kindly but firmly, will explain she's busy. (She's making a doll out of a sprouted onion, with a toilet-paper dress. She's set up a Barbie tanning salon, using our broken toaster oven.) I think back to my six-year-old self (who would have run upstairs first thing after school every day to play with a house like Audrey's), and realize (with interest, not pain) that my child and I are not as totally alike as I have sometimes thought.

□

Time was, I told my children about the world. I held their hands when I took them places, and told them the names of butterflies or rocks. Sometimes I'd go away—for an after-noon, or longer—and come home with stories for them about my adventures. It didn't have to be much to thrill them: Maybe I saw a porcupine cross the road, or a fireman bringing a cat down off a roof. I'd bring home a bagel from the city, or a helium balloon from my dentist, or a bar of soap from an airplane ladies' room, and they were happy. What they learned about life beyond the edges of our driveway they mostly got from Steve and me.

But I've begun to see the tables turn. I can still make the room come alive for Willy just by walking into it. But more and more, lately, I am the one who stays home (sitting at this desk of mine, looking out the window a lot, and eyeing the clock, waiting for them to come home, waiting for the stories they'll have for me). I see how it is for my friend Jessica, with her children grown and gone now, free to do the work she had to put off nearly twenty years, while she raised them. How she looks forward to the occasional weekend when her children are all, once again, briefly sleeping under her roof. I begin to see, though my children are much youn-ger, how she must feel. Now they walk in, and I light up.

I felt it pretty keenly on Audrey's first day of school—the way the mothers (and I was one) lingered on the playground after their children filed into the school building. Scuffing our feet in the dirt, studying the class lists for any clue they might yield about what our child's year would be like. Hud-dling together, surrounded by empty swings and teeter-totters, comparing notes on teachers—who looked nice, who looked tough. I'm not proud of the fact that one or two of us (and again, I was one) could not resist walking past our child's classroom just to catch a glimpse inside before finally taking off.

It's not that we're idle, that our lives are empty. Most of these mothers (and the few fathers who were there in the schoolyard that first day) have jobs, and a life separate from their children. We design buildings, draw up legal documents, build houses, counsel patients, write books. Our lives are full. But an hour after school starts, my phone rings, and it's my friend Erica (who also has a job she likes, a husband she loves, interests and concerns beyond motherhood), and she's saying "Well, what do you think?" And I know she's not talking about economic sanctions in South Africa or trade talks with Japan. She's talking about our daughters' new second-grade class.

Charlie is just four, and already it's happening with him too. I drop him off at his nursery school and kneel for a kiss, and he gives me one. But it's fleeting, and a little distracted, and I can tell, as I hug him afterward, that he's looking over my shoulder and eyeing the boys in the block area. "I'll be back for you in a couple of hours," I tell him (not that he's asking). "Yup," he says gruffly, over his shoulder. "Bye."

Of course there were children, that first day, who wept and clung to their mothers' legs. Even Charlie has his moments, still, when he climbs into my lap, afraid of a daddy longlegs in his room, or needing to hear, one more time, that dinosaurs are extinct. He still needs me to drive him places, to pour his milk, to do up the fasteners on his overalls. And he still depends on me to walk him across the street.

But there are also some things my children know that I don't. It starts with silly, odd bits of information: the various types of Care Bears available, which He-Man figures are good and which are evil. Then, gradually, it gets a little closer to home, and before a person knows it, her children are explaining photosynthesis and teaching her how to make an origami box. Which is just what we all want to happen, of course. Still, when it does, it's a shock.

One morning I notice Charlie putting on his socks and

fastening the velcro on his sneakers unassisted (and I wonder whether, in part, he has been humoring me, every morning, when—without thinking about it—I've dressed him). I speak, in some story I'm making up, about "a deadly tarantula," and both Audrey and Charlie correct me: A tarantula bite, to a human, it turns out, is hardly worse than a bee sting.

Charlie can transform a GoBot; I can't. At our local ski slope Audrey rides the chair lift to the top of the mountain while I stand at the bottom watching, amazed, with Willy in my arms or toddling close beside me. But even with him, I know, the days are numbered before he moves on and I'm left standing in his dust.

These are the very early stages, still, of a process all our parents and grandparents have witnessed clear through its completion: from the point at which the child is entirely dependent on the parent, to the place where it's the parent who looks to and counts on the child. We are, most of us, overtaken by our children in our lifetimes. (If we're lucky.) They will be not only taller, and longer-lived, but smarter, stronger, more handsome and more beautiful, happier (that's the hope) and wiser, their lives even more full than our own.

So already I see it beginning. Today, with Audrey at school and Charlie off playing at a friend's house, and only Willy left with me, I stand in my doorway, at one minute after three, waiting for the first glimpse of Audrey as she trudges around the last bend in our driveway and up the last little hill to our house. Swinging her Snorks lunchbox and her backpack, singing a song I didn't teach her. She breezes in the door as I turn to fix her a cup of hot chocolate. "Tell me about your day," I say, trying to sound casual. "Later, Mom," she says, blowing me a kiss. "I've got a really great game of Barbies going upstairs. I'll tell you about things later, I promise."

"Well," I say, turning to Willy. "Shall we put on Cyndi Lauper and dance?" I am still, briefly, his favorite partner.

□

A half mile down the road from our house there's a wide, rushing brook. In summer we swim there, in a place where the brook widens, and in the fall we sometimes have picnics along the banks. In winter the brook mostly freezes over, but because of the rocks and the speed of the water as it crashes over them, the ice forms thick blocks that fracture into jagged chunks and pile up, one against the other. Every winter—standing on the stone bridge over our frozen swimming hole and staring down at the way even the trees on either side have frosted over with the moisture from the brook—I think: "This has to be the most beautiful time of all." Then comes spring: The snow melts, the ice blocks break apart and dissolve, the fiddlehead ferns stick up through the ground, watercress begins to grow in the icy water, and the brook runs so fast I can hear its roar from my back porch. And I remember that there is nothing I like better than this brook, just as it is right now.

Always, though, my love of this spot is mixed with something else, and that's fear: Fear that when my son tosses his pebbles in to make a wish, he will lean too far over the railing and fall into those swirling waters. Fear that someday, like their father, they'll want to jump off the high boulder at one side of the swimming hole (where, if you don't position yourself just right, you could land on stone and break your back). On a walk one day with Audrey, when she was very small, we saw a gust of wind swoop down and lift her red cowboy hat right off her head and carry it down into the water, never to be seen again. And last fall, when a neighbor's puppy disappeared, we all eventually concluded that the dog had probably gone for a dip in the brook and that he'd been pulled under by the swift current.

Every spring, I try to make boats with my children and sail them in this brook, the same as I used to with my father, in a different brook, when I was young. With three children now, it's not always easy to hit just the right combination of good weather, good moods, good sailing conditions, and free time. Last Saturday everything fell into place.

It was, for starters, a beautiful day. We had a couple of friends' children over—Ben and Aaron, around the ages of Audrey and Charlie. Everyone was getting along. Nobody was wearing the kind of shoes that couldn't get wet. I brought out my giant box of boat-building supplies (Popsicle sticks, fabric scraps, Styrofoam blocks saved from various small-appliance purchases, odd bottle caps and old curlers) and let everyone loose with the glue. Forty-five minutes later, we had five small craft—each design as distinct as its creator—and we headed for the brook.

We found a good spot for launching: a place where the water was choppy enough to make for an exciting course, but not so rough as to capsize our craft altogether. There were enough broad flat rocks that we could step across to dislodge a vessel if one got stuck on a twig or hung up on some leaves. And because the brook flowed reasonably straight there, we could follow our boats downstream a little way, instead of losing track of them in a moment when they rounded the first bend.

I want to describe these boats because each one told something about the child who made it. Charlie's, unnamed, had a single mast, a red and black flag, the silver cap from an old shampoo bottle stuck on right in the middle. He worked very hard making this boat, and put a lot of thought into the placement of each feature. When he was all done, he announced he didn't want to sail it. He'd rather just hold on to his boat and keep it in his room.

Aaron had chosen a more elaborate boat design, with cardboard tubes from used-up toilet-paper rolls and bits of foil and a balloon and bottle caps all over the place, attached with liberal amounts of glue. Ben, his big brother, had actually gone so far as to consider flotation factors in his design. Willy cared only that he have some Styrofoam object, with a balloon attached, to fling into the water (and I was concerned chiefly with insuring that only the boat, and not Willy, got dunked). Audrey had made a kind of yacht, named *Amelia*, with a lifeboat, a captain and crew member made out of clothespins with glued-on yarn hair, a cabin, a couple of sails, silver streamers, a purple feather sticking up from the mast, and a few forsythia blossoms at the prow. She was willing to launch her masterpiece, but attached a long string so she'd be able to retrieve it.

I'm not sure I myself understand the source of the excitement produced by seeing a boat you've constructed actually making it from one point on a stream to another point a little farther down that stream. We all know water flows. We all know Styrofoam floats. But launching a boat, seeing it bob along, racing along the banks to meet it, and reeling it in again farther down—well, all that is not a whole lot less thrilling to me now, at age thirty-two, than it was at age eight.

For over an hour we launched these boats and watched them go, and dislodged them from the rocks, ran ahead, met them as they came by, reeled them in, then launched them all over again. And of course Willy did get soaked. And of course the toilet-paper rolls on Aaron's boat did get waterlogged. And the sails fell off, and the balloons came undone. None of the boats looked much like boats after a while (and in truth, we didn't look much like sailors, either).

It was getting late. Willy's pants were so wet that I was

wringing them out like a dishtowel. I told Audrey we'd take one more run, and then we'd better head for home.

But the *Amelia* hit a trouble spot: a little eddy of swirling water that sucked her pink balloon ballast over a rocky drop-off, causing her to capsize. Audrey managed to rescue the boat, but when she did, I heard her let out a wail. The captain and crewperson were missing, lost in the muddy depths of Beard Brook, along with the purple feather. Losing the feather Audrey could bear. It was losing those two little wooden people that made her weep.

So I put my arms around her and we talked about bodies of water and boats. How our small brook flows into a river, and how that river flows into an even larger river, and that large river flows into the sea, which stretches all the way to England. I suppose some people might think those two clothespin people will simply end up buried in the muddy brook bed or snagged on a stick a little way downstream. As for me, I picture them washing ashore on some African beach or bobbing across the English Channel some day, round about next August, where surely there will be someone waiting to receive them, with joy and wonder.

And that, it occurs to me, is pretty much how I feel about launching children into the turbulent waters it will be up to them to navigate. Their father and I will put our mark on them, for sure: we'll lower them gently, run along the banks a ways, step out on the rocks to get them unstuck when necessary, reel them in, even, a time or two. And then they'll be off, toward some distant and unknown destination, while we stand on the shore, waving and cheering, watching them go.

GROWING OLDER

□ *Sixteen* □ *Joan Baez Concert*
□ *The Baby Stroller* □ *Selling Our*
Land □ *Greg and Kate Have a Baby*

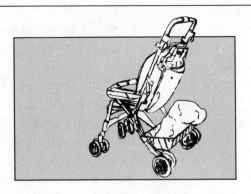

Steve and I had just come home from the movies. I was paying Jennifer, our babysitter; Steve was outside in the car, waiting to take her home. She mentioned that she had celebrated her sixteenth birthday the other day. She's taking driver's education now, of course. She'll have her license by summer.

Well, it's sixteen years since I was sixteen years old. Hard to believe: I don't feel that different. I can still remember so clearly the day I got my driver's license. The freedom I felt, getting into my parents' hulking Oldsmobile for the first time and pulling out of the driveway alone, with a thousand miles of highways stretching before me.

When I was sixteen I got my first real boyfriend. Bud was his name: a big, curly-haired boy, a year older than I— admired and even loved by nearly everybody in our school.

He liked to fish and he had a passion for soccer. He drove a Model A Ford with a window shade in the back. He kept a plaid blanket in the trunk, and a flask of rum. He had a hearty laugh and a marvelous wit, but also, more than once, I saw him cry. I love my husband, but I would probably still melt if I ran into Bud tomorrow.

I had always been the kind of girl parents call reliable. A daughter my parents could feel easy about leaving in a house with a full liquor cabinet. A much-sought-after babysitter. An A student, headed for the college of my choice. Probably the worst thing I'd ever done, my first fifteen years, was show up at school tardy once or twice.

Bud got me onto a six-person toboggan, on an icy hill. He got me to jump off a rope swing into the river. I cut classes with him: He taught me it was a crime to study Latin on the first warm day of spring. In his basement rec room, late at night, he played Jimi Hendrix records and fingered an imaginary guitar. I bet we put a thousand miles on his Model A, after school and weekends, just driving around. Every time I drink rum, I think of him.

He wasn't what you would call a bad boy. Didn't drive drunk. Would never have destroyed property, or hurt a soul. What he did was simply give me a chance to leave the comfortable, safe life I had been living under my parents' roof and venture forth for a few hours every Saturday night. And he made possible some leaps I might never have taken if I hadn't met him. He threw open a way of living that was a little riskier, a little less comfortable, more filled with possibilities. There are some things mothers and fathers just can't teach their teenagers about, though if they're smart they'll recognize it's not necessarily a bad idea if someone else does. Many of those lessons I got from Bud.

Our school soccer team won the state championship that year, with Bud as goalie. The team retired well before the first snowfall, but spent all the rest of that year celebrating. I have watched a lot of ball games since then, but I have never seen a group of players so tightly linked, so much a team. Skinny Joe, the left wing. Heartbreakingly handsome Nick, the forward. Gangly Kevin, a guard. Broad, laughing Bud, seeming almost to fill the space between the goalposts. They looked nothing alike, but went through life like brothers. Every time I saw them, it seemed someone had a soccer ball, and it was always in midair.

They were all graduating that June, going to the state university in our town or to jobs. I was a year younger, but I was leaving too: heading to a private prep school where, I'd been told, I would meet up with the best, brightest young minds in the country. It was understood, between Bud and me, that we would most likely go our separate ways come fall. Certainly I was way too young to make a commitment to anyone, even if I loved him. I wanted to begin my new Ivy League life with my heart unspoken for. I even thought that when I got to my new school I'd go by my middle name (Daphne). I was going to be a whole new person. Arty, sophisticated. Intellectual. How could I be those things, as long as I was spending my weekends driving around, listening to the radio and hanging out at Packer's Falls? But meanwhile, that summer, I kept looking forward to Saturday nights with Bud.

Late that June—a night I had stayed home—there was a car accident. Two carloads of kids smashed into each other when one of the drivers failed to negotiate a turn, and all seven were killed instantly. Bud was not in either of the cars, but three of his teammates (Joe and Nick and Kevin) were.

The next night, a Saturday, he picked me up as usual, and we just drove around for hours. Sometime around midnight we ended up in a field outside town, where we spread out his old blanket, as usual, leaned against each other, and wept. All the rest of that summer, I remember wondering if I would ever, in my whole life, feel right again.

We went out together a few more times after that. It's strange I can't even remember the last time clearly, and I guess that's because after the accident Bud and I drifted apart. He did go on to the state university that fall. I did go to prep school. (Where I kept forgetting to answer to the name Daphne, and eventually went back to Joyce.)

There was a soccer team at my new school. There were boys with whom I discussed record albums and SAT scores. And there were several I knew who talked a lot, that year, about the importance of what they called "the real world," which was why they were applying to an alternative school that gave college credit for farming. But it was years before I met anyone else who made me laugh the way Bud did, or just asked me if I'd like to jump in the brook. (When some-one did, I married him.)

It's hard for me to comprehend that I am not much closer to sixteen now than I am to fifty; that if I could somehow meet up with one of those dead boys from the old soccer team (all of whom are forever seventeen), they would proba-bly call me "ma'am." I drive cautiously now, with my littlest son in the car seat and my two other children buckled in among the groceries. The sixteen-year-olds honk at me as they whizz by me in the passing lane.

"I hope you drive safely," I tell our babysitter, Jennifer, as she gathers up her books to go. But my advice seems insuffi-cient and insubstantial. I could tell her all sorts of other things, about falling in love, growing up, taking some risks, resisting others. But of course I know better. All I do is ask her if she's busy next Saturday night.

□

I think I was ten years old the first time I went to hear a live concert. The performer was Joan Baez; I doubt if she was even twenty then. My sister and I had ridden a bus from

New Hampshire to Boston just to see her, after playing her records so many times we knew every ballad by heart: "Silver Dagger," "All My Trials," "Barbara Allen"—stories about love and loss, passion, heartbreak. I guess I was in the fifth grade then, but listening to Joan Baez sing about those things, I felt I understood all there was to know about life. Her voice was so clear and pure: I remember sitting in the auditorium that summer and shivering. When the concert was over, my sister and I gathered up our Greek shoulderbags and our ticket stubs (we would keep them forever) and headed for the Greyhound station. First thing the next morning, we were practicing the guitar.

I played folk songs for a few years—wore my hair long, bought every record Joan Baez and Judy Collins made. But there were other kinds of music developing in those years, and I branched out. The Beatles (hard to understand, looking at photographs of them, why their hair seemed so shocking back in 1964; now they look clean cut). The Rolling Stones, of course. Bob Dylan. With his scruffy clothes and his raspy voice, and his wailing harmonica, he was everything Joan Baez wasn't, but we loved him too, my sister and I—and, we read, so did Joan.

It was a time when performers—those performers, anyway—stood for something besides the music. Every folk concert came with a message, and usually several. (About the war in Vietnam. Poverty. Nonviolence. Peace.) Even the rock musicians, who seldom lectured on those things, conveyed a kind of stand. There was a world out there, of parents and business people and government, called the Establishment. And though few people in our country were doing bigger business or becoming more successfully established than rock performers, they were on the other side. They would never be conventional. Never be old.

When I was sixteen I sat in the front row at a Janis Joplin

concert. I saw the Rolling Stones on tour, and a lot of bands I can't even remember anymore. I lit a match—along with several thousand others—in a pitch-black, packed arena—while Dylan played an electrified version of "Blowing in the Wind." I didn't go to Woodstock, but of course I saw the movie—more than once. And there was Joan Baez again. By this time she was married to man named David Harris (I still followed the mythology), who was going to prison for refusing the draft. She was pregnant, and beautiful as ever.

I went to college. Folk music wasn't so popular there as rock, but I listened to both. Baez recorded an album, while her husband remained in prison, full of songs about how she awaited his return. The same moon shone on both of them, she sang: he in his prison cell, she, with their baby son, on her California mountaintop. "I live one day at a time," she sang, her voice as clear and pure as ever.

I left college after one year. I went through a period of listening mostly to classical music, and old tunes from other eras. Forties jazz. French torch songs.

Then, around age twenty, I thought my heart was broken, and the only kind of music that seemed to apply was country, hard-core country. George Jones singing "Stand on My Own Two Knees." Dolly Parton singing "I Will Always Love You." I read that Joan Baez's husband had got out of prison, but things didn't work out between them and they got a divorce.

I moved to New York City. I had a boyfriend who was very up on rock music, and I went to lots of concerts and clubs with him. He taught me the trick of stuffing wadded-up paper napkins in my ears to protect my hearing. He took me to a real hole-in-the-wall called CBGB's—thick with smoke, standing room only—to hear a much praised new group called Talking Heads. No possiblity of sing-alongs there.

I met Steve, and we moved back to my home state of New Hampshire. Audrey was born, and when she cried, I put on records—sometimes Dolly Parton, sometimes Bob Dylan, sometimes Benny Goodman, sometimes the Beatles—and danced her around our kitchen. That almost always worked. We had a few Sesame Street records, and, for Christmastime, Alvin and the Chipmunks singing "Rudolf the Red Nosed Reindeer." But mostly what I played for Audrey was the music I myself loved best. She knew the words to "Yellow Submarine" and "Dead Skunk in the Middle of the Road." She liked Stevie Wonder singing "Isn't She Lovely," and she loved the Solid Gold Dancers. Just because Steve and I were parents now didn't mean we were old. When babysitters came to our house, I always made a point of showing them how to work the stereo.

We went to Disney World on Ice in Boston, and to the circus, but we didn't go to concerts much. We did, once, drive to the city to hear one rock performer we liked, when I was eight months pregnant with Charlie. Steve and I were the oldest ones in sight, and certainly I was the only mother in evidence. The music was amplified very loud, and I had no paper napkin with me. I can still remember the extraordinary feeling of Charlie, in my belly, motionless through every number but kicking wildly every time there was applause. Around the third song, the audience got up on its feet, and stayed there the rest of the evening. My ankles hurt, so I stayed seated—fuming at the thoughtless behavior of the younger generation, that made it impossible for me to see.

Two years later, when I was pregnant again (with Willy), I got a magazine assignment to fly to England and interview the rock singer Elvis Costello. I spent a week listening to Costello tapes, bought myself the most new-wave maternity outfit I could find, and hopped on the plane. I was staying at a hotel frequented by a lot of rock singers: in the dining room, the next morning, my coffee was served by a waitress with a purple streak in her hair. Two tables away, a man in a black leather jacket and mohawk was eating French toast.

It had been a long time since I'd been out on an assignment like this—not since before I was married—and I worried that I wouldn't seem sophisticated enough. As it turned out, Elvis Costello (wearing a jacket and tie) behaved pretty much like any businessman. After the interview was done, I walked back to his house with him, to meet his wife and son. Their kitchen looked a lot like mine. Their son was getting ready to go camping.

That fall Charlie started going to a babysitter who got MTV, and he developed a passion for Michael Jackson. Every night after his bath, he and Audrey listened to the *Thriller* album—Audrey doing a graceful, restrained version of breakdancing, Charlie (still naked) going wild. It got so he could render a pretty convincing imitation of Michael, with a simulated moonwalk. He talked about Jackson all the time. (Charlie could spot his picture on the cover of a magazine in the supermarket from way over in the cereal aisle.) So when I heard the Jackson Five were going on tour, remembering what it had meant to me to see Joan Baez all those years back, I got myself an assignment to write about them so that I could bring Charlie and Audrey to the concert.

I thought we'd be among the oldest people in the hall that night, but it turned out there were many parents like us, bringing children. The crowd was orderly and there was no smell of marijuana wafting over the crowd the way there used to be in the concerts of my teens. This performance resembled a sporting event more than a concert. We all had a good time, but it also seemed to me that the best concerts of our youth were more powerful, more stirring.

But last night, Joan Baez came to a nearby city to sing,

and we got tickets. It was, I realized as I waited for her to come on stage, twenty-two years since I first saw her perform, when I was so excited I could barely catch my breath.

She has cut her hair (that happened a while back), and there's gray in it now. She was not particularly dressed up, but stylish. She is still a beautiful woman. And her voice, after all these years, is still marvelous.

She sang a few of the old songs: "Stewball," and "Farewell, Angelina"—giving us an imitation of Bob Dylan during one verse. She sang a song she wrote about her love affair with Dylan and one about her ex-husband. (Remarried now, I guess, and with another child. She herself never married again.) She also sang a song by Pink Floyd, and one by Elton John, accompanied by a grand piano. She brought up a few causes—Nicaragua, Libya—but there was a kind of detachment to the way she spoke about those things, rather like someone saying "here we go again." She has been crusading for close to thirty years now; she's seen plenty of causes come down the pike.

A lot has happened since those early days when she stood barefoot, with her guitar, wearing a dress that looked like a burlap bag, singing "We Shall Overcome." Times have changed: for her on the stage; for us in the balcony.

I think I had been a little worried when I bought my tickets: afraid her voice would be thinner, afraid she would seem old. (Afraid that seeing those things, I would feel that way myself.) But what I felt as we filed out, heading for home and my sleeping children, was wonder—and relief—at all the stages a person passes through, and all the things a person can survive.

□

There is a brand of baby stroller I've always wanted and never owned. I have had three babies now, and probably walked the mile from our house to the brook a little way down our road at least a thousand times with one or more small children in tow. But what I've been pushing all these years has been a cheap folding stroller, and though it's hardly the most difficult part of parenthood, let me tell you, pushing those cheap bargain models down that stretch of road hasn't been easy.

Our road is dirt, and very bumpy. There's a steep hill out here too, and so many rocks that sometimes I give up pushing altogether and simply lift the stroller in my arms, baby and all, and carry it over the roughest spots.

This road is hard on strollers. In all our years of parenthood Steve and I have gone through six cheap ones, where that one Cadillac of strollers might have lasted us right through: We've spent about as much on twenty-dollar strollers as we would have if we'd simply bought the good one in the first place. The problem was, we never had that much money all at once. But you know, in all those years of pushing our kids down our road (or sometimes watching well-dressed young professional-type city parents push their well-dressed babies in that brand of stroller I coveted), I don't think there was a single time I took a walk without wishing I had a good stroller and feeling a twinge of regret.

Well, for our youngest child there remains, at the outside, probably no more than a year of being strolled before he chooses to go wherever he is going on his own steam. I offer protestation (cannot bear the finality of this), but Steve tells me, firmly, that he's ready, with this third child of ours, to put having babies behind us. It has been hard, no question, and we both know our lives will be a lot easier once we have put away the stroller and everything that goes with it.

Already we are beginning to glimpse the light at the end of the tunnel of baby care. They're just fleeting glimpses, mind you: one morning out of twenty, when we're able to loll around in bed until six forty-five, without a single request for cereal, bottle, or book. The odd half hour when all three children are playing together, totally peacefully, without needing our intervention. I can sometimes duck into the bathroom unaccompanied now. I have begun wearing makeup again, and socks that match. We no longer spread newspapers on the floor under the table—to catch flying food—before every meal. And for the first time in ages, we are paying our bills on time, and going out to dinner now and then.

Last weekend, for instance, I thought I'd take the children to Toys R Us and let them each pick out a summer beach toy. Buckets, snorkels, swim fins, that sort of thing. No special occasion—I was simply celebrating the beginning of the beach season and the general easing up of our lives.

Then suddenly we were in the stroller aisle, and there it was: the one I always wanted and could never afford. The one our friends Tom and Diane had just bought, following the birth of their first child. (Unlike ours, a baby who was carefully planned for. For whom they waited several years, until the time was right.)

So I pulled over my shopping cart and just looked at it for a moment: the stroller of my dreams. I looked at the price-tag: $149.00. A lot of money, but still I knew I could write a check for that much. I was spending half that on plastic beach equipment and a backyard water slide that would probably be wrecked by Labor Day.

I lifted the stroller off the display stand and gave it a little push. (Smooth ride. Good suspension.) I tried folding it up. (That took about two seconds.) I ran my hand over the upholstery. I pictured Willy in the seat, waving a stalk of grass the way he likes to do on stroller rides, or a daisy with all the petals pulled off. And I pictured myself behind him, pushing up the hill so effortlessly I could manage one-handed.

I guess I'd been standing in the stroller aisle for several minutes, because Charlie began to get impatient. He could see the tricycles ahead, and pedal cars shaped like fire engines and police cars and rocketships. That's where he wanted to be.

Not Audrey. Audrey understood. Often these days (usually when I'm trying to get dinner on and the boys are pulling on my legs), I'll ask her to take her little brothers for a walk, with Willy in the stroller and Charlie holding onto the side. I pay Audrey a quarter to take the boys down our long driveway and back, and it's a job she likes—only partly because of the income she derives from it. The one problem is our stroller, which is so flimsy and beat up that even pushing it on level ground is hard for her.

"Look at that stroller," she said dreamily, as only a first child—a stroller pusher herself—could do. "If we had one like that, I wouldn't mind pushing Willy a hundred miles."

In the end, of course, I didn't buy the stroller. I bought our beach stuff and a Barbie doll for Audrey, for which she will pay me back over the summer by taking Willy for more walks.

About a week later Steve and I were driving down our dirt road without the children, to dinner and a movie. I was wearing the first new dress I'd bought in a while. Steve was talking about maybe getting away to the beach this summer, just the two of us. Making plans to put in raspberry bushes this year. Paint the house. Maybe we might begin looking into how much a used tractor would cost.

"I almost bought a stroller the other day," I told him, naming the brand I'd always wanted. I thought he'd laugh, or simply look horrified, but he didn't. He just nodded and patted my hand. Then we drove on to the restaurant, where dinner probably came to forty dollars. Not that anyone was counting.

□

I was taking a walk one day. This was a long time back—more than ten years ago, before I was married. I was on a dirt road near where we live now. No houses in sight, just woods. Through the trees was a path that looked as if it hadn't been explored in a while, and I took it. Where it led was a clearing filled with wildflowers. And beyond that, a roaring brook with watercress growing in the shallow parts, and beaver dams along the edges that made a pool deep and long enough to jump into. Which is just what I did that day.

Half a dozen years later—married and, very briefly, in possession of a little extra cash (I'd published a book that looked as if it might become a bestseller. It didn't.)—Steve and I heard that piece of land along the brook was on the market. Not just a few acres, mind you, but more than a hundred. More than we could comfortably afford—we knew that. "But we can always sell some off," we told ourselves. "It's a good investment."

Truth is, we are neither of us cagey investor types. We just loved that land. We'd spent a perfect afternoon tromping the woods along the banks. Rolled up our pants and waded across to the other side. Inspected the tree stumps the beavers had left, like well-sharpened pencils. Tried to identify mushrooms. Picked wildflowers.

We talked, that afternoon, about where we might build a house someday. How we'd keep a little boat on the beaver pond, and maybe build a sauna beside it. We had only one child then, but I pictured the others who would follow, and what a wonderful place this would be to grow up. Catching fish for dinner. Building tree houses. Inspecting frogs.

We bought the land, using our small lump of cash for a down payment and signing a ten-year mortgage for the rest. We had another baby, and I began to realize that writing

another book would be harder than I'd imagined. Steve
started taking on more and more house-painting jobs, to
come up with that monthly payment money. I stopped buying myself new clothes, started cutting my own hair. Steve
ran out of more and more colors of paints and didn't replace
them. "I think I'll just use black and white for a while," he
said.

There were fights too, and usually what they were about
(directly or indirectly) was money. We talked less about
building a new place down by the brook and more about
how to find more room in our existing house. By this time,
there was another baby on the way. We decided, finally, that
we'd put some pieces of that land on the market, and save the
largest, best one for ourselves.

Hard as it was coming up with the money every month to
make those payments, I loved owning that land. We didn't
get down there all that often, because it was pretty thickly
overgrown with brush, and hard for the children to manage.
But now and then we'd take them down for an afternoon of
fishing and a cookout by the water. A few times we set up
our tent and spent the night. (Waking, once, to the sound of
a beaver hitting the water and our dog Ron splashing in after
him.)

There had been an old sawmill on the site of the clearing
where we camped, and what remained of it was a enormous
pile of sawdust, perfect for children to climb on and jump in.
Audrey liked building little shelters out of twigs and moss
for dolls made out of acorns, with twig bodies and leaf
dresses. Charlie liked throwing stones into the water and
chasing frogs. Steve and I would sit by the campfire, sharing
a beer, looking out over the children and beyond them, to the
water, feeling no need to say a word. It was that place, those
moments, I'd seize upon and hold onto any time I wanted to
calm or comfort myself: during Willy's birth and at the funeral of my father, after a bad argument with Steve or on

some February morning when it seemed as if winter would never end. Our land—that's what I'd think of then.

We also headed down to our land every December to cut our Christmas tree, and though those trips were usually complicated some by my dissatisfaction with the spindly trees we found there, I always loved our tromps through the woods to find one. Last Christmas, a year after putting our land on the market (with no takers still) we found ourselves eyeing other smaller trees, for future Christmases, as we hauled in our spindly pine. Maybe we won't sell the land, I was thinking. Maybe we'll manage to keep it after all.

And then six weeks ago came the call. A young man and his wife, newly married, had spent the day walking our land (as Steve and I had, a few years back), and now they wanted to make an offer. Not on the smaller pieces we'd planned to sell, though. They wanted to buy the big piece—where we'd dreamed of building a house someday. The piece with the beaver pond and the watercress and our campsite and Audrey's twig villages and the sawdust pile.

Steve and I argued again. He pointed out—rationally, unsentimentally—how much easier our lives would be without that big payment to come up with every month. "You and I wouldn't have to work so hard," he said. "We'd have more time with each other and the children. More time for camping trips and swimming. Less worry and strain." Of course he was right, and of course I denied it.

It wasn't easy for either of us to think of parting with that land, and because of that we drove a hard bargain (I secretly hoping our prospective buyer would lose interest and go away). When he didn't (like us, he and his wife had already begun building a house in their heads, right there beside the brook), I cried. Knowing I was spoiled. Knowing we still have our house and our small piece of not-quite-so-breathtaking, but still pretty land on that brook. Knowing that in the scale of things, letting go of a beautiful piece of brookfront land is nothing, compared to all the sorts of things people have to give up all the time.

The day of the closing, as we drove down to the realtor's office to sign the final papers, we were both pretty quiet. "I feel as if a chapter of our lives is about to end," I said. "The most romantic, most hopeful part. It makes me feel old."

"You know," said Steve, "that piece of land was too big for us to get a handle on. We never could get around to thinning the trees or clearing a path along the brook for the kids. The land that's left is small enough to be manageable. We can make that parcel a real gem."

Which cheered me up. Better a few well-shaped Christmas trees you have time to look at than a forest full of spindly ones you never get to, after all. We're not old yet, I decided. Just mature enough to know what we can handle, what we can't. And what matters most.

□

Our friends Greg and Kate got together around the same time as Steve and I. But where we were married within months, and celebrated our first anniversary with Audrey in a high chair beside us, the two of them got around to making it legal only a couple of years back. And while, in the years we've been together, Steve and I have been largely occupied with having and raising children and keeping the home fires burning, Greg and Kate have always been the adventurers. They've swum in Morocco and off a remote Greek island and rented a cottage in a little Italian village. For a month every summer, Kate always took off on her own for an island in northern Maine, to write. They drive an old sportscar, with just two seats—a convertible. They don't have a lot of money, but every New Year's Eve they put on evening dress and hire a caterer to come to their New York City loft, where a waiter in tails serves them and around ten of their friends a midnight dinner that costs each guest a hundred dollars.

They invited us once to drive down to the city and join them for the big annual dinner, and I longed to say yes (only partly to know what a hundred-dollar dinner tasted like, and partly to prove to myself that three children had not totally robbed us of the spirit of adventure and romance we'd known in our younger, less domesticated days). But common sense and practicality got the best of us (as they usually do, these days) when we reminded ourselves of all the other things we could do with that money. In the end we used the two hundred dollars to buy a pair of new steel-belted radials for our van, and toasted the new year at ten because we were too tired to stay up until midnight. "Just wait," I laughed, a little sorrowfully, when we called Greg and Kate with our regrets. "Wait till you have kids."

Two weeks ago (with our youngest out of diapers now, and our oldest informing me that she's now reached the stage where she and I can begin trading clothes and accessories), Greg and Kate had their first child (a daughter they call Lily). And last weekend I took my own firstborn (now eight and a half) to New York City for a weekend—the first time we've had for just the two of us since her littlest brother was born. So, naturally, we paid a call on Greg and Kate and Lily. And where, so often, it had been Kate who blew in, in the red convertible, to see me (when I had one child or another in arms, or crying, or keeping me up all night), this time I was the footloose one—with my black sequinned evening jacket on and my arms full of shopping bags, heading to the theater—and she was the one who sat at the kitchen table in an old T-shirt, nursing the baby. And where once, (when it was me with the baby) I remember feeling wistful, seeing my friend so unencumbered and so free, (also so slim and rested looking), this time I felt a little wistful that the stage Greg and Kate are just entering may be permanently behind

Steve and me. It felt like a hundred years since I was the one in the rocking chair, crooning to an infant Audrey. We may or may not have another baby someday. But one thing is certain: We will never again have a first baby.

Everything about having a baby in the house is new for these friends: the little toes, the smooth pink soles of her feet. The way she startles every time they take her clothes off to bathe her. The brow, that wrinkles clear up to the hairline, and the belly button, so newly formed you can still see the last vestiges of her umbilical cord. Here is a person they will know and love for the rest of their lives. And they have yet to see her first smile. They don't know about Fisher-Price people or Esprit clothes yet, can't recite the words to *Goodnight Moon*, haven't been to Chuck E. Cheese, don't buy a new jar of peanut butter weekly. When I think of all the things we've already done that lie ahead of them, I feel weary and nostalgic, both at once.

Every couple I've ever been with, after the arrival of a brand-new baby, wants to tell about the birth. (Even years later, that impulse remains; I still savor the familiar stories of my three children's entrances into the world.) And so, because I love hearing friends' stories too, we spent a happy half hour or so going over the contractions, the trip to the hospital, the stages of dilation, the familiar feelings: "I can't go through with this." "There really is a baby in there after all." . . . And then the moment when the baby finally emerged. At which point in the story, these two good old friends just looked at Audrey and me—overcome—and shook their heads in wonder. "It was just—" they began, and then stopped, at a loss for words. And it doesn't matter that every day, every second, everywhere in the world, babies are born. The moment when the baby being born is yours feels like the first, the only, time something this extraordinary has ever taken place. And you're like those fifteenth-century explorers, charting new courses on never-before-traveled oceans. You have discovered the land of parenthood, and it's that strange and mysterious.

As for me, I'm an old veteran. I have to resist the impulse to offer my friends advice (on the use of a pacifier, on the inadvisability of playing with one's newborn when she awakes at three A.M.). I love and admire these two friends, as I know I will love their new daughter, but maybe (having got there first) I feel a certain need, at a moment like this, to stake out the territory (babies) as mine. (Just as, if we ever made it to Morocco, they might want to show us around.) But of course, when it comes to having children, we all have to learn the lessons, all over again, on our own. Steve and I are the world authorities on our children only, as Greg and Kate will be about theirs.

So Kate handed me the small package of Lily, and I held her close, walked her around the room, stroked her cheek, whispered in her ear, hummed for her the little tuneless series of notes I always hummed to my babies. I left my favorite new-baby activity for last: the sniffing of the top of her head—expecting to find there the faintly remembered smell my children had when they were new. And found, to my surprise, I could smell nothing. And then I realized: Lily's scent is for Kate and Greg alone, as Audrey's and Charlie's and Willy's were for Steve and me. I handed her back, with a combination of regret and relief. (I loved having new babies. But I also love seeing them grow up.) Then we said our good-byes, my eight-year-old and I, and took a subway uptown, to a Broadway theater where there were a couple of seats waiting for us for a musical I knew Audrey would love. And I found myself thinking that there are many ways to be a romantic adventurer: in a sports car, or a station wagon. And that there is no way to move forward without leaving certain things behind.

MARRIAGE – MINE AND OTHERS

I rode the rapids of the Contoocook river once, on a rubber raft in early spring, when the water was at its highest and most wild. I remember thinking my heart might burst, I was so terrified, as we crashed over the rocks and swirled down the river, with the water shooting into our faces. After it was over, somebody told me those were class-four rapids we'd traveled. More than one rafter has died on that same stretch of river. And of course, if I'd known that, I never would have set out in the first place.

Well, I am not as a rule a risk taker in life. I have spent most of my thirty-two years being cautious and fearful about many things: fast toboggan rides, high diving boards. But I plunged into my marriage and parenthood almost without a second thought or a backward glance, much as I entered the Contoocook that day: at a calm spot, the waters smooth and free of boulders, with the rocks and drop-offs concealed around the next bend.

I was twenty-three years old. I had come from New Hampshire to New York City the year before. I had a great job as a newspaper reporter, and good prospects. I had a penthouse apartment overlooking the park. It was the year of the bicentennial: I could stand on my balcony at night, sipping white wine, and see the Empire State Building lit up in red, white, and blue. I'd go out on a Saturday afternoon and pick up three new outfits at Bloomingdale's and a couple of new records. I bought myself African coffee beans and bouquets of calla lilies. I had plenty of friends; I went to lots of parties. Sometimes I went out on dates, and always, when I went out with a man, I tried to imagine myself married to him. But this was 1976; women my age—career women—weren't supposed to be thinking about marriage.

Sometime in the fall of that year, I started getting calls from a man named Steve whom I'd met briefly, years before, back in my one and only year at college. He was an artist, raised in the Midwest, who was supporting himself as a house painter and living in a downtown loft he shared with a struggling jazz singer. He remembered me from a bike ride we took together a half dozen years earlier, and he wondered if we could get together some evening.

I always put him off with one excuse or another: I had to cover a singles' convention for my newspaper. I was writing a story about celebrity bathrooms. I had to do my laundry. Really, though, I think I avoided Steve because—after dealing with all the men I had been meeting (who needed space, or couldn't handle commitment, or who simply disappeared, or didn't disappear, only I wished they would)—I had reached the point where nothing made me so suspicious of a man as to hear him say he liked me and wished he could see me again. Steve said those things, and he kept calling. (In New York, the city where, every thirty seconds, there's a new face coming down the street. Where no one's irreplaceable.)

I turned him down one weekend; he tried again the next. I told him, "Call me in a couple of months," and he did. I was seeing a food photographer at the time—a man who would, on occasion, spend an entire morning looking for the perfect anjou pear, or pour mug after mug of beer in search of precisely the right combination of bubbles and foam for a beer ad. A man who would eventually end our relationship, around eleven-thirty P.M. on Christmas Eve, drive off in his Porsche, and then return five minutes later to pick up his imported German fruitcake. It was sometime after the fruitcake incident, when Steve called again, that I remember telling a friend, "This guy is probably a psychopathic killer." He sounded so nice there had to be a trick.

He called me up one Sunday in February to ask if I'd like to go to a museum with him, and I don't know why, but that time I said yes. We spent the afternoon walking around the city, came back to my apartment, where (as usual, in those days) there was nothing in the refrigerator but a couple of eggs and a piece of cheese. He made us an omelet. Even that first night we talked about marriage and children, I think, in a way that strikes me now as reckless and crazy, knowing what I know now about those things. (How hard it is to be married. What an enormous and irreversible thing it is to take on the responsibility of a child.)

But we were twenty-three and twenty-five then—very different types of people, but both of us in love, both driven by a pretty unfashionable longing for family and home. Later (first, when I was pregnant with Audrey, and dozens of times after that) I would accuse him of marrying me only because of those things. "You just wanted me for a wife," I would say, as the clincher to a long list of accusations. "You just wanted to have a baby with me."

And really, I guess, there was some truth to that, for both of us—only it no longer seems to me like a crime. We were wildly in love, but neither of us was the person the other might have run off with to Bora Bora or the coast of France. Our work, our interests, our friends, our style of life, could hardly have been more different. (I loved to talk. He fell silent swiftly. I had spent my life sitting in chairs, thinking, analyzing. He would get restless if a day went by that he hadn't taken a run or played ball or fit in a ten-mile bike ride or a long swim. I looked at his paintings—large, abstract, undecorative—and didn't know what to say. He didn't ask me what I'd been writing about.) What we loved best about the other from the beginning, I think, was our dream of the family we could make together and the home we'd build.

We met in February, nine years ago. I quit my job a month later. In early April we rented a U-Haul truck, filled it with his paintings, my two white couches, his power tools, my designer suits, and moved to the old farmhouse in New Hampshire where we are living still. We had no money and few clear prospects for earning any. We hadn't met each other's families, didn't know the most basic facts of how the other spent the days. We instantly set about planning the wedding. (When Steve called his parents in Ohio to let them know, they were very happy. Then asked to speak to Karen, the girlfriend he'd been seeing the last time they'd heard from him.)

We were married early that summer, in a little church down the road from our house. Afterward we gave an out-door party for a couple hundred friends, back at our house. (In keeping with our approach to life back then, we had made no provisions for rain. None fell.) We left the dishes piled high in our kitchen that night and took off for the

Breezy Point Motel, six miles down the road. Came back the next morning to wash the dishes. Our daughter Audrey was born the following winter—a year and two days from the afternoon we first got together.

The seas we have been navigating in the years since then have been rough indeed—full of choppy waters, boulders, sudden drops—and we've sustained more than a few injuries along our course. We've laid some demons to rest. (I am less quick to argue. I've come to understand that days are finite. Time is precious. So is peace.) I no longer shed tears over my birthday present (I seldom get flowers, but I don't expect them). Some problems we've resolved. (He gets the car inspected. I do the cooking.) Some we no longer expect to resolve. We're more realistic, maybe. We've seen a lot of marriages break apart over the years we've held together. And what I feel when I hear the stories of those marriages, is never the lofty superiority of one who has it all sewn up herself. Only the recognition, felt, I think, by anybody who's been married a while, of how hard it is for two people to build a life together and how much more than love is required to make it endure.

□

Our friend Ursula's son A.J. blew into town the other day, and this morning he paid us a visit. We've known A.J. close to ten years now, though never well. Like his father, Andy, who died a few years back, A.J. is a large man with not a lot of small talk in him. Trained as a geologist, he has been working these many years as a carpenter instead. He was married around 1970 to a pretty red-haired woman named Julia with whom he lived in a little cabin out of town, without benefit of electricity or running water. A.J. grew a beard. Julia wore long dresses and long hair. Their first baby, Cassie, was born right there in the cabin, and the second one, Sara, came a year and a half later. They drove a beat-up truck and A.J. picked up odd jobs; Julia baked bread.

I didn't know them well back then, but they seemed like one of those couples—perhaps there were more of them, in those days—who lived by the creed "We ain't got much, but we sure have love." Sometimes I would run into A.J. and Julia in summertime, taking a dip down the road, at Gleason Falls, in the middle of the day—A.J. with a beautiful blond-haired baby in each arm. Around the time I met Steve, A.J. and Julia moved out West. A.J. had been offered a full-time construction job in San Diego. Sometimes, when I'd stop by to visit Ursula, she'd take out pictures from A.J. and Julia's travels cross country in the truck. They camped out in Baja California for most of that summer and part of the fall: more pictures of beautiful blond children (three of them now; there was a boy, Jesse), with golden tans, wearing bandanas on their heads.

After they moved West we mostly lost touch with A.J. and his family, except for reports from Ursula. They seemed to be doing well, though. First they had an apartment, then a house. Then a better job, in Colorado. A.J. had shaved his beard. Julia (always after A.J. to push a little harder in his construction business, be a better provider) was talking about getting a job herself. She was going on a diet. The children were growing fast—still blond and beautiful.

Every summer or two they'd come back to New Hamp-shire for a visit, and when they did we always had the chil-dren over to our house. I always liked those children: They were kind to each other, and kind to Audrey too. Some-times, months after a visit, we'd get a note from Sara, asking after pets, babies, news. Her family was moving again. (Texas this time.) They were buying a bigger house. She would take riding lessons. She was getting her own horse.

The new house was in a development called Pleasant Woods; I saw it on television, one time, when we were in

Ohio visiting Steve's parents, and Steve's father was watching a golf match televised there. The place looked green and perfect, and it turned out A.J. and Julia's house overlooked that very golf course. I tried to picture A.J. in a luxury housing development, not only building houses there but living in one. Hard to imagine.

Then we didn't see them for a few summers. ("Too busy, I guess," said Ursula, a little bitterly.) Ursula's husband, Andy, was dead by now. Julia had put the children in day care and got a job as a secretary at the Pleasant Woods resort complex, where she'd been such a success they'd made her executive secretary to the head of the whole place. She had indeed gone on a diet; the new photographs from Texas showed her in fashionable suits and a new short hairdo. A.J.—still a good-looking man, but considerably aged—had put on weight. Sara, the second daughter, was taller than me now and could've been a fashion model.

A couple of years ago they came back through town, in a rented Lincoln Continental. Sara came for a sleepover with Audrey, but there was a crisis when she misplaced a ring she'd just been given by her mother for her birthday. The ring was real gold. In the end we found it, but not before some tears were shed, with Sara saying, "My mom will just kill me."

A.J. and Julia were celebrating their anniversary that August: I think it was their fifteenth. As we stood on the lawn at Ursula's house, where they'd been married (Julia barefoot; the minister in an embroidered Indian shirt), they fed each other cake and Julia (in a pant suit) said something like, "Once you've made it together this many years, you've gone too far to quit. I know now we'll always be together." A few months later they split up.

Ursula called me one day early last spring, in tears, to say that A.J. had turned up at the housing development where Julia and the children lived, on the edge of the ninth hole, and he'd gone on a rampage—yelling, breaking things. He had just been committed to a mental institution. Julia had just called Ursula to say she feared for her life. "The man's gone nuts," she said. "He's crazy."

I told Ursula it didn't seem so crazy, to me, for a man who'd just ended a fifteen-year marriage and had been separated from his three beloved children, to flip out a little, but as for the homicidal part, I didn't believe it. He must be under a lot of pressure, I said. As long as he's getting good care, and he can get out when he's ready, it might not be such a bad idea for him to have a rest.

A few weeks later he started sending us poems. It was easy to recognize the characters: The poems were all about A.J. and Julia—the old days in the little cabin, lit by kerosene; and more recent history, in the house on the edge of the golf course that the bank had announced it was about to repossess.

The poems kept coming. It was odd, getting them: Steve and I had never really known A.J. all that well, but after reading a few batches of those typewritten sheets, with the hospital return address, he started seeming like a friend. And though they were odd poems—disjointed, angry sometimes, wistful—they were not the poems of a madman either.

He checked out of the hospital after a few weeks, when the insurance money ran out. He drove across country in his old truck, with a wooden bumper that had Sara's name carved in it. He took a carpentry job in Connecticut and kept sending us poems all summer.

A.J. came to New Hampshire from the Adirondacks a few times that summer. He'd show up on our doorstep, always unannounced. Once we were just heading out the door for our week's vacation in Maine, with the car packed and the children already buckled into their seats. Another time, when Steve was out of town, he knocked at the door just as I was getting the children into bed. I was so startled to see him, six feet tall and then some, looming in the doorway in the pitch-dark night, that I told him it was a bad time for a visit and closed the door before I realized he'd come over on foot from Ursula's house, where he was camping out.

His middle child, Sara, flew out to see him in the fall. She stayed with him at Ursula's for a week, seldom letting A.J. out of her sight. I tried to imagine our children without Steve, Steve without our children. I avoided seeing A.J. for a few days after Sara left, knowing it would be a long time before he'd see her again and knowing how torn up he'd be.

He came over this morning, just to visit. I fixed him a bowl of soup I'd been making, and he sat down and told us the story of how his marriage fell apart. Amazing, I thought to myself, that I ever took this man for the quiet type. I had been making a blueberry pie when the story started. I made a second pie so I could justify staying on to listen, and when that pie was done too, I started in on some cookies. As it turned out, I forgot to put salt in the pie crust (which has a more adverse effect on the pie than you might suppose), simply because I was so wrapped up in A.J.'s tale.

He has no home and no job and no money, and he sleeps in the back of a seventeen-year-old truck. He is back again to where he started, only now he's forty years old, with three children he loves more than anything, living two thousand miles away. I guess his is the old story: romantic, idealistic young love (the cabin in the woods), worn down by too much domestic reality. Designer jeans, horseback-riding lessons, summer camp, wall-to-wall carpeting: "We just got so busy getting ahead," A.J. says, climbing into the cab of the same ancient red truck he and Julia rode off in on their wedding day, back when they thought all they needed was each other. The last I see of him is his hand-carved wooden bumper, with his daughter's name carved in big capital letters (he made it the day she was born—on their bed, into his waiting hands). And then he disappears around the corner and out of sight.

□

Our old car needed a new muffler. That much seemed clear. And because the last one we'd purchased came with a lifetime guarantee, we were cheered to know we'd be out nothing more than the price of a new tail pipe to go with it. That, plus the sixty-mile drive to the muffler shop and back. We thought we'd combine the trip with a night at the movies: drop off the car, walk to the theater, pick up the car after the movie, drive home.

That was the plan. Steve made an appointment a week in advance for six-thirty on a Friday night. A few days before the scheduled appointment, he brought our 1966 Valiant into the shop for an advance viewing, in case the muffler installers might need to contemplate our particular tail pipe situation. We hired a babysitter. And finally the big night came: I set out the children's dinners, sleeper suits, a plate of brownies. We made a successful exit—no tears. We were on the open road, Steve patting the steering wheel with satisfaction, saying, "It's good to get this taken care of."

In theory I look forward to these long drives alone with my husband. There's been so little time to talk, lately, that sometimes I'm tempted to bring along a notebook with a list of subjects we need to cover. But the truth is, when I have him alone with me, captive in his seat belt, my tendency is always to raise large and troubling areas of discussion. Money comes up. Who has been sorting more laundry. Who last cleaned the car. I become icy. He grows silent. I may say, "Stop the car, let me out right now." Having heard this line probably once a month in our nine years of marriage, Steve calmly turns on the radio. I say nothing for ten miles or so, and then forget for a second that I'm mad, tell him something Charlie said today. A song we like comes on the radio. By the time we've reached our destination we feel like actors who have just finished auditioning for a Bergman film. Who did not—thankfully—play their roles well enough to get a part.

So when we walked into the muffler shop, we were friends again. Steve presented our six-year-old warranty and our car keys, reminded the manager about our tail pipe. And then the trouble began.

"We don't start repairs after six o'clock," the man said. I— who always anticipate trouble when it comes to cars— braced myself for a fight. Steve stayed calm, his voice friendly. " I made this appointment a week ago. The woman I spoke to said six-thirty would be fine."

"The girl was wrong. You know how they get mixed up." The manager winked in my direction.

Steve didn't have to look at me to know what I was about to say. He made the hand signal a policeman makes to indicate, "Slow down." I held my tongue while he talked the fellow into making an exception.

"Now about the tail pipe . . ."

"We don't have a tail pipe for that model in stock. You'll have to come back some other time."

I had begun pacing the floor a while back. Now I returned to the counter. "Leave this to me, please," said Steve, who is still pained by the memory of the time I took action when a commuter airline lost our luggage even though we were the plane's sole passengers. There is an entire airport we avoid these days, as a result.

Well, they had made a mistake. They had failed to order our tail pipe, and though they were equipped to make tail pipes at this place, the particular page in their instruction book giving the specifications for 1966 Valiant tail pipes was the one page missing from the book. No, they couldn't call another dealership: No one else in the state was open Friday nights.

There was a long silence as I prepared the speech I was about to deliver, and Steve, hands in his pockets, thought hard. "Please," he said to me. "Go outside now. Let me handle this."

I sat down and picked up an old copy of *Car & Driver* magazine, flipping through it in about the same manner in which Jerry Fallwell might handle a double issue of *Hustler.*

"Well, if all the muffler shops here are closed," said my husband, "let's call California. It's three hours earlier there."

The manager looked stunned. Was Steve kidding? Did he know what it would cost to call a dealer in L.A.?

About two dollars for three minutes, said Steve levelly, even cheerfully. "I'll pay."

"How am I supposed to get the number? What am I supposed to say?" This fellow had never made a long-distance phone call, from the sound of things.

"I'll make the call. I'll get the tail-pipe specifications."

Well, I'm going to skip over what happened after that, which was an endless debate involving telephones, mufflers, Valiants, reminders of the slogan from this muffler company's television ads—punctuated with occcasional, increasingly strained use of the word *buddy* on the part of my husband. I paced the office, scribbling notes, ostentatiously copying the manager's first name off his personalized shirt. He was just reaching for the telephone—gingerly, as if the receiver were a grenade—and he had the number for the muffler shop in Los Angeles, when he made one last grumble about how much time all of this was taking, and I lost control.

What about our time, I yelled. What about the sixty miles we drove? I don't even remember what I said, but somewhere in there a *Car & Driver* magazine ended up flung halfway across the floor, and a telephone receiver got slammed down. And a phone call wasn't made. And though we caught the second half of the movie, I have no recollection of what finally happened to Indiana Jones at the Temple of Doom—because all I could think about was our unrepaired car, our totaled evening. "That was a good idea about calling California," I said quietly as we made our way home in silence, except for the sound of our tail pipe rattling. Steve paid the babysitter seven dollars and drove her home.

It isn't that I learned, that night, that women should defer to their husbands in car repair shops. It isn't that I learned to suffer fools gladly. There were some lessons in there about counting to ten before leveling the first threat of a call to the Better Business Bureau. But what I really learned had to do with my precious freedom of self-expression that I guard so zealously, and that I certainly preserved, that night. Except the cost was too great.

One of the hardest things to learn in a marriage—and I'm still a long way from getting this right—has to do with sometimes putting aside one's self-interest for the good of this mysterious new unit, *the couple*. Who have a tendency to get all tangled up in details that never seem so important when they're going well, and then suddenly become vital when they're not.

□

Steve and I have known our friends Tim and Margaret for close to ten years—about as long as we've lived in this town. They're a bright, articulate couple, wonderful parents of two boys around the ages of our two older children, living just a couple of miles down the road from us; their paths and ours cross often. When they do, we always smile, wave, exchange news of kids and gardens, comment on how good it would be to get together. They have always seemed to me extraordinarily kind and generous, with the kind of conscience that extends not only to friends but also to strangers around the globe. I don't know many parents who spend more time with their children or display more tenderness. They have what has always looked to me like a really good and strong marriage. And one that's nothing like my own.

Tim is a long-distance runner who gets to work every morning by foot, not car, so we pass his tall, lean figure in a Day-Glo beanie on the road into town, no matter what the season. Margaret is a tiny, soft-spoken, very pretty woman with a lively sense of humor and one of the best gardens in town. I see her outside, tending it, when I drive by. Our children know each other less well, because while Audrey has been attending the big red-brick school in town, Tim and Margaret have chosen to school their two at home— partly because they would just as soon avoid conveying certain wordly lessons to their boys. They have no TV set, no He-Man figures in the playroom. On the Frisbee lying in their front yard are the words "He is the Lord."

Tim is a minister of the fundamentalist church in our town; Margaret carries her well-thumbed Bible wherever she goes, in a home-sewn case with handles like a pocketbook. It is their faith that shapes every aspect of their lives. Steve and I (who belong to the Congregational church, but don't always make it there on Sunday mornings) are less absolute in our convictions. We try to maintain, in our family, a strong sense of moral behavior (though, as a half Jew, I can never go quite so far even to identify what I am as strictly Christian). But you won't hear us talking about having taken the Lord into our hearts. The grace we sing before dinner—

a Shaker tune called "'Tis a Gift to Be Simple"—never mentions Christ.

Which has to mean that in Tim and Margaret's terms, we remain lost souls. I asked Tim about this once. "As far as you're concerned," I said to him sadly, "I guess you see me headed straight to hell." He looked at me kindly, and said he was praying for me.

We all like each other a lot. But the issue of religion keeps us from getting too close. What am I to do with the fact that one of the great achievements of Tim's career in town has been the creation of a crisis pregnancy center that denounces abortion as murder? What is he to do with the casual, eclectic background we provide our children? (A bible story here, a piece of Greek mythology there. A little Jesus, a little Santa, a little rock and roll.)

I read to our children, from our book of Bible stories, about Christ's Sermon on the Mount: "This man was wise and good and great, and we should live by his teachings," I tell them. (But so was Martin Luther King, Jr. So was Gandhi.) "Maybe God didn't literally create Adam exactly the way the Bible says, or Eve from his rib," I say (in a discussion of dinosaurs, cavemen, evolution). "The idea is simply that God made the world." If they heard me at a moment like that, Tim and Margaret would have to view us as the most lost-seeming of fence sitters—the watered-down form of Christianity we serve our children bearing about as much connection to the kind that governs their lives as Kool-Aid bears to nectar.

When our children were much younger, we invited Tim and Margaret's oldest boy, Ben, to come play with Audrey for the afternoon. When Tim came to pick him up, and the two fathers were animatedly discussing a ball game, Steve—who almost never swears—let slip a couple of words I'd almost never heard him utter, then turned bright red. "I don't

know what got into me," he said afterward. "I was so fo-
cused on not saying the wrong thing that I said it." I think
episodes like that one—combined with our mutual affection,
and our desire not to jeopardize it—have made us keep a
certain distance in the relationship between our two families.

Tim and Margaret invited our family over for Sunday dinner the other day, and all the things that had made us like
each other were present. Their boys proved to be the kind of
children I would have guessed they'd have—friendly, curious, lively, compassionate. Margaret had home-baked rolls
and a salad from her garden on the table. Their refrigerator
door was covered with kids' drawings, like ours at home,
only they also had a Bible lesson for the day printed in big
letters for the boys to read. When we sat down, we bowed
our heads together for grace, and I felt truly happy to see our
families together. Many of our values are so much the same.

The conversation came around to the counseling sessions
Tim and Margaret offer to couples about to be married. And
partly because Steve and I had celebrated our ninth anniversary just the day before, and because, even when it's not my
anniversary, I am always thinking about marriage and how
to make ours better, I asked them what sorts of issues they
cover in their counseling sessions. Child raising, finances, in-
laws—Tim offered a list of issues anyone who's been married a while would recognize as ones worth considering
—and ones Steve and I would have done well talking about,
more than we did, before our own wedding.

Then Margaret named another subject they deal with in
their premarital sessions, and I felt my teeth clench. "Headship," she said. "The principle laid out in the scriptures, that
the woman serves her husband, just as her husband serves
Christ."

Well, if I had liked this couple less, if I respected their
intelligence less, or knew less of Tim's respect for and devo-

tion to Margaret, I would simply have sat there in stony silence and beat a hasty retreat home as fast as I could. But I had to ask: How could they accept a notion like that?

Of course, this wasn't the first time someone had challenged them on the headship question; it's an idea that goes so totally against current thinking about men and women and their roles. And they both had some reasonable-sounding things to say: That nearly every decision they made was in fact made together, a product of both of them. And that, on the rare occasions when they were at an impasse, and his word overruled hers, nothing so humbled him, or earned her greater respect in his eyes, than to see the strength she possessed that allowed her to yield. Margaret added that Tim's position, as ultimate head of the household, protected her, made her feel safe. "I wouldn't want all the responsibility Tim has," she said.

Well, I am not buying it, and I am not buying it even though I know my pride, my willfullness, my headstrong need for control and equal responsibility in our marriage is the reason for at least seventy-five percent of the fights that take place in our household. Even though I know there would be a lot more peace and happiness in our house if we could accept a method of relating to each other like the one Tim and Margaret subscribe to. I can even see the reasoning behind a scriptural law that gives one sex ultimate power to overrule the other; the alternative (that exists in our household, for instance) makes for a lot of fights, a lot of impasses. Listening to Tim and Margaret describe their own system of living by the scripture, and the scripture only, I felt a kind of envy and sorrow. Because all around me—in their neat, bright, welcoming home, on their bountiful table, their blooming garden, and in the faces of their two fine boys— was evidence of how well it worked. And still, theirs is not the path for me. Steve and I will take the rocky road, with no one book offering all the answers, and I know from past experience that road will be filled with brambles and potholes, and even dead ends. I don't feel either of these two couples is wiser or better than the other (though I have a guess at who has the greater shot at pure happiness). We are simply different. Passing each other on the road, I know we'll always smile and wave, and wish the other well. And then, go our own, our separate ways.

□

There was a winter, a few years back, when I spent my days looking at real estate. As things turned out, we never bought any of those houses I tromped through, opening closets, inspecting basements. But every now and then Steve and I will be in some nearby town and we'll drive by a familiar-looking place, and it comes to me: I went there with a realtor. "$75,000," I tell him. "But it could probably have been gotten for less." "$160,000. There's a dumbwaiter in the kitchen." "$225,000. The walls were paneled in mahogany. And there's a bowling alley in the carriage house."

"You got a realtor to take you through a house that cost $225,000?" Steve says, not really surprised (we have been married for nine years), but faintly curious.

"I drove our good car to the appointment that day," I explain. Meaning our two-year-old Ford, and not our eighteen-year-old Plymouth.

"And what did you tell the salesman, after he'd taken you through this mansion?" he asks me.

"I was concerned about how we'd heat that third-floor tower room. Also, there wasn't enough land."

I remember well the winter when I went shopping for houses. Not just the prices of the houses I looked at, and which sellers would consider owner financing, and where interest rates stood. Charlie was not quite one year old then. Audrey was four. I wasn't working. Money was tight. One week our water heater gave out, and two weeks later it was the furnace. We were using our front hall as a closet, and even so, I had clothes boxed up in corners all over the house. The paint was peeling. Melting snow had leaked through the roof and onto the walls of the one room I'd papered. Every day a new layer of dust seemed to rise up through the cracks between our floorboards. The woodstove made my skin dry, and there were ashes everywhere. Our house is five miles out of town, at the end of a dead-end road. Looking out the window, all I could see was snow. Steve worked long days, and sometimes he was gone for a week at a time, house painting in the city. Days would go by that the only conversations I had were with children and real-estate agents.

So that winter I sat in their offices and told them about my dream house. It should have at least four bedrooms, I explained (there would be more babies. I knew that.) And bathrooms, lots of bathrooms (our own house having only one).

The house I was looking for was sunny. Had a big kitchen, with lots of counter space, everything built in, and room for a little desk in one corner and a comfortable chair to sit in and read to a child. I figured room for a refrigerator went without saying. In our house we have to keep the refrigerator in the pantry. And since the doorway to the pantry crosses paths with the front door and the doorway to upstairs, it's a frequent occurrence for a cook (me) to find herself clutching five eggs and half gallon of milk while she stands poised on the threshold, waiting for a couple of children and a dog to take off their boots, shake off a pile of snow, and finish arguing over whether they want miniature marshmallows or whipped cream in their hot chocolate.

Of course, when these real-estate agents heard that I also wanted land, and privacy, and a screened-in porch and plenty of closet space and a barn (for the horse we would someday own) and water nearby (if not on the property) and a first-rate public school district—they all told me you have to expect to pay a good price for such a place. Naturally, I concurred. And I didn't even blink when the realtor quoted me a price of two and a quarter (I, who had been putting off a trip to the dentist because I didn't know how we'd pay for my root canal).

I realize, telling all this, how thoughtless it sounds. I was taking up realtors' time, walking through people's houses—people's lives, actually. There was an old man, selling a huge old colonial he'd lived in forty years (the house he'd raised his children in). He showed me where his children built their tree house, where to find wild blackberries, where the good trees for Christmas cutting were. There was a big Dutch oven in the kitchen fireplace. He spent twenty minutes telling me how to cook a turkey in it. "You've never tasted a better bird than the ones my wife cooked in that oven," he said, with his eyes moist. His wife had died the summer before, which was why he'd put the house on the market.

There was a big modern solar house with one whole glassed-in side and a gourmet kitchen with a professional cookstove and a marble pastry board and a grill for indoor barbecuing and a stereo system built into the walls of every room. Dimmers on the bedroom lights, a balcony overlooking woods and a brook. Children's bedrooms (two of them), with custom-made bunk beds and a secret passageway. A greenhouse. A soundproof music room. So why was this family selling a place like that?

The couple got divorced is what happened. Neither one could afford to keep the place alone.

I guess I was pretty unhappy myself that winter (I can't

now reconstruct why, but after nine years I understand that even good marriages can sometimes seem impossible). That winter I certainly spent a lot of time arguing with Steve (who had always loved where we were living) about our house. It was too isolated. Too hard to maintain. Too small. Too dark. I get up in the morning (I would say), and the first thing I do is turn on the lights. Naturally I feel discouraged. Who could be happy, in such a dark house?

Of course I see now our house wasn't really the problem. We were simply living through some rough times. And during times like those it's easier to think about moving than it is to think about changing—easier to believe that what stands between you and happiness is a slate-floor kitchen with built-in skylight and a dumbwaiter (even if it carries a two hundred thousand dollar price tag) than to get down to the business of working things out in a too-small house with one bathroom and a toilet that only flushes if you jiggle the handle just right.

Well, in the end, we didn't buy a house or sell the one we had. It would probably be helpful to someone else (currently eyeing the real-estate listings) if I knew what it was that changed, but that's as hard to pin down as what was wrong in the first place. Some things I know: The new baby started sleeping through the night. Steve took fewer trips to the city. We sold the piece of land that had been driving us rapidly into debt. Partly what saved us may have been my husband's unwillingness to accept my vision of doom or my perception of our home as the wrong place to be. And it may sound too simple, but I think it's true that I also began to see—walking through all those other people's houses (houses I coveted that still hadn't made their occupants' lives complete or perfect)—that a good home must be made, not bought. In the end, it's not track lighting or a sunroom that brings light into the kitchen.

□

We've finally got all three children in bed, and Steve and I are cleaning up the kitchen. I'm scraping bits of spaghetti off a chair, he's washing dishes.

"I know you hated it when I gave you these knives," he says, drying off the blade of the one he used tonight to carve the chicken. It's one of a set of three he gave me one year, early in our marriage, for my birthday. And he's right. I cried the year he gave me the knives; the truth is, I have cried over almost every gift he's ever given me.

Not immediately, upon opening. (Then I always thank him, kiss him, tell him, "This is great.") It comes out later: "All I am to you is a wife," I said about the new bathtub, the stainless-steel spaghetti pot, the can opener, the knives. Eventually he got the message about practical gifts, so in recent years the presents have been perfume, silk stockings, jewelry, a skirt. But even those were never quite right. The skirt was horizontally striped and made me look thick around the waist. The stockings came from an expensive lingerie store I'd steered him to, specially, with hopes of a particular nightgown I'd seen there. I never wear perfume. Didn't he even know that about me, after nine years?

But the birthday he gave me the knives was a particularly bad one. I was twenty-four, mother of a new baby girl. I'd gained fifty pounds with that baby, and I still had twenty-five to lose. I lived in drawstring pants and loose blouses that buttoned down the front for nursing. We had almost no money. And here Steve had gone out and spent seventy-five dollars on knives. "All I am to you," (I said again, a few hours after the initial half-hearted expressions of pleasure when I first opened the box) "is a wife." Then, reaching for the largest knife to cut myself another piece of birthday cake, I'd sliced my thumb instead, so badly I had needed to rush downtown to the medical center for stitches. I still have the scar.

"It's true," I tell him now as he dries off that same blade, eight years later. "They're good knives. But I didn't think they were a good present." Meaning, there's nothing romantic about a knife.

"You know," he says, "I can still remember the afternoon I bought those knives." He was in New York City, having just finished a house-painting job, and he had a couple hundred dollars cash in his pocket. He was driving home to New Hampshire that night (to make it back for my birthday). He'd seen the knives in the window of a little store downtown, and he knew right off that was what he wanted to get me. He couldn't afford a complete set, of course. But the three knives he got me were the best made.

I remember that November too. We had just one car then, and Steve had taken it to New York, so I'd been home, alone with six-month-old Audrey, for five days. One afternoon I'd taken out all my old clothes from before we were married— back in the days when I was living in New York City myself, and working as a newspaper reporter, the days when I belonged to a health club and got my clothes in little designer boutiques. My silk blouses didn't even button. I left them in piles on the closet floor and fixed a large bowl of buttered popcorn for Audrey and me. I was about to turn twenty-five years old, and all I was was a wife and mother. (Which I now understand to be quite a lot indeed. But I was younger then.) What I needed, that year, was a new dress and a bottle of bubble bath.

"The man in the knife store could tell the situation," Steve says. "Young husband, not much cash, just starting out and wanting to give his wife a present that would last. He must have taken out three dozen knives, telling me about the uses for each one, helping me choose which ones would be best for us."

They chose well, Steve and the knife seller. I have used those three knives nearly every day for nine years now. Paring potatoes. Peeling broccoli spears. Slicing muffins. Carving turkeys. Making radish roses. Trimming pie crust. And because (a couple of birthdays later) Steve gave me a knife sharpener, the blades still cut as well as they ever did.

"I knew these knives would last forever," Steve says, hanging one up on the magnetic knife rack he gave me one Christmas.

"Durability," I say sharply. "That's your idea of romance."

"And to you nothing's so romantic as heartbreak," says Steve, not unkindly.

He has a point there. The truth is, I am a domestic type. I like nothing so well as making a home and raising children in it. But I guess I've always thought less of myself for being that way. I have looked curiously and enviously at those mysterious women who've resisted the impulse to follow my particular path. Wondering (I always will) whether they are remaining truer to their essential selves, while I've been compromising mine. I eye them from my kitchen—those passionate, reckless, footloose, undomesticated women who have been following their hearts all these years that I've been driving the car pool. The only time a woman like those ever sees a knife like mine is between some lover's teeth, as he threatens to slit his throat if she leaves him. There's romance for you. There's passion.

And maybe because I've always seen myself as a little too domesticated, because I've believed that unhappiness (or tumult anyway) was a more interesting condition than security or comfort, I've always done what was necessary to keep this domestic life of mine from ever coming close to running on an even keel. I don't just cry on my birthdays: There were whole years, for a while, when I cried almost daily. I have started nearly every argument that ever took place under this roof of ours. I have thrown dishes, dumped entire meals into the sink, stalked out the door, jumped in the car and driven away. I have asked myself, at least once a week, whether it's a good idea to stay married, and frequently I have concluded that it isn't. I have never stopped loving my husband or my children. But loving them has sometimes been about all I've been sure of. I have lived in the same house with the same man for nine years now. But there were plenty of times, there, when I didn't make plans more than a couple of days in advance, in case I wouldn't be around by then.

I shouldn't put absolutely all of this in the past tense either. I'll always have my flare-ups. But lately it has been occurring to me that I am in fact leading the life I want to be living, and that it's a good and lucky one.

"I think it's about time you realized you're happy," my friend Laurie said to me the other day (Laurie being the friend of mine who, more than any other, I would describe as having lived a nearly uninterruptedly happy life, a woman who tells me she has never allowed herself to consider, for an instant, the possibility that her marriage wouldn't last; the one who tells me, when I'm miserable, that I should start running again, or take up Dancercise). As for what she told me: I realized with shock that she was right.

I won't ever possess Laurie's kind of optimism and whole-hearted self-assurance. It's also true, I will always mourn all the other lives I couldn't lead, places I can't go, all the other babies I won't have. (With every child I've had, I've grieved for the other sex that wasn't born, even as I was rejoicing over the one I got.) I live in the country and miss the city. I love the husband I've got, but sometimes I imagine other kinds of marriages, other kinds of men I might have chosen. I have done the same one thing to earn my living since I was eighteen years old, and still, every week, I read the help-wanted ads in the paper. I will probably always feel ambivalent. I will want to change my life until the day I die. And all this time, through all my wavering and anxiety, all my husband has wanted was for our marriage to last as long as our carving knife.

"I never felt more romantic then I did the day I bought you those knives," says Steve, who has also been telling me, for years, that this is what life is like, this is how marriage is. "I loved giving you something that wouldn't wear out," he says.

And so far, anyway, he's been right. They've all lasted. The knives. The scar from the cut they gave me. The family we're forging here.

———

POSTSCRIPT

We were sitting at breakfast, all of us, watching Willy pour Cheerios down the front of his diaper, when Audrey piped up, "Imagine, some day Willy will be a dad! I wonder what kind of a dad he'll be."

There was a lot of laughter then as we imagined scenes: Willy playing baseball with his children—bonking them on the head with the bat, the way he hits Charlie now when the two of them play wiffle ball. Willy—the same size he is now, but sporting a moustache and wearing a miniature business suit—driving away in his car, standing up on the seat to reach the steering wheel. Willy reading his children a book—upside down. Serving them dinner by throwing the spaghetti noodles onto their plates from halfway across the room.

It was a good game, this future projection. Imagining myself as a grandmother, Steve as a grandfather. The children our children might have. Our children as parents themselves—that most of all. The scenes Audrey hypothesized were comical, but I could almost weep at the thought of my beloved offspring suddenly transplanted from the comfortable shade of childhood to the hot, unprotected sun of parenthood. Thinking of all the things we try to spare them, and what sparing them costs us. Thinking of our children, to whom we have given over so much of ourselves, someday giving themselves over to a set of little strangers whose faces I can't begin to imagine.

But of course, if they didn't—if my children chose not to become parents, if they chose to remain always (even into adulthood) our children, rather than somebody else's parents—I'm sure that would sadden me. Which is just one more example of the conflicts that dog me, always, in this life I love, and choose to lead, that drives me nearly crazy. I love having children. I want my children to have children. I also wonder, sometimes, whether there will be anything left of me, once my children are through growing up. Sometimes it seems to me that I'm not so different, really, from one of those animal species for whom reproduction is the final act before death.

Audrey's joke about Willy as a father got me thinking. The truth is, the image of our daughter someday being a mother, and our sons someday becoming fathers, is never totally out of our minds as Steve and I go about raising our children. When I teach Charlie how to break an egg, or put a dish in the dishwasher, or mop the floor, I'm thinking, "Someday they'll teach their children these things."

We are fathering and mothering our children, that's for sure. But what we're also doing is teaching our kids how to be a father, how to be a mother. The songs I teach our children, the tricks I use to get them into their pajamas or stop their tears, may be the songs and tricks they'll use with their

children. More than that, how we view them and our role as
their parents will determine how they will someday view the
idea of parenthood and the children who may someday be
theirs. I go about my days as a mother filled with the sense of
the continuum I'm part of. Knowing there must be things in
me that come from great-great-grandparents I've never heard
of. Knowing there will be things from me in great-great-
grandchildren I'll probably never meet. Ambivalence and
frustration—they'll be there, for sure. But I hope what we
pass on to our children about being parents—above all
else—is how much we love our job. What a joy it is to have
children. What I want to teach my spaghetti-throwing son,
in preparation for the day when he may be sitting across the
table from a spaghetti-thrower of his own, is that despite the
enormous mess they can make of our lives, we would never
choose anything different.

Sometimes, smack in the middle of things, it has seemed
to me that all I'm here for is to make peanut-butter sandwiches and clean up the crumbs. So much of the job of parenthood is taken up by mundane concerns, it's easy to lose
track of what the whole thing's for, easy to forget there is a
meaning and importance to the sum of those tasks that goes
way beyond what any one of them appears to possess,
viewed all by itself.

I once thought our life here was about nothing more than
getting through the days on a basically upward curve. We'd
have a baby, build a few bookshelves, put in raspberry
bushes, have another baby, reshingle the roof. Have another
baby, modernize the bathroom and clear land for a pond.
Someday we'd have time and money enough to raise sheep,
get a pony, take trips, concentrate on our work in a way
that's just not possible while one's children are young.
Meanwhile we'd go swimming every chance we got, Steve
would make paintings and play ball, and I'd grow zinnias
and bake lots of pies. And that was pretty much how it

went. We had plenty of hard times and plenty of good ones. There were times when I wondered if we'd still be married in six months, and times when I wondered how I could ever have questioned that we'd be together always.

We've learned some things along the way. We seldom had, in our ninth year of marriage, the kind of arguments we used to have (about who changes the diapers, who clears away the dinner dishes) in our first. By our tenth year—this one—we still argued some, but we had become more conscious of what every battle cost us, and the value of peace, of compromise. I no longer had to buy diapers; we were getting a regular eight hours unbroken sleep nightly. We had a family van that had never gotten stuck in snow, and full medical insurance coverage. When our old black-and-white TV set finally gave out, we even bought a color model and a VCR. Steve and I were still working hard, but I began to picture a life for us, within reach, in which we'd take vacations, put in a second bathroom. We had both scaled down our nearly infinite expectations some. And that might have been that. I might have lived out my life at the end of this dirt road, taking pleasure in watching our children grow up, tending my own back yard.

Then last January we were listening to the news (half listening only: Steve was reading to Charlie, I was chopping vegetables for a salad) and got the word that our town—the very piece of land on which our house sits, in fact—had been named by the federal government's Department of Energy as one of twelve proposed sites for a high-level nuclear waste dump, the single largest public works project in our nation's history. Over the weeks and months that followed we learned that there was no dump of the kind proposed for our town anywhere on the face of the earth. We learned that the waste they were thinking of burying in this back yard we'd been so busy tending included the most dangerous, most highly radioactive substances known. We heard a man from the Department of Energy explain that these radioactive wastes would probably not leak into our water systems "for thousands of years"—although, he added, there were no guarantees. We learned that our town could be subjected to as many as twelve years of testing before we'd know for sure whether the government would be buying us out. It was explained that the Department of Energy was not concerned with our grief and sense of violation at the prospect of having to give up our property to make possible the disposal of a private industry's waste, and the even larger outrage that our whole region could be contaminated for tens of thousands of years to come. Our home, a safe future for our children, everything we'd been working for, and everything that mattered most to us, were suddenly threatened. "If you don't vacate your house voluntarily," said the man from the Department of Energy, "then we'll call in the Army Corps of Engineers." At first all I could do, hearing that, was cry.

Then our little town got organized. We wrote letters by the hundreds and had meetings, mapped our historic sites and wetlands, made speeches, sought out television cameras, organized a truck convoy to the state capitol. I stopped cooking meals, I let the laundry pile up, I lost ten pounds from sheer worry. I was on the phone for hours, while Willy wound himself in my long telephone cord. Charlie woke in the night with dreams of dumps, bombs, explosions. (This was also the winter of the *Challenger* tragedy, and the spring that brought the Chernobyl disaster.) On the morning of her birthday Audrey woke to say, "Could I please not hear the word nuclear all day?" And though I tried, I couldn't even get through the day without breaking my promise. It was a draining, exhausting time.

But some good things came out of our dump crisis too. I loved seeing our community pull together, laying all our differences aside. I felt very sure of what we were doing—not a trace of ambivalence, for once. I realized, when I had to face the prospect of losing the life we have here, how dear it is to me. And though I had never before been conscious of having been a voiceless member of society, once I had become an active participant in the workings of my government I could no longer imagine functioning any other way. So even when the announcement was made, last May, that the search for a nuclear waste dump in our area had been "postponed indefinitely," Steve and I were incapable of going back to the old life of tending our garden and our garden only.

I was finishing this book the day I learned that the ground I was standing on might become the nuclear waste dump of the nation—and after the news sank in and changed our lives around here permanently, none of what I'd written up to then made sense anymore. Words written in the days of my innocent bliss ran through my mind like the film footage of the space-shuttle crew heading out to the launch pad the morning of the explosion. Like a bad and tasteless joke. My stories about cooking spaghetti sauce and arguing over replacing the car muffler seemed irrelevant, my old life meaningless. All I wanted to talk about was how our world is in danger, how our children might be deprived of their future.

But it has come to me, in the months since that first rude awakening, that our concerns here—before our nuclear dump ordeal and since—aren't different: Keeping the woodchucks out of our vegetable garden and keeping the Department of Energy off our soil. Making sure our children brush their teeth and stay a safe three feet away from the color TV and questioning the term "acceptable levels of radiation." Packing away the best baby clothes for future grandchildren and calling up my Congressman to register my support of a nuclear weapons test ban. Looking out for our back yard and beyond it as well. Neither can go on to the exclusion of the other. I will never become one of those people prepared to fast to the death for world peace, and I'll never make my children sit out in the rain all day with antinuclear placards, because it seems to me there's nothing left to fight for if, in the name of the cause, you sacrifice everything you love about your life. I still bake pies and I still grow zinnias, only now I think those small pleasures seem more precious to me.

A year ago our focus shifted radically here, from domestic affairs to global ones. (Not simply nuclear waste in my back yard, but nuclear waste in anyone's back yard. And the power plants that produce it. And the site in Nevada where the bombs are tested that have the capacity to destroy everything. And that invisible shield up there in space that we're supposed to believe protects us better than a total weapons ban would.) But it is not, in fact, that this new cause of mine has replaced my children. Just the reverse: Where I used to think that being a mother and taking good care of my children was reason enough not to be an actively involved citizen, I have come to see there is no dirt road so far out of town, no house so well protected by trees and woods, that the people who live there can escape whatever is going on beyond their stone walls and fences, and there is no way to be a good mother without also looking out for the world one's children will someday inherit.

I used to be home to tuck my children into bed and sing to them nearly every night. It wasn't a competing set of concerns and passions that took me away from them then, to go to meetings and make phone calls. It was only more of the same fierce longing every parent feels: to protect her children.

Charlie—who, at four, has perhaps registered the recent changes in our household more than either his older sister or his younger brother—asked me a couple of nights back, as I was tucking him into bed, "What will the future bring?" I told him how he'd grow bigger, make new friends, learn how to read and how to ride a two-wheeler. Someday he might play a musical instrument, someday he might sail across the ocean. He would find out what kind of work he liked to do, and have a job. He might fall in love, might marry, become a dad. It's the old dream—a variation on the one (Ozzie's and Harriet's, and Beaver Cleaver's) that always propelled me when I was growing up, and while the details change, it's still the one I believe in. Even large and lofty goals need to be grounded in small, earthly matters.

We were at an antinuclear rally a couple of months back. There stood Dr. Helen Caldicott, on a podium with the huge white dome of the nearly completed Seabrook reactor looming behind her, and a chilly April wind from the ocean blowing in her face as she spoke to the crowd on the grass (where I sat, with my sons on my lap, handing out the peanut-butter sandwiches). "There is only one reason we're put on this planet," she said. "And that's to save it."

What we are all concerned with here is the future, and our own small emissaries to it. Seeing to it that they are just as brave and strong and healthy as we can make them, for the day when we won't be there to wipe their noses and look both ways before crossing. Seeing to it that they will someday be able to have and raise children of their own.

I got a letter the other day from a reader of my newspaper column—a man, thirty-eight years old, married a few years. "I've been reading stories about your family life every week now for a few months," he wrote. "And I wanted to tell you" (at this point I reached for my coffee, to better savor the compliment I thought I was about to receive) "it was reading about your children that made me decide, once and for all, to get a vasectomy."

Well, I persuaded Steve to get a haircut once. I got Charlie to try asparagus the other night. But this was a new one.

And the thing is, these stories I'd been telling about my children and the frequent havoc they wreak on our home were mostly about times I wouldn't trade for the world. At midnight, finally sponging off the last counter, turning out the lights, heading upstairs, and finding Willy wide awake and sitting on the steps, in total darkness, with his toy chainsaw on his lap, his face beaming. "Happy New Year," he says brightly. (In fact, it is March.)

Who could be angry?

Although often, of course, I am. The other day (with Steve out of town, and the rest of us feeling a little lonely), I dressed the children up and announced we were going out to dinner. Put on socks. Tied shoes. Buckled belts. Sponged off faces. Sent the three of them outside, then raced to run a comb through my hair. Looked out the window: saw my two sons ankle deep in mud. Audrey rushing, in pink-satin Chinese slippers, to rescue her brothers, who were stuck. (Mud on dress. Boot in mud. Head in hands.) Everybody had to be cleaned up and dressed all over again, naturally.

"Are you mad, Mom?" asked Charlie, cautiously, after five minutes' drive in total silence on our way to the restaurant. And to my surprise (having been furious for a second there), I burst out laughing.

Our house has suddenly become overrun with mice, and after weeks of gentler (and unsuccessful) forms of mouse-deterrent efforts, Steve decides to set out traps. Audrey finds one, complete with dead mouse, and carries it outside, using corn tongs. Three days after the mouse burial (and the funeral, and the memorial service, and the construction of grave markers and funeral wreaths), Willy wanders into the kitchen, tightly clasping a mysterious muddy object in his fist. It's our mouse, raised from the dead (trap and all). "Look, Mom," he announces, triumphant. "He came back."

There is a day when Charlie, demonstrating a sudden leap in manual dexterity development, removes every lace from five different pairs of boots. Willy, who has been suspi-

ciously silent for half an hour, turns out to have pulled every
one of approximately three hundred children's books off the
shelves. "Bookland!" he cries, as he brings me to come see.

Charlie and Audrey have applied what was supposed to be
a press-on decal, featuring a life-sized image of Michael Jackson's head, not to Charlie's shirt but directly onto his belly
(where it remains, resisting all my best efforts at scrubbing,
through the next five baths and two trips to the YMCA
pool). Willy pours Rice Krispies into the bathtub. Audrey
loses her fifth hairbrush this year. Willy sets a new record:
spilling four glasses of milk at a single sitting.

If I went on at this, maybe they'd be forming lines at the
vasectomy clinics tomorrow.

Or not.

No question, there's disruption and disorder that comes
with raising children: physical commotion in early years,
followed, I guess, by turmoil of a more emotional nature.
But truthfully (though you will never hear me admit to it the
morning I'm down on my hands and knees sorting through
the pieces of seventeen different jigsaw puzzles Willy has
seen fit to dump on the playroom floor—"puzzle land," he
called it), frustration, disruption, exasperation—despair,
even—are surely necessary parts of the whole process of
raising children. If one can say of hiking the Appalachian
Trail that it's the journey, not the arrival, that matters, the
same is surely true of child raising. The point is not getting it
done and over with, but doing it. And if there were no spilt
milk—no need, ever, to peel off the snowpants, untie the
double-knotted boot laces, pull off the boots (all so the seams
of the socks underneath can be lined up, just so, along my
son's five toes)—well, life would be easier going, and less
tiring, but less mysterious and rich.

It's ten o'clock at night. I am standing over Willy's crib,
which contains not only Willy but a stack of about twenty

Little Golden Books, a pile of stuffed animals, his chainsaw, his football, his skis, an avocado seed, a fireman's hat, a plunger, and his riding motorcycle. I am singing to him, for the third time tonight, his current favorite song—a made-up number we call "'Willy's Riding in a Truck." I am so dead tired I start to fall asleep, standing up, in the middle of the verse about the windshield wipers, but it doesn't matter—Willy finishes the song for me. "Night, Mom," he says, signing off. (We'll hear from him again around six A.M.) "Happy New Year."